The ALTERNATE CELEBRATIONS CATALOGUE

The ALTERNATE CELEBRATIONS CATALOGUE

Milo Shannon-Thornberry

THE PILGRIM PRESS   NEW YORK

Library of Congress Cataloging in Publication Data
Main entry under title:

The Alternate celebrations catalogue.

  1. Holidays—United States. 2. Gifts.
3. Cookery. 4. Simplicity. 5. Handicraft.
I. Shannon-Thornberry, Milo, 1937-
GT4803.A64   394.2′6973   82-3638
ISBN 0-8398-0601-6 (pbk.)   AACR2

Photographs by Jacqueline Gill
Design by Irwin Rosenhouse

The Pilgrim Press, 132 West 31 Street, New York, New York 10001

To
    Colleen,
       the Alternatives staff,
        and
          all those whose experiences
          are shared in this book,

Who
    have taken responsible
    living and celebrating
      from theory to practice.

CONTENTS

The ALTERNATE CELEBRATIONS CATALOGUE

1.

INTRODUCTION

There is a spirit movement among the peoples of this land: ★ born of a longing for more integrity between our spiritual and economic values; ★ born of a resentment that national and international issues, as well as the most personal aspects of our lives, are the objects of manipulation by a society whose values are closely interlocked with consumption; ★ born of an anger that our most sacred celebrations are spiritually bankrupt, their meanings prostituted by the notion that the only vehicle for expressing joy, gratitude, love or sorrow is purchased with money; ★ born of a sense of estrangement among families, friends and communities because the values of human relationships have been replaced by crass materialism; ★ born of a sense of alienation from the land, and a fear that our world is well on the way to committing ecological suicide; ★ born under the judgement that the precious limited resources of the earth have been exploited for the sake of the few privileged at the expense of the many without privileges.

This movement has its immediate roots in the self-imposed alienation from contemporary American values by young people in the 1960's, various social struggles (civil rights, anti-war, women's rights, hunger, environmental, consumer protection, and others) and the ideal of the "simple life" represented in the Mennonite and Brethren traditions of the Christian church. The movement toward responsible living, or voluntary simplicity, combines commitments to consuming less with personal self-reliance, and to achieving principles of global social justice and ecological balance.

Other realities, which only in the 1970's became part of the American consciousness, have contributed to the movement toward responsible living. These realities have undermined the unquestioning confidence on the part of the middle class in the viability of the American way of life, especially since after World War II.

First, runaway inflation has created a financial insecurity not experienced by the middle class since the Great Depression. Such insecurity has always been, and continues to be, the lot of poor people. In the 1970's people in the middle class began to see how tenuous their own financial security really was.

Second, awareness of the limits of natural resources together with the social and ecological costs of maintaining an affluent lifestyle have contributed to a growing lack of confidence in the old assumptions about bigger and better. It is especially manifest in the absence of the old assumption that we will, of course, have larger houses and cars than our parents had.

Third, that so many of our most prevalent health problems are linked to the "All American Way" of living and eating—heart disease, gastrointestinal disorders, blood diseases, obesity, tooth decay, and even some forms of cancer—has done much to undermine confidence in that way of living and eating.

Before the 1970's, for example, with a sense of economic stability, unlimited natural resources and superior health, there was little general concern ■ that of more than $150 billion spent on farm-produced goods in 1975, about $100 billion was spent just getting the goods from the farm to the table; ■ that to get the food to us it had to travel more than 3.2 million miles of intercity highways alone while fifty years ago most of the food eaten by city people was grown within a fifty mile radius; ■ that in 1950 farmers used 50 million pounds of pesticides with a preharvest crop loss of 7 percent, while by 1979 farmers were using 700 million pounds of pesticides with a preharvest crop loss of 13 percent.

By the end of the 1970's the environmental/economic/health costs of food have become a significant issue for middle-class Americans, as they have always been for poor people. The above examples of food and agriculture can be duplicated by other basic necessities: shelter, clothing and transportation. The larger costs and risks (economic, ecological and social) are pushing people to consider alternatives to lifestyles based on mindless consumption and convenience.

For many Americans, especially those in the churches, the impetus for movement toward new levels of responsible living has come from the emergence of two related moral dilemmas, brought into sharp focus by the attention given to the problem of hunger in the last half decade: ➤First, although the natural and technological resources are available to prevent it, malnutrition is the greatest cause of death and disability in the world. ➤ Second, the high levels of consumption by 30 percent of the world's population are directly related to the continued impoverishment of the other 70 percent.

A multi-billion dollar advertising blitz will result in over $20 billion spent in America for Christmas in 1982, and this becomes a moral issue. In 1969 the total U.S. arms sales amounted to less than $1 billion; by 1980 sales were over $30 billion to underdeveloped countries alone. This too becomes a moral issue. Twenty-six million Americans by the government's own standards do not earn enough to provide an adequate diet for themselves, and are now asked to bear the burden for this country's anti-inflation policies. These are all moral issues directly related to the way we live.

Many people across the United States have determined to take a new kind of responsibility for their relative affluence, to resist the suffocation of pervasive commercialism and consumerism, to take a holistic approach to devoting themselves more fully and effectively to the work of humanizing society for the benefit of all its members.

Enter Alternatives ★ Helping to shape the movement, and being shaped by it, has been Alternatives, a non-profit organization founded by Bob Kochtitzky in 1973. Although long committed to discovering new more responsible ways of living, it was his frustration with Christmas that prompted him to act. Listen, as Bob described his journey in the first *Alternate Christmas Catalogue* in 1973:

Eight years ago, in December I said quits to Christmas. Not the Christmas that symbolizes love, brotherhood, justice and peace and not Jesus' birthday, the Man of Peace with few possessions.

What I said NO to was Christmas as the year's best money-making season ...Christmas that hustles $8½ billion dollars out of our family budgets...Christmas of plastic Santas and aluminum trees and $3 extra for shiny metallic paper and machine-tied ribbons on your package. (At the time I was unaware that many people had already done the same thing.)

My antagonism against the prostitution of the Holy Season was slow to build, as water takes a while to boil. I can't even remember the drip by drip process which finally broke the dam. What I do remember is the anxiety I felt over how my family would take this radical departure from custom. The response was cool but accepting.

In 1965 I'd never heard of ecology or limits to growth. But I knew the material things of the world had been unfairly distributed leaving millions of people in misery and poverty. And I knew that we were a middle-class family who really didn't need all the clothing and appliances and gimmicks which we gave each other. If the celebration of Christmas was showing our love with a gift that the other person *really needed*, then I wouldn't give up gift-giving. I'd just change the form of the gift. There was no question what my family really needed: a world without war, racism, poverty and oppression.

Well, I couldn't pull that off with $100, but I could divide the money up among organizations which I felt were moving us in the direction of a non-violent, cooperative world. I sent checks to three groups.

In the spring of 1973 Bob, and a small band of friends, organized Alternatives and set these goals:

1. To help organizations working for justice, peace and the environment to improve their financial situation through a new source of revenue.
2. To motivate individuals and families to reduce or eliminate their consumer purchases for celebrations and to donate that money to people- and earth-oriented projects.
3. To encourage people to develop a celebrational lifestyle which is more simple, less consumption oriented and more supportive of justice and peace.
4. To get people to purchase the products, usually handcrafts, of cooperatives and community-controlled companies run by Chicanos, American Indians, Blacks, Eskimos, Appalachians and others; to get people to purchase Third World craft items imported by such groups as SERV (Sales Exchange for Refugee Rehabilitation Vocations).

Alternatives produced the *Alternate Christmas Catalogue* that year as the key tool in implementing its goals. That first 60-page catalogue was both a resource on alternative celebrations and a presentation of organizations working for justice, peace and a better environment. People were encouraged to live and celebrate in such a way that new funds could be diverted to these and other organizations. Testimony to the hunger for such a resource as this was seen in the fact that by April 1974 19,000 of the original 20,000 catalogues printed had been purchased.

Enlarged to 128 pages with the ideas that poured in response to the first *Catalogue*, the second edition, *The Alternate Catalogue*, made its appearance in the summer of 1974. Over 46,000 copies of this edition were sold before a yet larger edition with new ideas on many different celebrations and responsible living appeared. By the time the 4th edition appeared in 1978, as the *Alternative Celebrations Catalogue*, more than 100,000 *Catalogues* were in circulation. It is impossible to tell how many persons changed their living and celebrating patterns, or how much money was diverted to other causes, as a result of the *Catalogues*. It is clear, however, that Alternatives touched a nerve in a significant minority of people in this country, people who are, indeed, looking for a better way.

Why Celebrations? ★Celebrations are the ritualized interruptions in the continuum of daily life which remind us of who we are, where we came from and where we are going. Our need and desire to celebrate are powerful drives. Celebrations should be vehicles for nurturing the human spirit. Too often they become a stable of indentured servants for commercial interests. If it were not that the drive to celebrate were so strong, celebrations would not be so attractive to exploit for profit.

Celebrations are important points of beginning changes in the way we live

because it is often in those celebrations we are reminded of the conflict between those values we hold most dear and those current in our society. Nowhere is the crass materialism of our culture and its seductive appeal more visible than in the use of religious symbols and sounds to persuade us to buy at Christmas. In the prostitution of our most sacred holidays we are able to see with greater clarity the values that really govern our society and our lives.

As we celebrate, so do we live. The ways we celebrate are more than symbols of the ways we live: they are of its very essence. Spending $17 to $18 billion to celebrate Christmas is more than symbolic. Spending over $1 billion for Easter finery and half that for Easter candy is more than symbolic. Such spending represents a collective disregard for the world's poor and a disrespect for the earth, whose scarce resources make such overconsumption possible and whose environment will be polluted by the waste this creates.

If the drive to celebrate can be channeled into activities that truly nourish the human spirit, express our solidarity with all of earth's people, and respect the environment, celebrations can be a powerful means to change the ways we live generally.

Alternative Christmas Campaigns ★ In order to reach persons beyond those who had the catalogues, Alternatives began national Alternative Christmas Campaigns. Beginning in 1979, an annual "Best and Worst Christmas Gift Contest" was started to focus the attention of the public at large on the abuses and creative possibilities in our Christmas celebrations. This discordant note in the mass media during the Christmas season has proved immensely popular, testimony both to the high levels of frustration experienced at that season as well as to the increase of persons discovering alternative ways to celebrate.

1980 saw Alternatives embark on a special Christmas Campaign for congregations. Under the theme, "Whose Birthday Is It, Anyway?" resources were provided to congregations who wanted to change their celebration patterns and call their members to change theirs. Almost 3,000 congregations responded the first year and more in 1981. Churches are responding positively to the question, "If it is not the Church's business to call for responsible Christmas celebrations, whose business is it?"

Beyond Celebrations ★ Even in the first catalogue the aim was to change the whole of our lives. In each succeeding edition attention was given to responsible living beyond celebrations. That's how Alternatives got into the mail-order book service. After the publication of the first edition, people began to write asking for additional resources on lifestyle. At first, five or six titles were offered. This service has continued to grow so that by 1982 over 100 books, games and audio-visuals on lifestyle-related concerns are offered to those interested. In addition to titles from other publishers, Alternatives itself publishes a curriculum for study groups, a filmstrip on alternative celebrations, alternative celebrations planning calendars, packets, bulletin inserts for special holidays, a quarterly newsletter on responsible living and celebrating, and other resources.

Beyond providing up-to-date reliable lifestyle materials, Alternatives offers consultation on Responsible Living and Celebrating Workshops. Opportunities to explore perspectives and possibilities in personal, family and institutional lifestyles can be offered in workshops.

The Best of The Catalogues ★ At the initiative of the editors of The Pilgrim Press, we started a process to select the best resource materials in each of the four editions of the catalogues and combine them in this one volume. The result is a comprehensive collection of resources for alternative celebrations of all the major holidays and rites of passage, as well as resources for responsible living personally, in families and in the community at large. The concluding essay looks at some of the emerging issues for responsible living in the last two decades of this century. While we must assume responsibility for its final form, this volume would not have been possible without the efforts of Bob Kochtitzky and the Alternatives staffs who produced the earlier catalogues.

What is not included in this volume are the "ads" of the organizations working on justice, peace and environmental issues which were an integral part of the earlier editions. For earlier catalogues, lists of currently available resources from Alternatives, information about the Celebrations Campaigns, consultation on workshops, or other concerns, readers are encouraged to write us at:

ALTERNATIVES
P.O. Box 1707
Forest Park, GA 30051

Milo Shannon-Thornberry

2.

LA MERE

Births

For years I have been conditioned to feel the necessity of sending a gift whenever friends have a baby. I have recently found that there are ways of showing your love and joy without sending a blanket or silver spoon or cup—many of which never get used. I first learned about alternate "baby gift" ideas from Nancy Gilbert, who sends checks to UNICEF or similar organizations which help children. Recently we have started sharing our "retired" baby clothes with close friends when they have a child. Naturally this alternative soon runs out.

Perhaps the old cigars and candy habit is no longer practiced. If it is, wouldn't it be much more life-supporting, especially if your baby is healthy, to send $10 to the Easter Seal Society, the Cerebral Palsy Association or the local school for retarded children?

One very successful idea was to give an "alternate baby shower," at which the mother-to-be received promises of help, time, meals for her family, a poem, and so on.
Paul and Marie Grosso   Washington, D.C.

On the occasion of the birth of our daughter, our congregation wanted to give us a shower to mark her birth. I agreed on the condition that the guests bring children's or baby's clothing to be given to Church World Services in Sarah's name. Everyone had a great time, and left the party feeling a closer tie with the less fortunate of the world.
Connie Hansen   Malden, Massachusetts

We sent the money given to our new child to support a nonprofit day care center which serves the local community. We notified our friends as to where the money would be going, and asked them to let us know if they preferred another channel for their gift.
Mrs. Paul Rothfusz   Atlantic, Iowa

Think about the idea of godparents "adopting" a child overseas on the occasion of their godchild's baptism. There are many organizations that will accept monthly contributions to support a needy child overseas.
Rev. Susan Thistlethwarte   Durham, North Carolina

Rites of Passage

Rites of passage are those celebrations marking changes in individual and family life.

The word on alternate celebrating seems to have spread internationally, as these Birth Announcements from Holland and the US show!

Pauli and Pim have a son: Pepijn. He was born on January 19th in the Saint Catherine Hospital in Eindhoven where he will stay with his mother for another week. Our Pepijn will not lack anything. However, many children lack even the most necessary things. UNICEF tries to do something about this. Please help them. The children of Asia, Africa, and South America will be happy with your gift.

The birth of a child is a joyous event. It is also a time of reflection. As we prepare to provide for our new baby, we are reminded that one of the greatest gifts for our children would be a better world in which to live. Therefore, if you plan to send the baby a gift, we hope instead that you would consider a contribution to UNICEF, or some other organization dedicated to easing the problems of hunger, fear, and the ever-increasing ravages of war. We hope that because of the birth of our child, life for others may be a little better.

Birthdays

There's a movement under way to take the icing off birthday cakes, the prizes out of children's games and drastically reduce the number of presents received.

Unpopular as this sounds, it is an effort to dematerialize that ultra-personal holiday, the birthday, and return to its deep personal significance.

In many religious traditions throughout the world a birthday is a time of prayers and blessings as well as one of feasting and gifts. But the American child's birthday party, in recent years, has taken on a strong commercial flavor, often involving bigger productions each year, hired entertainers, and catered food. Even in modest circles, the American birthday party tends to bring out a child's greediest and most acquisitive nature.

That's just the opposite of the day's original significance. A birthday properly celebrated should renew life, surround the celebrant with life-supporting influences, highlight his or her uniqueness, and symbolically insure for him or her a good year to come.

The need to celebrate birthdays dates back to ancient times. Historically, birthday celebrations have involved feasting and gift-giving, often including cakes with lighted candles, games, singing and dancing.

It appears we have strayed too far from the original significance of birthdays: the unique life of one person and how that can be surrounded with love and support.

Birthday party games often foster competitiveness and violence. For instance, a group of five-year-olds with balloons tied to their legs, viciously kicked each other trying to break the other fellow's balloon, the object of the game. Another example was a treasure hunt "game" where children knocked each other down to find hidden prizes. Although the mother meant well, she had set in motion circumstances which actually encouraged the violation of the unique worth of each child as part of the group.

Nearly anyone with a child can recite similar horrors. No one seems to have a very good time at the traditional American child's birthday party. Waiting and anticipation is unbearable for birthday children, dressing up and remaining clean is a struggle. Since they are overexcited, they may forget any good manners they have learned, grabbing the gift and ignoring the giver. The

getting and opening of the gifts is the thrill and the contents don't interest them much. In fact, the contents are tossed aside, scattered, sometimes lost before the day is over.

When my first child was five I gave my first and last party of the traditional sort. I introduced a few games and prizes. My overexcited child insisted on being first in every game and winning all the prizes. I found myself threatening to send the honored one to his room before the party was half over. I resolved never to have competitive games and prizes at a children's party again.

But ceremonies and games are important to birthdays. They are a symbolic wiping out of the past and a starting anew. Trials of strength and skill measure the growing child's progress. Even that old favorite birthday game, Pin the Tail on the Donkey, is symbolic. Beginning the game with a blindfold on is like beginning the new year, not knowing if one will be successful. At the end of the game, as at the end of the year, you can see how close you have come to the mark or goal.

In *A Manual on Nonviolence and Children,* published by the Society of Friends Committee on Nonviolence and Children ($5.00 from Alternatives Bookstore), the subject of children's games is taken up in the chapter entitled "For the Fun of It." Games are described and listed in such categories as "Games that Encourage Laughter" and "Cooperative Games."

The introduction points out that "elimination games are really only 'fun' for the coordinated and fast players...that means that the majority of people are not playing for most of the game while the 'better players' are competing for the prize."

The Friends' Committee, feeling competition

among children has been overemphasized, has focused on games that foster a spirit of cooperation. "We have tried to weed out any games that leave people out, force children to compete against each other or participate unequally. With these 'no win' games, we hope to create a kind of environment where everyone can work and play together without winning or losing being a criterion for success."

So how do you plan an alternative birthday party? In previous Catalogues suggestions included asking guests not to bring gifts, taking children on an outing such as a camping trip, museum, circus, or ball game. Try handmade gifts, "recirculate" toys, books, and sports equipment in good condition. Starting with these alternatives at an early age is easier than a transition after peer pressure has made the celebrant rigid.

If your child is going to a party where gifts will be given, discuss with him or her sending a check to a charity which helps children and let him or her write a note explaining that this is a family tradition.

If you decide to buy a gift, consider seeds, a terrarium, plants or a book which says something about life, cooperation or the gifts of different cultures. Write a letter, a poem, a song, make a banner, promise your child a block of time once a week, give "coupons" for future favors.

Ask party guests to bring one of their own toys or books, gift-wrapped, then have a drawing and everyone gets one gift. Have the birthday child plan and make favors and decorations for his or her own party.

Take a beady-eyed look at birthday party food. If your meals don't normally run to hot dogs and chocolate icing, why cave in because it is a birthday? Cakes can be made with honey and whole wheat pastry flour. Whipped cream can substitute for icing. Ice cream is available made with honey only. Hot dogs can be found without additives. Or natural peanut butter can be substituted. Raisins, peanuts, and popcorn can take the place of candy, and unsweetened fruit juice in place of soda.

Children are direct and will ask you why you don't have "regular" food. Tell them you used to have "regular" food until you discovered this food makes everyone stronger, slimmer, and more beautiful. Don't say healthy and good for you.

Our family prefers outings for birthday celebrations. Memorable ones that come to mind include a camping trip for nine-year-olds, an eight-year-old's sight-seeing trip to New York shortly after we moved there, a trip to a children's game show for three seven-year-olds (our son got to watch himself on TV a couple of weeks later); all-day trips to the beach; dinner at a good restaurant where the waiters sing "Happy Birthday."

The very best birthday party we ever had was in honor of our daughter's seventh birthday. I gave her the choice of an outing with one or two of her friends or a backyard barbecue with anyone she liked. She chose the barbecue and invited her family, a few friends her own age, several neighbors including adults, and at least two infants. In addition, she asked if she could invite the young man who taught her swimming class at the local pool.

I felt sure she would be disappointed but that charming young man accepted her invitation, appeared at the party, ate a hamburger, and gave her his second-best lifeguard whistle as an absolutely memorable gift for a seven-year-old.

We made hand-cranked ice cream and had bowls of soap suds for blowing bubbles. There were no games. The children ate and ran about and watched the stars come out. Everyone enjoyed it.

Carolyn K. Willett   is a free-lance writer and poet in Larchmont, New York

For our daughter's fifth birthday, we struggled with the traditional party where kids bring presents to a girl who already has enough. So we sent a note to the families asking that they not buy a gift, but that the children create their own thing as a gift of themselves to Tracy. The response was great. All the children made "creations"—painted rocks, pictures, artificial flowers out of pipe-cleaners potted together in an English Leather bottle cap, etc. And our daughter greatly appreciated and enjoyed receiving a part of her friends that way instead of through a commercial gift. The parents liked it, too! We have taken the idea a step further for this Christmas and have suggested to our family relations that we use our talents and create rather than buy something for each other.

Jan and Ed Spence   Aztec, New Mexico

My siblings and I and now our children have what we consider our "birthright" (rite)—our favorite menu and being released from our daily chores for that one very special day. When my sisters and brother and I were growing up (30s and 40s) my parents would never have dreamed of indulging us in an orgy of parties and presents. Even if they could have afforded it, they would have felt it wasn't good for us. But our special menu for the day was really special. Whatever we wanted (within reason, of course) we could order for breakfast, lunch, and supper....And being released from chores made us feel like a king or queen. With my own children we've continued this custom and they love it. Also, the book *Happy Birthday to You*, by Dr. Seuss, is great for young children on their birthday....Another thing I've done with my children is to buy each one a nice book on their birthday, and over the years they've accumulated a pretty good library.

Mrs. Charles Jackson   Madison, New Jersey

Our daughter will take a gift to present to her class (something everyone can use and enjoy) in honor of her birthday rather than bring in a candy treat. If everyone did this individually or the class got together and decided something they could get for their room or the school they could contribute something plus cut out the sweets.

Jeann Schaller   Midland, Michigan

Our house is a commune, a collective, an extended family of 12 folks and as you would expect, one of the main sources of celebration is each other's birthday. They take various forms, some very much planned, some not, but all having the same creative caring as well as casual informality. They usually focus on particular aspects or interests of the person.

When a drama instructor recently had her birthday, we put on a scene from one of her favorite plays. The scene was exaggerated, and hilarious adaptations alluding to special events in her life were added. When a pancake and strawberry fanatic had his birthday, you know what we had for dinner. When the founder of our house had his birthday, we covered the dining table with a roll of shelving paper and each person drew a representation (symbolic or otherwise) of some special event that took place between them.

Some of our favorite birthday gifts include: a concert for Dad's birthday (I arranged a song so that each of the children could play an instrument, then we practiced it and performed it for my husband for his birthday), a promise to the children for lessons in riding, gymnastics, etc. My brother-in-law, my husband and myself "share" a birthday card. It's about 5 years old now, and we are able to send it back and forth because our birthdays alternate.

Frances M. Hraster   Wheaton, Maryland

We hold "Mystery Night" for each other or for other couples on birthdays. They are asked to reserve a particular evening on or around their birthday, with only a suggestion of how to dress for the evening. We make plans to do something unusual—always a surprise!

Paul and Linda Hartman   La Mesa, California

We recently celebrated my father's 80th birthday and invited many of his friends. One of the guests played the piano, and all sang songs, most of which were 70 or 80 years old. The older people there were encouraged to tell tales of their lives as we all sat in a big circle. Our 11-year-old daughter gave a gift to her grandfather which was to learn to play "Happy Birthday" on her flute and then to play it at the party. Our 8-year-old made his grandfather a crown and a birthday flag. I wrote my father a poem which covered events in his life and the feelings that I have for him.

Katie Barker   Lake Oswego, Oregon

To eliminate wrapping paper and create a personalized gift wrapper use large scraps of cloth cut into proper shape or sew smaller pieces together. Make these gift cloths for each member of the family and use them over and over again. Some of the history of the person could be recorded on the cloth by embroidering birthday and holiday events like "First Bicycle," etc.

BIRTHDAY PARTY FOODS

A child usually wants the "in" thing to eat at a birthday party. Party food in vogue with young people includes sweet gooey cakes, coke, and candy—all causes of tooth decay. However, there are alternatives. Take a stand. Serve a nutritious cake that's made without chemical additives and an excessive amount of sugar. Serve nuts, raisins, and popcorn instead of sugar-laden candy. Serve lemonade, apple juice or ice water instead of coke.

The change from chemical-ridden screaming yellow zonkers might be slow at first. Talk it over with the children, or the birthday child. Be assured that you are giving yourself and the birthday child a lasting gift of good nutrition, good health, and good eating habits.

To avoid heavy sugar icings, you can simply sprinkle a little confectioner's sugar through a sieve and shake over the top of the cake. One alternative is whipped heavy cream, but a more interesting variation is creme fraiche. Start by mixing one teaspoon of buttermilk with one cup heavy cream in a jar and sealing it with wax paper or plastic wrap. Thickening will occur at room temperature—between 60 and 85 degrees. On a hot day, the cream will turn in a few hours. In cold weather, it takes longer, as much as two days. Then, put your precious jar in the refrigerator where it will keep for several days and be useful with many desserts.

A child's birthday is always special and years after he or she will often remember the menu of a particular party. The wise parent makes the menu nutritionally sound as well as memorable.

WHOLE WHEAT NUT WAFFLES

2 cups whole wheat flour
2 tsp. baking powder
½ tsp. salt
3 eggs
1½ cups milk
¼ cup melted shortening
½ cup chopped walnuts

1. Mix the flour with the baking powder and salt.
2. Beat the egg yolks and add the milk and shortening. Add to the flour mixture and mix until all flour is moistened. Add the nut meats.
3. Fold in the stiffly beaten egg whites.
4. Bake in a hot waffle iron and serve with melted butter and topping.

Suggested Toppings

HONEY BUTTER

½ lb. soft butter
3 Tbsp. honey

Mix honey and butter together until well blended. Pack in a crock or jar and chill.

ORANGE BUTTER TOPPING

½ cup soft butter
1 cup honey
6 Tbsp. (½ of 6-ounce can) frozen orange juice concentrate thawed, undiluted

Beat honey, 2 Tbsp. at a time, into butter until thoroughly blended. Gradually beat in undiluted orange juice concentrate. To reuse, soften at room temperature and beat to re-blend into uniform texture.

BREAKFAST SYRUP

½ cup molasses
½ cup honey
½ tsp. vanilla
pinch of salt

Mix ingredients. (Chopped pecans or walnuts may also be added.)

Waffles would also be a birthday treat with whipped cream and fruit on top or a mixture of heavy cream and sour cream with assorted fruits (perhaps strawberries or blueberries in season or canned pineapple at other times of the year).

GREAT SPECKLED PANCAKES

1 cup unbleached white flour
½ cup whole wheat flour
½ cup cornmeal
4 tsp. baking powder
1 Tbsp. raw or brown sugar
   (optional)
½ tsp. nutmeg
½ cup nonfat dry milk solids
2 eggs, lightly beaten
¼ cup oil or melted butter
1–2 cups water

1. Sift the unbleached white flour, whole wheat flour, cornmeal, baking powder, nutmeg, sugar, and milk solids together into a bowl. Tip the coarse remains in sifter into the bowl.
2. Using a rotary beater, beat in the eggs, oil, and enough water to make a creamy batter that pours. Thicker batter will give thick, puffy pancakes; a thinner batter, thinner crisper pancakes.
3. Pour batter onto a hot, oiled griddle and cook until browned; turn and brown the second side.

MOLASSES AND ORANGE WAFFLE SAUCE

½ cup unsulphured molasses
¼ cup brown sugar
⅓ cup orange juice
¼ cup butter
1 tsp. grated orange rind

Combine all the ingredients in a small saucepan and heat, stirring until mixture is smooth and well blended. Serve warm over waffles.

These easy cake recipes can replace packaged birthday cakes.

BANANA CAKE

1 ¼ cups unbleached flour
1 cup sugar
½ tsp. salt
1 tsp. baking soda
½ cup margarine
¼ cup wheat germ
3 small ripe bananas (1 cup puree)
2 eggs

1. Mix dry ingredients in bowl.
2. Put margarine, bananas, and eggs in blender and blend smooth.
3. Add pureed ingredients to dry ingredients and mix only until moistened.
4. Spoon into lightly oiled 9-inch square pan and bake in preheated oven at 350 degrees for five minutes; loosen edges, turn out to cool right side up.

GINGERBREAD RAISIN CAKE

⅔ cup sugar
⅔ cup molasses
⅔ cup boiling water
2 Tbsp. butter
1 tsp. baking soda
½ cup raisins, washed and dried
½ cup chopped walnuts or pecans
1 egg well beaten
1½ cups flour, unbleached
1 tsp. cinnamon
1 tsp. ginger
¼ tsp. cloves

1. Preheat oven to 350 degrees.
2. Mix together the sugar, molasses, boiling water, and butter in large bowl. While the mixture is hot, stir in the soda. Cool.
3. Add the raisins, nuts, and egg.
4. Sift the flour, cinnamon, ginger, and cloves together. Stir into the molasses mixture.
5. Bake in 9-inch square pan for 35-40 minutes.

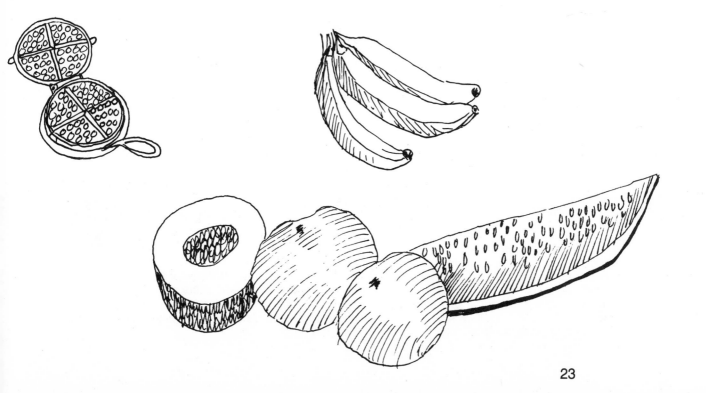

Bar/Bat Mitzvah

Jewish celebrations, older in tradition than any other religion in America except the rites of the American Indians, suffer the same commercialism the gentile world is plagued with. Our research turned up an aggressive movement within Judaism toward celebration simplicity, and it refreshed our souls. We touched spirits with outraged rabbis and offer here some of their alternatives.

Concerned with the materialistic abuses resulting from the "catered synagogue," Rabbi Lawrence Kushner, Congregation Beth El, Sudbury, Massachusetts, wrote:

[the caterers] … are not bad people. It's just that they are businessmen whose business success depends upon their ability to convince us that we need what they sell, when in most cases we do not.

While we, on the other hand, trustingly allow some of the most sacred events in our lives to be determined by those businessmen so skilled at twisting our modest goals to expensive necessities. They often benignly exploit our native insecurity that we are still low-class peddlers at heart in need of a high-class collaborator to tell us how to entertain.

All too often they capitalize on our parental love which must say, "For my kid, do it just right" and convince us to spend hundreds and even thousands of dollars on invitations, plastic flowers, monogrammed paper napkins, engraved matchbooks, decorated mints, souvenir yarmulkes, and a seemingly endless array of garbage. Thanks to their business skill and our social gullibility, moments of what should be holy family celebrations are transformed into affluent suburban versions of the potlatch ceremony, an old Northwestern Indian ceremony in which families in a tribe, having become fabulously wealthy due to unprecedented demand for animal furs, would have a contest to see who could destroy the most wealth and thereby gain higher social status.

I think our congregation should offer to assist families in phrasing truly individualized invitations in Hebrew and English (if they want them at all) and arrange for an ongoing relationship with a local printer to further reduce costs. I think our congregation should organize its own catering service. Let any kiddush or luncheon held in the Temple be catered by members themselves. Since the most expensive part of anything catered is the help, and since every family who had a Bar/Bat Mitzvah during the year would promise to help out at two others, the result could be every bit as nice, twice as cheap, and infinitely more communal.

We found that caterers will not give prices over the phone. Florists were freer with information. For an average party with 100 guests, centerpieces for 10 tables would cost $200. Some celebrations have 500 guests and the flowers cost $900.

The Bar/Bat Mitzvah is perhaps the most commercialized Jewish celebration next to the wedding. The words translate "son/daughter of commandments" and the rite was originally conceived as deeply religious in purpose, content and in ceremony. The boys experience Bar Mitzvah at age 13 plus one day, the girls at age 12 plus one day. The young person recites or chants prayers and Bible readings as the first public demonstration of his/her new role as a full member of the congregation.

It is a traditional family gathering and there is a get-together after the ceremony. An old Jewish tradition is to give food or a donation to the poor on the occasion of your child's Bar/Bat Mitzvah.

Here is a description of a Bar Mitzvah which took place in the eastern U.S.:

Luncheon for 100 guests, dinner for 143 guests in synagogue hall. Food catered. Bill for food— $2800. Florist bill—$300. Invitations—$200. Music—$525. Total cost including side expenses and several costly gifts to son—$6200! The mother who gave us this information admitted *the motivation was the father's ego!*

Rabbi Albert Axelrad at Brandeis University believes that "Bar Mitzvah ceremonies as we know them at age 13 are ridiculously premature" and would be far more meaningful at an older age. His concern has produced what he calls a "Belated Bar/Bat Mitzvah." He described one held for a Brandeis senior as a part of the Sabbath morning *havurah*. Thirty friends joined in the singing, *davening*, and Torah reading and the young man's *derasha* (preaching) on the convenant highlighted the event. The *Kiddush* was catered by his friends.

Art Waskow of the Fabrangen Community in Washington, D.C., told us of a very creative joint Bar/Bat Mitzvah which took place in a kibbutz in Israel. During the 13th year the boys and girls engage in 13 creative projects (field trips, directing plays, writing poems). The years-long process of creativity instead of a crash event symbolizes the rite of passage into responsible adulthood. Previous to this year the father is responsible for the child's deeds. After it, the teenager takes responsibility.

Other alternatives include designing and making invitations at home; serving homemade food or sharing the task with the congregation; having joint services with other families to share expenses and joy; creating decorations at home; using puzzles, games, and rented movies for entertainment.

A growing number of rabbis have set limitations on weddings and Bar/Bat Mitzvahs for the sake of simplicity and religious integrity. Rabbi Axelrad favors Jews making contributions to worthy causes in honor of observances, events, honors, and celebrants. Included are Hillel, the day school movement, Breira and the Jewish Peace Fellowship, PIPA (Peace between Israel, Palestinians, and Arab States). He also favors tree-planting as a fitting alternative, either in Israel via Jewish National Fund or Southeast Asia via Trees and Life for Vietnam in Washington, D.C.

Alternative Weddings

Before inflation really began punishing every American, including fathers of brides, *Business Week* advised that "an elegant wedding for 250 runs $10,000 to $15,000." The breakdown is also mind-boggling. "Your biggest expense," the article says, "will be the catering. For the full treatment—hors d'oeuvres, beef dinner, cocktails, champagne, wedding cake and gratuities—count on $40 per person…Flowers can easily run another $1000 … allow at least $500 for the photographer… Invitations are $25 to $50 per 100 these days…"

And while the parents are nervously totalling up the cost of such "necessities," what about the young couple? They, too, are being besieged by venders who "know" what every bride and groom must have. The pitch begins as soon as the word "wedding" is even whispered aloud. Perhaps it begins even earlier. There is a devilish board game now on the market. "The Bride's Game," it teaches girls, aged 8 to 14, that they cannot "reach" their goal—The Wedding—without ring, gown, cake, flowers, presents, etc.

Marketing people in the industry speak of "bride-generated" purchases. To understand what that means, you need only pick up a copy of one of the bridal magazines. There are page after page of ads for china, crystal, and silver—to say nothing of vacuum cleaners, luggage, electric cookware, photographers, tuxedos, and bridal gowns. The travel industry doesn't drag its feet, either. In one recent issue I counted more than fifty ads for honeymoon hideaways—with slogans such as "Days You'll Always Remember"… "Pure Joy" and on and on *ad nauseum.*

It is no wonder then that these magazines can confidently estimate that the average first-time bride begins her married life with 120 major new purchases; that she will spend some $3500 to furnish her first home. The bride, like her father, has been subtly persuaded that all these things

are necessary if she is to be happy.

The merchants do not stop with the father-of-the-bride and the newlywed couple. Their lures are out for the hapless wedding guest, too. Marcia Seligson points out that Americans spend $200 million on wedding gifts every year. The entire wedding ritual—including, in some cases, the ceremony itself—is dictated by the industries that fill their coffers by encouraging such "traditions" as engagement parties, showers, gift registries, lavish honeymoons, and Complete Homes. The American wedding has, in short, become a rip-off.

The sad part of the business—and that is a most appropriate word—is the essential emptiness of the whole show.

Perhaps the most poignant words on the subject come—unwittingly—from a recently married Ohio couple. Groom: "I took out a loan for $4000 to cover our honeymoon … But I wanted us to have a good start. We'll be paying bills for the rest of our lives anyway so what's one more?" Bride: "When I looked at myself in the mirror before I left for church, I thought, "This is it. From now on it's making beds and washing dishes." Stacey, as I'll call her, spent more than $400 for her gown and veil, much more than she could afford, but, "It's only once in your lifetime and it's worth it."

This couple, like many thousands of others who will be married this year, has been conned. They've been told over and over again that to enjoy the happiest day in your life you must "spend, spend, spend." And they've come to believe what they've heard.

Isn't it time to start fighting back, to wrest control of this most important event from the jeweler, the baker, the florist, and the social director? Isn't it time to return the wedding day to the bridal couple, their families and friends?

Happily, some young couples are striking out on their own and have put together alternative kinds of weddings where ritual and tradition are not abandoned but pomp and circumstance are.

Many young couples have already celebrated alternative weddings; many others, however, are just beginning to plan and need practical suggestions. What follows, then, is a compendium of alternatives, a variety of more personal, life-supporting, noncommercial ways to celebrate marriage. Use whatever suggestions you wish; adapt them; let them lead you somewhere else. Be free.

BEFORE THE WEDDING

Engagement. The engagement period is historically one in which the couple has time to prepare for the marriage—getting to know one another and their families; gathering together belongings for the household; being advised about the joys and responsibilities of marriage by their elders. Ideally, it is a period in which they discuss in depth the shape they expect their lives to take, the priorities they each have and the goals they agree to work for. But too often it is occupied by preparation for the wedding ceremony rather than for the marriage itself. To help the couple explore their future together, many churches require that they engage in a series of conferences with a member of the clergy. Some couples have taken family life education courses together, in which they discuss lifestyles, the pros and cons of children, etc. Couples in the Oregon area, and in other states as well, have profited from Engaged Encounter, a weekend designed primarily for couples being married in the Catholic Church, in which they are guided toward private dialogue with each other on all aspects of their married life— their strengths and weaknesses, desires, ambitions, goals, attitudes about money, sex, children, family, their role in the church and society. For information, write Engaged Encounter, 1330 Corum, Eugene, OR 97401.

Engagement Ring. According to Howard Kirschenbaum and Rockwell Stensrud, authors of *The Wedding Book: Alternative Ways to Celebrate Marriages,* the custom of giving an engagement ring was probably handed down from a time when marriages were arranged (as they still are in some parts of the world) and a groom made a down payment on the agreement by giving land, livestock or other valuable items. It's certainly not necessary, and many couples have found alternatives that more nearly state their own commitment to marriage—a regular time they agree to share each week in working for an individual or organization of their choice, a tree or garden they can plant and tend together, making a living gift of the investment that would have gone into the engagement ring. They find out what the weekly payment would be, for instance, and use that amount to entertain friends one week or to donate to a worthwhile cause the next.

If a ring is really important to you, however, there are alternatives to the diamond most people buy for the sake of tradition, investment, or status. Family rings may be exchanged, or lovely rings can be found at auctions and antique jewelry stores. Also, local craftsmen may help you plan a ring or other piece of engagement jewelry that makes a very personal statement and at the same time supports a friend rather than an impersonal business.

Parties, Showers. The first round of pre-wedding buying and spending often begins with showers to supply the bride with household needs—and

luxuries. They can create an unnecessary financial burden for friends and relatives, who are also expected to "shell out" for a wedding gift, as well as leave the bride with several items she can't use.

A shower can provide necessities for the couple who is young and without resources. However, many of today's couples are marrying later and have had their own households—or shared them— prior to marriage. If friends want to celebrate a coming marriage, there are ways to do it and to provide thoughtful necessities without emptying the pocketbook.

"Theme" showers have always been popular, with guests asked to bring items for a kitchen, a bathroom, or any other selected area. Instead of giving gifts, why not give ideas? Recipes, information, and hints can be cleverly packaged and shared. Or you might shower your friends with IOUs which can be collected at a specified time. A catered dinner or picnic would be fun, or an IOU for homemade breads, soups, preserves, or garden foods.

One *Catalogue* reader, Anne Doerfert McGoey of Taos, New Mexico, shared the following alternative with us:

"When the women (in my home church of Aztec, New Mexico) said they wanted to give me a shower I was apprehensive...imagining all sorts of electric frying pans, electric can openers, electric blankets, etc. So I wrote...expressing my concern about exploitation of natural resources and (saying) I would prefer it if items which were used but still good could be given as gifts—as a form of recycling. I also included a list of items we needed, such as wooden clothes-drying racks, garden tools, trash cans.

"...We didn't receive anything that was useless or wasteful, but we did receive practically everything on the list. The most wonderful part was that nearly everything was stuff people had had tucked away in closets for years and no longer used, or the gifts were handmade by the women.

"Also, none of the gifts were wrapped. Instead they were arranged cleverly around the room. It was a lot of fun just to see how the women had used their imagination—the gifts themselves were the decorations.

"...There were women of all ages at the shower. However, it seemed that the oldest women were the ones who showed the most enthusiasm.

"...Most important...a new channel of communication evolved between myself and the women who came to the shower. From the love generated during that very special wedding shower, they stepped partly into my world, and I into theirs again ... there has been some constructive communication, and I have learned much."

Invitations. Today we rarely see the traditional wedding invitation, which is impersonal, stating most clearly the expense the bride's family has gone to in choosing it. It is also ecologically unsound, with its excess of tissue paper and inserted envelopes.

Many couples still use printed invitations, but new processes making duplication easy and relatively inexpensive have broadened their choice. Any number of things may be pasted on paper (recycled, if possible) and printed, with excellent results. Printers will often help you decide on

This Is My Beloved

And

This Is My Friend

—*Song of Solomon 5:16*

Because you are special,

we would appreciate the joy of your presence

at our

Worship Service celebrating Holy Christian Marriage

on Saturday, July 26, 1975, at 2:00 p.m. at

Central Park Presbyterian Church,

1700 B Avenue NE Cedar Rapids, Iowa.

Reception will immediately follow at the church.

Bonnie Kay Myhre   Bruce Douglas Williams

While realizing the frequent tradition of gifts following a wedding announcement, we request —given the problem of world hunger at this time—that you consider the option of alternate giving with funds going to CROP, The Community Hunger Appeal of Church World Service, c/o The Reverend J. Joseph Trower, P.O. Box 1073, Jefferson City, Missouri 65101. Thank you.

typesetting, script, or layout. You might use works of art—silk-screen, lithograph, photographs, even potato stamps or woodcuts, if you'd rather do it yourself but have few artistic talents. Handwritten notes are another way of extending personal greetings to the friends with whom you want to share the beginning of your marriage. The message can be anything from a simple "Y'all come!" to an original essay or a favorite poem that expresses what your wedding means to you.

Individual invitations aren't necessary, of course, if there are other ways of communicating with your friends. Some couples have used commercial or handmade posters, announcements in church bulletins or company newsletters explaining that no invitations are being sent but that all are welcome. Others have made lists of guests and divided them among friends who agreed to telephone and extend a personal invitation. One couple who used the phone method reported that their wedding was much friendlier than it otherwise would have been—their circle of loved ones was wide, but few knew others in the circle, and the telephone conversation had paved the way for several new friendships.

Whatever invitation you choose, be sure and give your guests an idea of appropriate gifts and attire. The more information they have the more comfortable they will be and the more festive your celebration.

THE WEDDING DAY

Like any other event, a wedding must be carefully planned or it may turn into a catastrophe for everyone concerned. The most informal event needs some planning, even if the two of you are the only ones present. And the more people you expect to participate, the more help you'll need in preparing for them. You might find a member of the clergy who is interested in out-of-the-ordinary weddings, or a friend who has helped others plan theirs. There are even a few alternative bridal consultants, who charge small fees for planning simple celebrations. Whomever you turn to, take the time several weeks ahead of time to sit down and talk it through. Then you'll all be able to relax and enjoy it.

Place. Wedding ceremonies and receptions can be held just about anywhere from a great hall to a barnyard, provided arrangements are thought out and made well in advance. Think about a place that has special meaning for both of you to share with friends and family. If a major support of your marriage will be participation in a church family, then the church building may be an appropriate place to begin. If you share a love for camping or nature walks, then a garden or park may be fitting. Or if the sea beckons you, then a boat may be your answer. Or a beach at sunrise. Wherever you choose, contact the owner or manager and find out what kind of arrangements you have to make. At public facilities, for instance, you often have to arrange for a law officer to divert traffic. And, if you pick a spot that's off the beaten path, make sure your guests know how to get there, that it's as convenient for a crowd as it is for two, and that your crowd won't damage the environment.

Dress. Many brides—or perhaps more accurately many brides' mothers—wouldn't feel they were married without the traditional bridal dress and veil. It seems to be one of the biggest money wasters around—buying an expensive outfit that can be worn for only one occasion in a lifetime. Many couples are choosing alternatives, either because they think other ways of spending the money they have is more beneficial to them or because they feel any money spent for things they don't need should instead be given to people to obtain things they do need. Some, of course, use grandmother's, mother's or friend's dress—just as brides have done for years for sentimental reasons. Others buy next-to-new dresses at a fraction of their original price in local shops which buy up worn-only-once garments and resell them, either for profit or for charity. Still others find the classified ads include at least one "wedding dress" for sale almost any day.

No rule says long bridal dresses are essential. Choosing something you're comfortable in, something that reflects your personality, is what's most important. Handmade dresses have long been popular, and many brides are choosing styles and materials they can wear after their marriages. Others are choosing ethnic costumes—either reflections of their own cultural roots, or costumes that will emphasize their unity with peoples throughout the world. Other parts of the wedding are internationalized, as well, with an explanation to guests of what each means. If you expect your marriage to emphasize understanding and acceptance of other cultures, this may be an exciting way to share your beliefs with your friends. Couples can also "come casual" and wear jeans or other informal attire—if, for instance, they want to make a strong statement that it doesn't matter what one wears but how one acts toward one's fellow human beings. But if you plan to deviate from what your friends would expect, you should explain to them what you're doing and why, so they can be more comfortable about making their own choices.

What holds true for the bride holds true for the groom and any other members of the wedding party. The men don't have to wear matched tuxedos; in fact, they don't even have to wear suits. Nor do the brides' attendants have to wear matching dresses. Ask yourself what's most important to you. If you like creating a pretty picture, then you'll probably want some blend of styles and color tones. If you want attention directed to the ceremony rather than the costumes, you won't choose outfits that will shock your guests. On the other hand, you won't choose breathtaking beauties by Priscilla of Boston. You'll choose clothes that make you comfortable, that make you feel radiant and festive, that can be used more than once, that make a personal statement about your lifestyle.

Decorations. It's possible to have a wedding without decorations, but just as a lifestyle of voluntary simplicity would be drab without celebrations, so celebrations would be drab without decorations. The environment sets the mood for the occasion, and the more festive the decorations the more festive the celebration. What kind of mood do you want to share with your guests? A thoughtful one? Then keep your decorations simple—traditional arrangements of greenery done by a friendly florist (and there are those who don't charge an arm and a leg!) or an artistic friend, wildflowers or other natural materials from woods or sea. A gay one? Then use banners, balloons and other party ideas. A reverent one? Then try only candles and the cross, or candles and the *huppah.* (marriage canopy)

The Ceremony. If there are parts of the traditional wedding ceremony that mean little or nothing to you and thoughts you'd like to include that say more about your own marriage, feel free to explore this with the person you choose to perform the service. There may be fewer requirements than you thought. All that is required in the United States for a legal marriage is the signature on a validated marriage license of a member of the clergy, judge, sea captain, or other qualified person. Various requirements are imposed by individual states to obtain a validated marriage license—witnesses to the signing, a blood test, birth certificate, and waiting period being most common. Various denominations also make certain portions of the vows a required part of the service, though one mainline Protestant minister in San Francisco makes it a practice to ask a couple into his office and talk with them about their feelings and plans. If they appear ready for marriage, he informs them at the end of the interview that they are married and, except for civil requirements, they need do no more.

But for most couples who choose a nontraditional wedding, the ceremony is the heart of the matter because it is here that you can express your most cherished thoughts. The

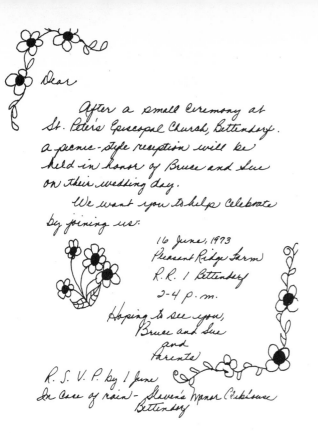

Dear

After a small ceremony at St. Peter's Episcopal Church, Bettendorf, a picnic-style reception will be held in honor of Bruce and Sue on their wedding day.

We want you to help celebrate by joining us:

16 June, 1973
Pleasant Ridge Farm
R.R. 1 Bettendorf
2-4 p.m.

Hoping to see you,
Bruce and Sue
and
Parents

R.S.V.P. by 1 June
In case of rain — Steven's Manor Clubhouse Bettendorf

traditions of some faiths or officials may limit your choices, but most will work with you to make the celebration meaningful for you.

Since the prelude and the processional are the first elements of a traditional ceremony, it makes sense to talk about music first. Its association with weddings dates back to the days when noise was thought to keep the evil spirits away, but whatever the reasons for its use, its effect is to evoke emotion. In other words, it can get people into whatever mood you want to create, which should be reflected in the other elements of the ceremony. If you want a feeling of community, a processional hymn is a good choice. One couple chose to begin with the joyful old Shaker song, "'Tis the Gift to be Simple," as sung *and* danced by talented friends. Other couples prefer the tranquility of classical selections or the informal notes of jazz. And one couple, as they turned from the altar for the recessional, asked their guests to join them in a rousing rendition of "I've Got That Joy, Joy, Joy, Joy Down in My Heart." Church musicians are good people to contact first. Even if they're not eager to discuss possibilities with you, they'll usually direct you to other musicians in the community who will be able to explore new ideas with you. One note of caution: music is marvelous as a part of the ceremony, but too much of it may change the wedding to a concert and overshadow what you want your wedding to say.

Other introductions to the ceremony generally include some explanation of the reason we are gathered together, like the following examples:

Reading by minister:

Julie and Kevin have honored us by inviting us to be with them during this time that will make them husband and wife. They wish to dedicate themselves unto each other pubicly today. The wedding they perform will not join them; only they can do that through an awareness of the spiritual bond which already exists between them; the ceremony is only proclaiming that fact.

It is fitting and appropriate that you, families and friends of Julie and Kevin, be here to witness and participate in their wedding, for the ideals, the understanding, and mutual respect which they bring to their marriage have their roots in the love you have given them.

What Julie and Kevin mean to each other is obvious in their lives but not easily expressed in the language of a ceremony. To convey the sense of what they wish their marriage to mean, they have requested their good friend Marty to read from Kahlil Gibran's *The Prophet.*

> *You were born together, and together you shall be forevermore.*
> *You shall be together when the white wings of death scatter your days.*
> *Ay, you shall be together even in the silent memory of God.*
> *But let there be spaces in your togetherness,*
> *And let the winds of the heavens dance between you.*
> *Love one another, but make not a bond of love;*
> *Let it rather be a moving sea between the shores of your souls.*
> *Fill each other's cup but drink not from one cup.*

The Rite of Dionysus
a festive celebration of Wine & Revelry honoring the Marriage of

Julie & Kevin

*Give one another of your bread but eat not from
    the same loaf.
Sing and dance together and be joyous, but let
    each one of you be alone,
Even as the strings of a lute are alone though
    they quiver with the same music.
Give your hearts, but not into each other's
    keeping.
For only the hand of life can contain your hearts.
And stand together yet not too near together,
For the pillars of the temple stand apart,
And the oak and cypress grow not in each
    other's shadows.*

II

(used in a Jewish/Christian service)

We are gathered together today as family and friends of Earl and Ellen. They have honored us by choosing us to be with them and rejoice with them in making this important commitment, which will make them husband and wife.

The essence of this commitment is the taking of another person in his or her entirety, as lover, companion, and friend. It is therefore a decision which is not made lightly, but rather undertaken with great consideration and respect for both the other person and oneself.

A marriage that lasts is one which is continually developing and one in which both persons grow in their understanding of each other. Deep knowledge of another person is not something that can be achieved in a short time, and real understanding of another's feelings can fully develop only through years of intimacy.

While marriage is the intimate sharing of two lives, it can enhance the differences and individuality of each partner. We must give ourselves in love, but we must not give ourselves away. A good and balanced relationship is one in which neither person is overpowered or absorbed by the other.

We are here today then, to celebrate the love which Earl and Ellen have for each other, and to give recognition to their decision to accept each other totally and permanently. Into this state of marriage these two persons come now to be united.

III

(used in a Protestant/Catholic service
and shared by Rev. Edward J. Wynne Jr.,
Caldwell, New Jersey)

Greeting

Dearly beloved, we are gathered together here in the sight of God, and in the presence of these witnesses, to join together Patrick and Janet in holy matrimony; which is an honorable estate, instituted of God, and signifying unto us the mystical union which exists between Christ and his Church; which holy estate Christ adorned and beautified with his presence in Cana of Galilee. It is therefore not to be entered into unadvisedly, but reverently, discreetly, and in the fear of God. Into

this holy estate Patrick and Janet come now to be joined.

Scripture Lessons

Old Testament Lesson. So God created man in his own image, in the image of God he created him; male and female he created them. And God blessed them. (Genesis 1:27-28)

It is not good that man be alone. (Genesis 2:18)

Therefore a man leaves his father and mother and cleaves to his wife, and they become one flesh. (Genesis 2:24)

New Testament Lesson. I may speak in tongues of men or of angels, but if I am without love, I am a sounding gong or a clanging cymbal. I may have the gift of prophecy, and know every hidden truth; I may have faith enough to remove mountains; but if I have no love, I am nothing. I may dole out all I possess, or even seek glory by self-sacrifice, but if I have no love, I am none the better. Love is patient; love is kind and envies no one. Love is never boastful, nor conceited, nor rude; never selfish, not quick to take offense. Love keeps no score of wrongs; does not gloat over other men's sins, but delights in the truth. There is nothing love cannot face; there is no limit to its faith, its hope, and its endurance. Love will never come to an end. Are there prophets? their work will be over. Are there tongues of ecstasy? they will cease. Is there knowledge? it will vanish away; for our knowledge and our prophecy alike are partial, and the partial vanishes when wholeness comes. When I was a child, my speech, my outlook, and my thoughts were childish. When I grew up, I had finished with childish things. Now we see only puzzling reflections in a mirror, but then we shall see face to face. My knowledge now is partial; then it will be whole, like God's knowledge of me. In a word, there are three things that last forever:

faith, hope, and love; but the greatest of them all is love. (I Corinthians 13—*New English Bible*)

Homily. (Meditation Concerning Marriage adapted from *The Common Ventures of Life* by Elton Trueblood)

Of all the human events, none more easily becomes an occasion for rejoicing than does marriage. Even the dullest person alive can hardly fail to have a sense of wonder as he sees a man and a woman take their places before an altar and pledge their lifelong devotion to each other.

Science and art are efforts to find unity in diversity...but marriage not only discovers unity, but undertakes to create unity. Two lives, belonging to different sexes, and often with widely different biological backgrounds, come together in the sight of God and before their friends to inaugurate something never seen in the world before—their particular union of personalities. They join their destinies in such a manner that sorrow for one will be sorrow for the other, and good fortune for one will be good fortune for the other. Marriage has a mystical quality because it combines the flesh and the spirit in remarkable unity, the closest physical intimacy that is possible. Moreover, the normal expected result of their union will be the coming into the world of new persons, who apart from this union, would never have been granted the possibility of existence. Marriage, then, is a sharing in the entire creative process and a window through which the meaning of human existence shines with unusual brilliance.

A charge to the couple, and sometimes to the congregation, is common. Involving your friends in the ceremony usually makes the occasion meaningful for all of you, as in the following dedication made before the exchange of vows:

A Dedication: (P-Pastor, C-Congregation)

P- This couple comes together out of a community of friends and relatives. They ask our support as they together begin the adventure of married life.

P- We come today to join in marriage————and ————. It is our fondest hope that their separate lives may together explore new dimensions of love.

C- We dedicate ourselves to the continuing task of helping them in all ways possible to build a deep and abiding love.

P- We ask for them the excitement of new discoveries and new creations, that their lives may be an adventure together wherever they may go.

C- We dedicate ourselves to the continuing task of helping them in all ways possible to live the most fully human life.

P- We know that love is not a state of being easily achieved. We ask that————and ————find the courage and the patience to overcome any obstacle to open a profound communication— the very cornerstone of all relationships of love.

C- We dedicate ourselves to the continuing task of helping them in all ways possible to meet the challenge of a marriage pledged to honest struggle, open words, and shared lives.

P- And finally, we recognize that love is not limited nor can it be contained. We ask that the love ————and ————feel for each other reach out beyond themselves—to their family and to the world in which they live.

C- We dedicate ourselves to the continuing task of helping them in all ways possible to let their love so shine that it touches all who know them; and may their lives be lived not only for themselves but for all humanity.

Personalization of vows has become a common practice, even in the most traditional ceremonies. The suggested Lutheran vow, for instance, is open to one stipulation being that the "as long as we live" sentiment remains. The two obvious ground rules for writing original vows are that they be a sincere expression of your feelings for each other and that they be worthy of the occasion. They need not be identical. In fact, if you're taking a standard vow and adding your own touches, why don't you both try making the changes without consulting the other? The vow each of you develops could be the one you use as your promise.

Some vows are quite short, like the examples shown below. Others take the form of a contract specifying the understanding and expectations each partner has about the marriage. Some have included agreements on finances, child-rearing, in-law relations, careers, even provisions for separation—though that seems to insert a defeatist attitude about the marriage from the start. Others have been short, general statements of purpose—often lettered and illustrated by an artist friend—designed to be read and/or signed at the ceremony.

We think of contracts as a modern innovation, but in ancient times the Ketubah, a legal contract, was used in Jewish marriages to set forth in writing the terms of the marriage agreement—thereby protecting the woman by discouraging the man from divorcing her. Today it is still used in Jewish ceremonies, but in most cases it has become wholly symbolic.

Vows

———, I take you as my wife (husband) and equal. I pledge to share my life openly with you, to speak the truth to you in love, I promise to honor and tenderly care for you, to cherish and encourage your own fullfillment as an individual through all the changes of our lives.

(MH-Maid of Honor; BM-Best Man;
  B-Bride; G-Groom)

MH-Love is a growing thing ...

BM-...a growing awareness of the meaning of "otherness." Another self who stands outside your self, whose life is a mystery and a challenge, a vexation and a thing of wonder.

MH-It comes from involvement, and grows in living with a person, sharing with him, and building something with him. It requires energy and imagination.

BM-It is impossible for superiors and inferiors to love, since the superior can only condescend and the inferior only admire. Love means recognition between two equals, not exploiting each other's strengths or weaknesses, but rejoicing in each other's presence.

MH-Love must be a bond and yet not binding, else our freedom is stifled in the name of love, and with our freedom, our humanity is lost.

BM-It is a relationship of greater possibility and greater risk, for the power to create is the power to destroy.

MH-Marriage, then, is not a bond made of words or promises or the clauses of a contract.

BM-For no set of rules or promises can possibly exhaust the demands love may come to make on you.

MH-It is a special spirit or style of life between two people. And if it is there, no possible words will make it more sacred or worthwhile.

BM-If it is not, no special phrases will make it exist. The words are an affirmation of that spirit, not a substitute for it.

MH-Marriage is an affirmation of the possibility and power of forgiveness.

BM-It must have permanence. It should be something to depend on, a rock to anchor against the storm, a place to come home to.

MH-Yet its permanence is not that of a wall which shuts things out or seals something in. It should be free and open to the winds of God.

BM-It is a stage on the road of friendship and love and discovery.

MH-It means opening yourself a little more to the possibilities of another self and life itself.

BM-Finally, it was meant to be a continuing celebration of the gift of life and love. For it is in sharing and in joy that it is fulfilled.

G-I, ———, having full confidence that our abiding faith in each other as human beings will last our life time, take you, ———, to be my wedded wife; I promise to be your loving and faithful husband; in prosperity and in need, in joy and in sorrow, in sickness and in health, and to respect your privileges as an individual as long as we both shall live.

B -I, ———, having full confidence that our abiding faith in each other as human beings will last our life time, take you, ———, to be my wedded husband; I promise to be your loving and faithful wife; in prosperity and in need, in joy and in sorrow, in sickness and in health, and to respect your privileges as an individual as long as we both shall live.

"All that I have I offer you. Wherever you go I will go. What you have to give I gladly receive. I pray God will grant us lifelong faithfulness, and so I take you for my husband (my wife)."

Minister: ———and———, if it is your intention to share with each other your laughter and your tears and all the work and pleasure the years will bring, by your promises bind yourselves now to each other as husband and wife.

The couple faces each other, joins hands and repeats:

I take you (name) to be my (husband/wife) and I promise these things:

I will be faithful to you and honest with you;

I will respect you, trust you, help you, listen to you and care for you.

I will share my life with you in plenty and in want;

I will forgive you as we have been forgiven; and I will try with you better to understand ourselves,the world and God;

so that together we may serve God and others forever.

In one wedding, the following was inserted in the wedding program, and each person present had the opportunity to reaffirm his or her marriage vows:

"I,———, joyfully acknowledge you,———to be my friend and wife/husband. I promise, before God, to try to be honest and to appreciate your honesty...to maintain my individuality, yet share all my growing and feeling with you...to understand, appreciate and respect your growth and your needs...to live up to the values we share, and respect each other for them...to be aware of the world around us and of how it affects our lives and our neighbors' lives...and, above all, to be a person you can trust and depend upon as I do you. These things I have promised to try, but there is one promise I can make with some certainty; that I will love you even more deeply in the years to come than I do today."

The blessing of rings or other symbols of the couple's love and faithfulness, the pronouncement of marriage, and the closing prayer or statement generally conclude the ceremony. But one couple, feeling keenly the breakdown of emotional supports in the society around them, included the role of paraclete in the wording of their ceremony and asked an older friend to fill the role, pledging to offer them advice and support throughout their marriage, either individually or as a couple.

According to Jewish law the giving and accepting of the ring in the presence of witnesses is the most important part of the ceremony, and the marriage is legalized when the groom places the ring on the bride's finger and pronounces the formula, "Behold thou art consecrated unto me with this ring, according to the law of Moses and Israel." But it was the ancient Egyptians who gave us the concept of the ring as symbol of the unending circle of love. Whether you choose to use this symbol or any other, of course, is up to you.

The following are closings you might want to consider:

I

(used in the marriage of Jim Goetsch and Marian Waltz)

The couple exchanges symbols with these words:
This is a symbol of my love and faithfulness.
Minister: As Marian and Jim have declared their love and their convenant before us and before God, let us acknowledge and rejoice in their marriage.
Minister and People: Jim and Marian, we affirm and announce that you are husband and wife, in the name of the Father, and of the Son and of the Holy Spirit. AMEN.

(At this time the minister, couple, and people exchange the greeting of peace. Turn to another person and greet him/her with "Peace be with you" and the person should respond "and with you." Shake or hold hands or embrace.)
Minister: Let us pray and bless God for all the families throughout the world:

Faithful Lord, Father of Love, pour down your grace upon Jim and Marian that they may fulfill the vows they have made this day. Make your

purposes of marriage known to all the families of the world and especially to us who celebrate at this wedding. Enrich husbands and wives, parents and children, more and more with your grace that, strengthening and supporting each other, they may serve those in need and so move the world closer to the fulfillment of your perfect kingdom, where with your Son Jesus Christ, and the Holy Spirit you live and reign, one God throughout the ages.
Minister and People: Our Father in heaven, holy be your name. Your kingdom come, your will be done, on earth as in heaven. Give us this day our daily bread. Forgive us our sins as we forgive those who sin against us. Do not bring us to temptation but deliver us from evil. For the kingdom, the power and the glory are yours now and forever. AMEN.

"What greater thing is there for two human souls, than to feel that they are joined for life—to strengthen each other in all sorrow, to minister to each other in all pain, to be with each other in silent, unspeakable memories at the moment of the last parting."

George Eliot

33

Benediction: (Everyone should light candles)
Minister: The Lord bless you and keep you. The Lord make his face shine on you and be gracious to you. The Lord lift his countenance on you and give you peace.
People: AMEN (All leave with lighted candles down center aisle).

II

The Giving of the Rings:

Receive this ring as a token of love and faithfulness. With this ring I wed you. With my body I honor you. And may God help me become your true husband (wife).

Pronouncement of the Union:

Because_____and_____have desired each other in marriage and have witnessed this before God and our gathering, affirming their acceptance of the responsibilities of such a union, and have pledged their love and faith to each other, sealing their vows in the giving and receiving of rings, I do proclaim that they are husband and wife in the sight of God and man. Let all people here and everywhere recognize and respect this holy union.

And Go Forth Together:

"Go placidly amid the noise and the haste, and remember what peace there may be in silence. As far as possible without surrender be on good terms with all persons. Speak your truth quietly and clearly, and listen to others...; they too have their story. Be yourself. Especially do not feign affection. Neither be cynical about love; for in the face of all aridity and disenchantment, it is as perennial as the grass...nurture strength of spirit to shield you in sudden misfortune. But do not distress yourself with imaginings. Many fears are born of fatigue and loneliness. Beyond a wholesome discipline, be gentle with yourself. You are a child of the universe...the universe is unfolding as it should. Therefore be at peace with God...in the noisy confusion of life, keep peace with your soul." Go in peace. (Anonymous)

Benediction and Circle of Love

III

Place ring on finger and say, "This is my beloved and this is my friend."

Forasmuch as Julie and Kevin have pledged themselves to each other in the presence of this company, sealing their vows with the giving and receiving of rings, I do pronounce that they are husband and wife.

"To live content with small means; to seek elegance rather than luxury and refinement rather than fashion, to be worthy, not respectable and wealthy, not rich."

IV

Minister: In order that the first words of_____ and_____as husband and wife might be those of prayer, would you join with them as we pray together the Lord's Prayer.
All present: Our Father, who art in heaven, hallowed be thy name. Thy kingdom come, thy will be done, on earth as it is in heaven. Give us this day our daily bread. And forgive us our trespasses, as we forgive those who trespass against us. And lead us not into temptation, but deliver us from evil. For thine is the kingdom, and the power, and the glory forever. AMEN.
Minister: May the joy and peace which only God can give, and which cannot be taken away by anything in this world, be yours today and in all of life's tomorrows. AMEN.

Bibliography

Abingdon Marriage Manual. Perry Biddle, Jr. Nashville: Abingdon, 1974. Contains extensive guidelines and suggestions for conducting weddings and making the service more personal, seven contemporary services of various denominations, recommended wedding music, summary of marriage laws in each of the 50 states.

Write Your Own Wedding. Mordecai Brill (Jewish), Marlene Halpin (Catholic), William Genne (Protestant), eds. New York: Association Press, 1973.

The Wedding Book: Alternative Ways to Celebrate Marriage. Howard Kirschenbaum and Rockwell Stensrud. New York: Seabury, 1974.

The New Wedding: Creating Your Own Marriage Ceremony. Khoren Arisian. New York: Random House (Vintage Books), 1973. Humanist orientation.

The Joyful Wedding: New Songs and Ideas for Celebrations. Nick Hodsdon. Nashville: Abingdon, 1973. General Protestant orientations.

The Creative Wedding Handbook. Wendy Somerville Wall. New York: Paulist Press, 1973. Liberal Roman Catholic.

Marriage: An Interfaith Guide for All Couples. Raban Hathorn, William Genne, Mordecai Brill, eds. New York: Association Press, 1970.

The Folklore of Weddings and Marriages. Duncan Emrich. New York: American Heritage Press, 1970.

We Can Have Better Marriages if We Really Want Them. David and Vera Mace. Nashville: Abingdon, 1974.

Together for Life. Joseph Champlin. Notre Dame: Ave Maria Press, 1970.

The Future of Marriage. Jessie Bernard. New York: World Publishing, 1972.

Funerals

Averaging $3,100 each, funerals are the third largest purchase (after a house and car) most Americans make. As a study for the Wharton School of Business concluded, "(we) can think of no parallel case where such a large consumer expenditure is contracted for under such pressures of time, by persons having so little knowledge of the area in which they are dealing, who are not in the fullest possession of their normal judgement." Funerals can be genuine celebrations which express appreciation for the person's life—and for LIFE itself.

Last year we urged people to contribute to health research organizations rather than giving flowers to funerals. Mr. Howard S. Anderson, Director of the Florist Information Committee of the Society of American Florists and Ornamental Horticulturists wrote in protest and it is useful to print part of his letter:

> The implication of these statements ("Stop sending flowers"), demeaning the role and purpose of sympathy flowers at funerals is that the money spent on funeral flowers can be better spent for some other humanitarian purpose.
>
> Florists and funeral directors having long experience with human death and serving bereaved families know that there is *no substitute for flowers* (emphasis added)...to symbolize sentiment, the expression of love, affection, compassion and heartfelt sympathy of people reaching out to communicate their support for a bereaved family....
>
> Flowers are truly the handiwork of God...and without flowers a funeral service is cold, vacuous, and a depressing experience for the bereaved. (People) deeply resent being told not to express their feelings of esteem and respect for the deceased...but rather to donate money intended for flowers to the XYZ fund....
>
> The florists of America fully subscribe to worthy memorials, but not in lieu of flowers at the funeral service. Both serve their useful purpose, and one cannot be substituted for the other.
>
> ...[T]he florists are offended by the article in your magazine that belittles funeral flowers, and fails to present the true and indispensable role of flowers in the funeral service.

Our response to Mr. Anderson's arguments is first to point out that the only thing flowers are indispensable to are the profits of florists. Traditions and social customs change when human need requires it. Translated, Mr. Anderson's argument amounts to this: It's always been done this way and the effect upon the profits of florists would be damaging. Our answer is that florists can make up the difference by selling small living plants for birthdays! And if flowers are needed at funerals to brighten the occasion, then take them out of your yard! Whatever you do, don't be bulldozed into guilt feelings about funeral flowers.

Be bold and stop sending them so you can give the money to help the living.

ALTERNATIVES

Recently, a small but growing interest in funeral reform has proven that dying can be an inexpensive and useful experience for the living. In Washington, D.C., the St. Francis Burial Society published the first issue of its Quarterly. The society provides simple pine boxes and ash containers—assembled or in kit form. Write to 3421 Center Street, N.W., Washington, D.C. 20010. Membership, including four editions of the Quarterly, is $12 for individuals.

Rabbi Ian Wolk of Temple Shalom, 8401 Grubb Rd., Chevy Chase, Maryland 20015, has written a beautiful book entitled *A Guide to Jewish Funeral and Mourning Practices*. The book is a result of years of disaffection with funerals which are ostentatious and deviate from Jewish traditions. Copies may be obtained by mailing a $1 donation to the Temple.

One of our catalogue readers sent in this description of a very beautiful funeral:

> The young daughter (25) of a friend of ours died of cancer. Instead of a funeral they had an open house, pot luck one afternoon between 1-4 P.M. People came together out of love for this girl to talk and share their feelings. They were encouraged to speak to the group about their memories and feelings. Some of her friends were black and a few sang songs she had enjoyed. The ashes of her body were later scattered in a beautiful wooded area in a private ceremony.

Beth Brownfield   Golden Valley, Minnesota

We at Alternatives encourage you to think seriously about making your dying a life-supporting event. Join or start a memorial society. Make plans to give your organs to help the living. Consider cremation as a way to avoid the cost of cemetary, casket and funeral home.

The material which follows is reprinted with kind permission from Ernest Morgan, author of *Manual of Death Education and Simple Burial.* (9th edition, Ernest Morgan. Available from Alternatives.)

ON DEALING WITH GRIEF

In my youth I lost, through cancer, a beloved aunt who had cared for me from infancy (my mother had died when I was a baby). Sadly bereft, I meditated deeply on life and finally decided that the best thing I could do for her was to carry on her life. Not necessarily her habits or her ideas (I didn't always agree with these) but the quality of her life, which was characterized by integrity and a profound human dedication. After that my grief went away.

In the course of time I was appointed chairman of the Burial Committee of our Friends Meeting, where I would have to deal directly with death. I accepted this as a disagreeable chore, but found it to be a profoundly meaningful experience. At last I had grasped the nettle, and was maturing in an important way. Soon I became involved in the memorial society movement, and this too I found rewarding in terms of personal growth.

In my wife's death from cancer I had the privilege of nursing her during her last months. We talked freely of her approaching death, and she remarked to me how much it helped her to have the family accept it. Far from avoiding her, visitors came in a steady stream. She expressed to me the concern that her death might upset the students at the Arthur Morgan School, which she had founded. Accordingly I prepared a talk, to be given to the students, telling of her approaching death and discussing life. After working it over with her to our joint satisfaction I gave the talk and it seemed to serve its purpose well.

Following her death I sought active involvement. I helped lift her body into the box and myself drove the station wagon that took it to our little burial ground. At the grave I helped lower the box, after which I recited a favorite poem of hers, albeit with some difficulty. At the memorial service I spoke for more than an hour telling of her life. This did me a world of good. My own health being shaken by her death, I as quickly as possible arranged a sales trip of several weeks' duration, to give me active involvement with people and with work. My health soon stabilized.

No one can really tell another how to handle grief but sometimes one can, by sharing some of his or her own experiences, help light the path of another.

THE SIGNIFICANCE OF SIMPLE BURIAL

Because death is a universal experience, and because it almost invariably has a profound emotional and social impact on the survivors, the customs and practices associated with it are very important.

To many religious people of all faiths, and secular-minded as well, the preoccupation of a funeral with the dead body represents a misplacing of emphasis, no matter how thoughtful the sermon, how impressive the surroundings or how gracious the funeral director. Further, the competitive social display implicit in a "fine" funeral ("expected of the family because of its position in the community") is itself a negative and unworthy manner in which to signalize death.

A simple procedure, whereby the body is removed promptly and with dignity for immediate cremation or burial, after which one or more memorial gatherings are held, can minimize the negative aspects of death and emphasize the deeper meanings and positive values of the occasion. The economy of simple burial is not the central issue.

All memorial societies and funeral directors agree that each family should be free to choose the type of funeral or memorial service it wants, and which will best fill its needs and express its religious ideals, without pressure from any organization, business, or social group. Such freedom is basic to our way of life.

ABOUT FUNERAL DIRECTORS

The funeral director (don't call him or her an undertaker) has been the object of much unkind criticism because of his or her tendency to encourage ostentatious and extravagant funerals.

There are nearly 2,000,000 deaths each year in the United States. Divide these among 20,000 morticians and you have only two funerals per week. However, the majority of funerals are

36

handled by a tiny fraction of the 20,000 morticians, leaving nearly half the morticians of the country with less than one funeral per week. The situation in Canada is much the same.

A community which is adequately served by one bank, one printshop, and one lumber yard will commonly have several fully equipped mortuaries,

firms provide the desired service. They also assist those who wish to leave their bodies for education or their eyes or other tissues for transplant or therapy.

With the guidance of these societies thousands of families are now being helped to secure dignity, simplicity, and economy in their funerals.

all of them standing idle most of the time. A printer whose plant stands idle even half the time can hardly survive in free competition. His prices will have to be too high. How do the thousands of morticians manage whose plants are idle over 80% of the time?

They manage because they can and do charge the overhead of days or weeks of living expense and idle plant to a single funeral. This is possible because competition does not exist in their business in the same way it does in other businesses.

THE NEED FOR PLANNING

We have, in the United States and Canada, an amazing custom of displaying dead bodies in a costly and elaborate routine. Each year, in response to this custom, nearly two million American families put themselves through an emotional ordeal and spend upwards of two billion dollars doing so.

When death occurs in a family in which there was no planning, the survivors find themselves virtually helpless in the face of entrenched custom, and dealing with a funeral director who expects them to follow this custom. Through planning, however, a family can have the precedent, information, and moral support needed to get the type of service it wants.

To help with advance planning, nonprofit funeral and memorial societies have been formed in some 130 cities in the United States and Canada. These societies cooperate with funeral directors, sometimes by having contracts with them and sometimes by advising their members as to which

ABOUT FUNERAL AND MEMORIAL SERVICES

There are now Memorial Societies in 130 cities in Canada and the U.S., representing some half a million members. The Canadian societies are united in the Memorial Society Association of Canada, 5326 Ada Blvd., Edmonton, Alberta. The U.S. Societies belong to the Continental Association of Funeral and Memorial Societies, 1828 L St., N.W., Washington, D.C. 20036.

The two groups work closely and membership is reciprocal between them.

How Funeral and Memorial Societies Work

Q. What is a memorial society?
A. *A memorial society is a voluntary group of people who have joined together to obtain dignity, simplicity, and economy in funeral arrangements through advance planning.*
Q. Is it run by funeral directors?
A. *No. It is an organization of consumers that helps its members to make dignified funeral arrangements at reasonable cost.*
Q. How is it controlled?
A. *It is a democratic organization managed by an unpaid board of directors elected from its membership.*
Q. Who organizes memorial societies?
A. *Usually they have been started by a church or ministerial association; occasionally by labor, civic, or educational groups; sometimes by a few concerned individuals.*
Q. Is membership limited?
A. *No. Membership is open to all regardless of creed, color, occupation, or nationality, even*

though a society may be organized by a church or other group.

Q. How are memorial societies supported?

A. *Most have single modest membership fees for individual or family memberships. A few have annual dues. Some receive gifts or bequests. Some make a small charge which is remitted to them by the funeral director at time of death.*

Q. Who does the work?

A. *The members. Most societies are run by unpaid officers and committees, some by church staffs. A few larger ones have part or full-time paid secretaries.*

Q. What happens when you join?

A. *The society lets you know what kinds of funeral service are available and at what cost. You talk it over in your family and decide on your preference, then fill out forms provided by the society.*

Q. Can these plans be cancelled or changed?

A. *Certainly. Any time.*

Q. How does preplanning help at time of death?

A. *In several ways:*
1. You know what you want, how to get it and what it will cost. You don't have to choose a casket or negotiate for a funeral.
2. Your family understands what is being done. Simplicity will reflect dignity rather than lack of respect.
3. By accepting in advance the reality of death, and by discussing it frankly, you and your family are better able to meet it when it comes.

Q. Does planning really save money?

A. *The amounts vary greatly, but memorial society members usually save several hundred dollars on a funeral.*

Q. What is the basis of these savings?

A. *Simplicity. A dignified and satisfying funeral need not be costly if you are not trying to demonstrate social status or compete with the neighbors. There is also the element of collective bargaining in your favor and the advantage of knowing where to go to get the desired services at moderate cost.*

Q. How do I join a memorial society?

A. *Write the Continental Association or the Canadian Association to find out if there is a society that serves your area or if one is being formed. If you are interested in helping start a society, the Association will supply information and frequently local contacts as well.*

Q. How can I tell the real thing from the imitation?

A. *In two ways:*
1. Virtually all genuine memorial societies are members of one of the two Associations. The Associations screen their members with care.
2. A bona fide society has no commercial interests. Membership rarely costs over $20. If an organization calling itself a memorial society tries to sell you a cemetery lot, or if it asks a large membership fee, you had better investigate it carefully.

Q. Is there any essential difference between funeral societies and memorial societies?

A. *No. Both types of service are arranged by most societies. In every case, however, the family is encouraged to make the type of arrangements most congenial to its background and religious beliefs.*

Q. Is embalming mandatory?

A. *If the body is to be kept several days for a funeral service, or is to be transported by common carrier, yes. Otherwise embalming serves no useful purpose and except in one or two states is not legally required.*

Q. Why then is embalming usually practiced in this country?

A. *Funeral directors presume that unless otherwise advised, there will be viewing of the body, and a service in its presence, and that embalming and "restoration" are desired. If this is not the case, the funeral director can be instructed to omit embalming.*

Q. What appropriate disposition can be made of a body?

A. *There are three alternatives:*
1. Earth burial was once the simplest and most economical arrangement. With increasing population, rising land values, cost of caskets, vaults, and other items usually required, it is becoming more and more costly.
2. Cremation, a clean orderly method of returning the body to the elements, is economical and is rapidly increasing in use.
3. Bequeathal to a medical school performs a valuable service and saves expense. In many areas there is a shortage of bodies for the proper training of doctors. Many public-spirited people leave their bodies for this purpose. A number of body parts can now be transplanted or otherwise used to promote medical research, restore sight, or save a life. To facilitate the gift of body parts at time of death, a "Uniform Anatomical Gift Act" has recently been passed by most states and provinces. Everyone is encouraged to cooperate.

HOW THE DEAD CAN HELP THE LIVING

There are many ways in which socially concerned people can arrange while they are living to serve the needs of their fellow men and women after they have died. Many lives can be saved, and health and sight can be restored to thousands through the intelligent "salvaging" of organs and tissues from persons who have died. Medical and dental training requires thousands of bodies each year, for anatomical study. Medical research, too, needs our cooperation, in the form of permission for autopsies (not permissible if the body is left to a medical school) and the bequeathal of special parts, such as the earbones of people with hearing difficulties.

If we truly accept our own mortality and genuinely identify ourselves with humanity, we will gladly help in every way we can. These ways are steadily increasing.

Permission for an Autopsy
Such permission should routinely be granted except when the body is destined for a medical school. Autopsy is often very helpful in improving the knowledge and experience of doctors and in some cases is more valuable than bequeathal. Sometimes it directly benefits the family.

Bequeathal of Ear Bones to a Temporal Bone Bank
More than 18 million people in the U.S. alone—three million of them children—suffer partial or total deafness. Since 1960, thanks to the John A. Hartford Foundation and other financial donors, research into the causes and cure of deafness has been greatly accelerated.

Persons with hearing problems are urged to bequeath their inner ear structures for research. A medical history is valuable. (Some normal ear structures, too, are used, for transplant purposes.) The removal is a specialized task and advance arrangements should be made. For more information and for the necessary forms, write: The Deafness Research Foundation, 366 Madison Avenue, New York City 10017, or the National Temporal Bone Banks Center, Baltimore, Maryland 21205.

Bequeathal of Kidneys
Several thousand kidney transplants have been made. Next to eyes and skin they are the most frequently transplanted tissue. A kidney transplanted from a brother or sister has a survival expectation of about 90 percent. The survival chances from an unrelated donor are now 50 to 60 percent. More kidneys are urgently needed. Transplants are coordinated by the National Kidney Foundation, 116 East 27th St., New York City 10010.

Regional Tissue Banks
This is a recent development, typified by the Northern California Transplant Bank, 751 South Bascom Ave., San Jose, California 95128 (408-998-4550; after hours, 408-289-8200). It is a unified regional approach to the problems of procurement processing, storage, and distribution of tissues for transplant. Included in the organization are transplant units concerned with bone, ear, eye, heart, heart valve and artery, renal, and skin. A donor to such an institution can be assured of maximum "recycling." We will appreciate learning of similar institutions.

Pituitary Glands
An estimated 5,000 to 10,000 children in the U.S. are suffering from serious pituitary deficiency. Each of these children needs the hormone extracted from about 300 pituitary glands to maintain normal growth for one year. Only six or

seven hundred children are getting it. An estimated additional 50,000 to 100,000 children have a partial deficiency and would be helped by growth hormones. Pituitary glands should be "harvested" whenever possible. They can be kept frozen, or in acetone, and sent periodically to the National Pituitary Agency, Suite 503-7 210 W. Fayette St., Baltimore, Maryland 21202.

Donor Clearing Houses
The Living Bank, P. O. Box 6725, Houston, Texas 77025 (713-528-2971) is a nonprofit registry which coordinates the disposition of anatomical gifts. It supplies donor cards and records donor data for instant retrieval.

Medic Alert, Turlock, California 95380 (209-632-2371) is also a nonprofit registry. It supplies its members with a necklace emblem or a bracelet if preferred, engraved with personal health data such as blood type, allergies, etc., and also donor information. Data is kept on all members, for instant retrieval, which can save precious time.

The Naval Medical Research Center

The Tissue Bank, Naval Medical Research Institute NNMC, Bethesda, Maryland 20014 (202-295-1121) is reported to be doing an outstanding job and will accept donations of anatomic material, particularly from persons under 35. Ordinarily transportation limits acceptance to donors near Washington, D.C. The bodies must be cremated or buried at the family's expense.

Skin for Dressing and Grafting

For persons suffering from serious burns, skin taken from a person who has just died can be extremely valuable. Such skin commonly constitutes the most desirable kind of dressing, and in some cases can be successfully grafted.

Blood for Tranfusions

In 1971 about 6½ million units of blood were given in America to about 2¼ million patients, resulting in nearly 70,000 cases of hepatitis and 8,000 deaths. These figures come from Dr. J. Garrott Allen, Professor of Surgery at Stanford University Medical Center, and are backed by solid data. Over 90 percent of these cases and the resultant deaths can be traced directly to the use of "commercial" blood, for which the "donor" was paid, rather than blood from volunteers.

Authorities agree that properly selected cadaver blood is desirable, but they differ sharply on the practicality of obtaining it. Having listened to both sides, the writer withholds judgment but strongly urges further study of the possibilities.

Other Rites of Passage

TOOTH RITES

The day that our six-year-old's first tooth came out, we suddenly realized that we either had to go along with the ritual of the "tooth fairy" or invent a new one. Whatever the original purpose of this rite, we felt its present connotation was negative. So we created a new family "rite of passage." When our son came home from school a sheet covered the entrance to the dining room. On it was a drawing of a tooth and the phrase "out with the old, in with the new." At supper, to signify that he had reached a new level of growing up, he was seated in daddy's chair and given a crown inscribed with the words, "The New Man." Before eating, a word was said about the added responsibility of growing up (losing a tooth) and it was suggested that he was now old enough to make up his bed each morning. That night he put his tooth under the pillow expecting 25 cents to be there in the morning. Instead, I wrote a note, "A surprise is coming" and the next day some books I had ordered came in, among them The Selfish Giant.

GRADUATIONS

I had completely forgotten about graduations as a celebration until someone at the Sign of Jonah Gift Shop came up with a great idea. There is a ritual in our society called "the senior trip" which consists of cramming 50 students in a chartered bus, driving to Washington, D.C. (or someplace else), sleeping four to a room in a hotel, eating hamburgers at McDonald's, and visiting scores of buildings, monuments, and statues. As a more creative way to celebrate graduation and prepare a student for what is ahead, it was suggested that parents or grandparents make it possible for the student to attend the Washington Youth Seminars program (1734 P St. NW, Apt. 6, Washington, D.C.). The program deals with how our government works, the vital social issues of our day, and what people can do about them.

Is the wearing of a cap and gown crucial to the graduation ceremony? Certainly it adds to the pomp and ceremony. But think of the creative things which could happen if the money spent on caps and gowns was diverted to help people. A student body of 500, assuming they were each paying $10 to rent the equipment, could generate $5000 as a class gift for local or national projects working on prison reform, drug rehabilitation, racial justice, economic development, or environmental action. Or they could set up a scholarship loan fund for students needing funds to go on to college.

ANNIVERSARIES

Does anyone still use that list of items to give on wedding anniversaries? You know, it begins with paper and concludes with gold on the 50th year of marriage. It would be interesting to know who created that list. Probably some imaginative business person. Remembering your marriage partner on the anniversary date can be very meaningful. But there are better ways than through consumerism. Paint a room, repair a lamp, refinish a piece of furniture, write a poem, cook a favorite recipe. For your parents' anniversary make a gift like the calendar with the grandchildren's pictures on each month.

40

3.

Surviving the Holidays

The Christmas season is a happy and significant one for numbers of people. Quite a few people with whom I talked look forward to the holidays with great anticipation and look back on them with pleasure. A few reacted with surprise when they learned I was writing on *surviving* the holidays. "I never think about *surviving* the holidays," they said, "I just love them!"

But whether or not one likes Christmas, the traditional holiday celebration produces stress in our lives—more decisions, more demands, more excitement, more social activity. Inevitably, the contradictions of our complex society and compelling community pressure to observe Christmas in a particular way produces strains and tensions which have a negative effect on us, both physically and psychologically.

For instance, the Berkeley Mental Health Adult Outpatient Clinic sees more problems among out-patients around the Christmas holidays than at any other time of the year. Depression—brought on by unfulfilled expectations, loneliness, feelings of alienation, despair resulting from family discord. Problems created by the special family closeness we associate with the holidays—increased friction; arguments caused by conflicts in values; disagreements over rituals; disappointments regarding expected behavior; hurt feelings concerning gift exchange.

There are ways, however, that we can reduce the stress of the holiday season. By adapting our holiday style to fit what we're comfortable doing we can avoid being overburdened, protect ourselves from exhaustion and illness, and create a holiday that's more enjoyable for ourselves and others.

Our complaints about the holidays are characteristic of an affluent society. Most of us dislike the high prices, fighting traffic, the annual commercial orgy, and the competitiveness of buyers. The "canned" music on the streets assaults our sensitive ears. Gift exchange has gotten out of hand. The bad taste exhibited in holiday advertising and the covetousness of

Getting Through the Holidays

children and adults take the joy out of living. There never seems to be enough time for preparing and mailing gifts and cards. We resent the details of planning and complain that we cannot look forward to a relaxed holiday because we are weighed down by the duties of "having Christmas" for the children or the relatives.

What I frequently see is the individual (usually a woman) who grew up in a well-heeled family where the mother's role demanded that she bake dozens of fancy cookies, fruitcakes, and gingerbread men; have all the relatives for both Thanksgiving and Christmas dinner; address hundreds of Christmas cards; do most of the shopping and gift wrapping; take part in the Christmas bazaar, contributing handmade gifts carefully spangled with sequins late the night before; attend an annual holiday party or two; and stay in happy spirits with the in-laws, her husband, and children without batting an eyelash. This super-mom follows her mother's example, but with today's incomes, it often leaves the family budget in shambles, with the costs spread out in payments through the year until the next season. There is no record of the number of family quarrels resulting from this issue alone—much less those caused by exhaustion, drinking, differences with the in-laws, exchanged gifts, and deflated expectations.

Super-moms like these usually survive but hide their scars of resentment, migraine headaches, and standing-up nervous breakdowns, at least until all guests have gone. Some wind up sobbing on an analyst's couch. Others let go and have a "screaming mimi." Still others push their exhaustion and bitterness down into their grinding teeth at night or turn up with vague psychosomatic symptoms at the clinic.

It is easy to fall into the "victim" trap and go along with the expectations or demands of others. It is difficult to say "no" and stick by our guns when we feel we are "hurting" others. It is easy to be manipulated into doing something we would rather not do or get into the position of engaging in activities that load us down with responsibilities we come to resent. But while we cannot deny our responsibilities to our families and loved ones, we must realize that we have some responsibilities to ourselves and that we have the freedom to choose which ones will create in us a more joyful holiday spirit.

Some things should be made clear here. I am not suggesting that Christmas be abandoned. But I *am* suggesting that we take a long, realistic look at what we are doing and what it is likely to be doing *for* and *to* us. Neurotic self-concern is not the answer. Rather, part of the key is self-transcendence—finding meaning outside ourselves in the larger family and community.

Also, although the Thanksgiving-Hanukkah-Christmas-New Year season exacts the greatest toll from our American population, trauma is not confined to these holidays. Birthdays, Easter, Valentine's Day, Mother's Day, Father's Day—any time loaded with expectations—have their share of victims.

Holidays are not to blame, however; it's what we do with them. We generally cause *ourselves* the suffering, with the help of commercial advertising and the media.

We cause ourselves trouble mostly by our expectations of ourselves and others. We remember how these holidays used to be celebrated—or worse, we are told by mass media how they are "supposed" to be observed—and we approach them laden with all kinds of plans, demands, and presumptions. Then if we lack the money, time or energy to do all we planned, we blame ourselves or others, and the war is on.

In the past our holidays festivities were fashioned around the extended family. More often than not parents and grandparents, aunts, uncles, and cousins lived within driving distance of each other. Before the onslaught of expansive radio and TV commercialism, less emphasis was placed on "store bought" gifts, and the entire family joined in the making of gifts and ornaments. Before women went to work outside the home, mother and the children had time to make goodies for the special occasions. When our population was less unwieldy, an entire town might join in creating a parade or pageant celebrating a momentous event. There were no cash prizes; just the warm special glow of pride which comes from a job well done and community spirit.

We are no longer living in such times. Our extended family is scattered across the continent or even around the world. Our grandparents are in rest homes instead of in front of our fireplaces. Our mothers are working at outside jobs, with hardly a day off to rest, let alone time for all the old preparations. Our TV sets seduce us to buy all sorts of gifts, from cars and refrigerators to electric saws and vacation cruises. Recent inflation has shrunk even the thrifty, plan-ahead person's savings fund. Fuel shortages make long-distance visits ill advised. Our children are active in groups outside the family which demand our money, our energies, and our time. Divorce and separation leave families divided. The friends we loved have moved to another state or remarried into a different social set. Everyone seems too busy and preoccupied to take the time to get together "like they used to."

Many of us are caught up in impersonal office parties, competitive decorating, pressurized giving to nameless families, collections of money for the boss's gift, anonymous cocktail parties, name-drawing for gifts to unknown fellow employees. This almost always leads to deep feelings of emptiness, despair, loneliness, and alienation. We get depressed and long for the "good old days," but are mesmerized into going along with the crowd. Idealization of the past leads us to nostalgia. We dream of and wish for something in our past which, if we could relive it, wouldn't be the same at all.

Our fluctuating social standards and economic uncertainties place stresses upon us all, making it difficult to arrive at confident, healthy, positive decisions about our lives. But if we want to combat conflict and unhappiness we must develop attitudes and activities which are effective, productive, and emotionally satisfying.

You may decide to change things, or you may not. In any case, giving your celebrations serious thought and talking it over with your family and friends can help keep things in perspective. We all need to develop our individual styles, restructuring the holidays to fit our abilities and interests. If we are comfortable with one particular tradition or way of celebrating, we can keep it. If not, we can forget it, no matter what others say about it—provided, of course, that we do not step on others' rights in the process.

Clarence Rivers, in a beautiful book called *Celebration*, holds: "There must be a close connection between liturgy and life.…From the point of view of psychology, liturgy will fall flat unless it helps man to discover his identity…We must know what we are doing—not merely cerebrally but deep within our being…Our rituals are doomed to failure if followed slavishly."[1]

If we could all disconnect ourselves from our traditions long enough to make choices about our holiday activities, if each of us could rethink our holidays to show who we are, perhaps we could be like the instruments of an orchestra—each different from the other, but playing our part in the score, in key, in harmony, creating together a beautiful composition that glorifies our humanness.

M. Deane Walters   is a free-lance writer in El Cerrito, California

[1]*Clarence J. Rivers, Celebration (New York: Herder and Herder, 1969), p. 5.*

Celebrations belong to the people. They are not natural resources to be strip mined each year for the sake of profit

The Hidden Price Tag

We make a grave error when we think that the only cost of our celebrations is the price tag on the gift. The *actual* cost includes the effect on the environment and our natural resources, taxes, and the human and social cost. How many manufacturers and merchants think about the *actual cost* when they unleash their massive advertising campaigns for Christmas, Mother's/Father's Day, weddings, and other celebrations which are ripe for sales? How many celebrators have considered these costs to society when they perpetuate consumption-oriented celebrations?

"Celebration" is big business! Almost $18 billion in retail sales last November-December were credited to "seasonal variation." Over 50 percent of this figure came from department and variety store sales.

The effect of $18 billion in Christmas/Hanukkah sales on our Earth's resources and the lives of Earth's people is devastating. Irreplaceable resources are exhausted. Think of all the coal and oil tied up in the production and operation of the thousands of nonsensical electric gadgets we buy as "gifts"; or the plastic and metal decorations the Chambers of Commerce erect shortly after Thanksgiving; or the miles of Christmas lights we trail over our buildings and trees. Consider the ravaging effect on land and communities of strip-mining for these energy resources.

The gift items and paraphernalia we purchase also embody work hours of productive effort along with hours of creative energy spent on trying to convince us that we must buy these things. Our labor resources could be better used in more life-supporting and enriching pursuits as housing, health, safety, and the eradication of poverty.

Our grandchildren may never see living jaguars, leopards, fur seals, or crocodiles if we continue to support the market for these skins. The Christmas trees we use for a few weeks and then throw away represent lost wood and timberland. The packaging, wrapping, trim, and cards that accompany our gifts also use up wood pulp and energy. 80 percent of the 300 million tons of annual household garbage we throw away comes from virgin resources and 40 to 50 percent of all municipal waste is paper. (In addition, there are 160 million tons of industrial waste and 2 to 3 billion tons of agricultural and mining wastes per year.)

What price tag can justify the value of the human lives that are lost or destroyed due to the increase in accidents, suicides, psychic strains, and highway holiday carnage that surround our "celebrations"? How do you say "Happy Fourth of July" to a boy who's blown off his hand with a firecracker? Our insurance rates reflect this holiday carnage even if tragedy doesn't strike us personally.

In addition to the cost of wasted resources, we burden ourselves with increased social costs and taxes. The number of broken homes and troubled children could be reduced if more love were expressed in the home. Family love and closeness can't blossom fully when plastic toys and money gifts are all that are exchanged between family members. The unique pleasures of creating, sharing, and self-involvement are lost when a gift is chosen from a store shelf that contains 100 items just like it. The people we love are special to us, yet so often we express this special love by sharing gifts that are mass-produced and not unique. We pay for our consumer orientation (in contrast to people orientation) in the form of the increased social costs of supporting juvenile courts and homes. We also pay for the waste generated by our consumption through increased taxes. The rate of our consumption of material goods is increasing faster than the rate of population growth, so that there is an increasing rate of garbage being generated per person. If taxes aren't raised to meet the increased costs of

45

collecting and disposing of our ever-growing pile of trash, then the costs of removing that trash will have to be at the expense of other municipal services such as schools and parks.

In our celebrations we exploit not only ourselves, but the resources and quality of life of the rest of the world. Limited land and mineral

resources are devoted to export by the Third World countries while their people struggle at, or below, subsistence to feed our insatiable consumption. African resources provide our gifts of exotic furs and diamonds. South American minerals are formed into cars built with planned obsolescence in mind. These same cars and electrical gadgets then

demand the importation of energy resources to keep them operating.

Richard Easterlin, professor of economics at the University of Pennsylvania, surveyed the relation between happiness and income and came to a paradoxical conclusion. In the U.S., the average happiness level in the 1970s was not much different from that of the late 1940s, although average income (adjusted for taxes and inflation) could buy 60 percent more things in 1970. Satisfaction doesn't come from the number of goods we can buy, but from how this number compares to what we think we need. What we think we need depends on our social and cultural impressions and experiences.

Our materialistic orientation has us running on a treadmill, seeking new pleasures and goods to maintain old levels of subjective pleasure. Happiness and human fulfillment are not conceived on Madison Avenue, produced in Detroit, and delivered at your local store.

Although we can't buy happiness, we can give gifts whose effect supports life, conserves the earth, enhances the human spirit. For example: educational toys give pleasure to a child and also enable the child to learn and develop new skills. Giving to nonprofit and social service groups helps not only their functions, but may also allow them to increase their staff, training, and out-reach programs so that job, skills, and new opportunities are opened up for more people. Our usual response to a child's "Trick or Treat" is the empty calories of a sugery treat. Better for Halloween to result

in UNICEF feeding the hungry then your dentist drilling out cavities. One child's nickel diverted from a candy bar to UNICEF has a tiny but positive impact on the world. Imagine the possibilities that our $18 billion worth of holiday retail sales could have if spent in life-supporting celebrations.

Why don't we do it? We've been indoctrinated with the virtues of growth as measured by increased consumption and are led to believe that unemployment results when we don't buy what our labor churns out. Greater demand for people-orientated goods and services would just involve a shift in work power resources. Dislocations would not be severe because the gifts we buy are primarily produced with machines rather than people. Social service groups need people, but usually don't have the funds to pay their wages. Diverting our dollars to these groups helps them hire permanent staff, as opposed to the temporary holiday help of retail stores. Also, the "products" of social service and self-help groups improve the quality of life much more than "plastic" gifts off an assembly line.

It's possible to shed the burdens, stresses and costs we tolerate and impose upon our world by our traditional celebrations. We can affirm life and our love and care for each other and the world with alternative celebrations. We have nothing to lose and a whole world to reclaim. Let us celebrate life!

Kathy Hoffman

The Psychology of Consumption

HOW TO KICK THE HABIT

The neighborhood kids had stumbled onto an ominous situation. Through electronic surveillance with their modernized Dick Tracy spy devices they had overheard revolutionary talk. A small group of people in their own neighborhood actually fomenting a revolution!

On the surface, the "revolutionaries" looked innocent enough, in fact, nothing more than a single family group. But the words picked up by the kids indicated that something far bigger than the little family was going on: words like "refusal to be conned," "quiet resistance," and "lifestyle of protest."

REFUSAL TO BE CONNED

The kids heard this part of a conversation: "You know why I wouldn't buy that magazine? It would have been a vote for it. That's 'cuz our economy assumes that buying reflects taste which reflects rational judgment. See, I didn't want the publishers assuming their magazine itself was getting a vote for being tasteful. But was that thing ever advertised! That's how we get conned all the time into buying stuff we don't need. My refusal to buy was a refusal to be conned."

Conning requires two things: gullibility and deception. An idle or lazy mind allows advertising through continuous bombardment to deaden us to any issue other than possession and accumulation.

Deception is the trick of saying happiness is possessing and accumulating and then redefining everything as marketable to make possible more and more buying and, therefore, "greater happiness." But much of human satisfaction is of a noncommercial nature. Consider such unsellable satisfaction as competently managing a home, gardening organically, walking in the woods, thinking creatively, giving sensitive and sensible advice, conversing with others, and praying to God. Everyone knows that such satisfactions are not included in the Gross National Product (GNP). But not everyone knows that certain miseries are. The GNP actually reflects detractions from human satisfaction, by including expenditures such as those for police protection, pollution control, emergency accident treatment, and methadone maintenance programs. The GNP is not the great quality of life indicator it is cracked up to be!

The goal of deception is to convert all noneconomic satisfactions to economic ones, to sell everything—including natural highs. So being a competent home manager is no longer good enough: replacement value must be computed, to prove worth in terms of dollars. Gardening becomes a small business for the accumulation of more money for the purchase of more possessions. Even self-love is being marketed these days, through a wild variety of programs for self-improvement. It's called the growth industry, and really brings in the money. And then there is the leisure industry...

"Let me say this before rain becomes a utility that they can plan and distribute for money. By 'they' I mean the people who cannot understand that rain is a festival, who do not appreciate its gratuity, who think that what has no price has no value, that what cannot be sold is not real, so that the only way to make something actual is to place it on the market. The time will come when they will sell you even the rain. At the moment it is still free, and I am in it."[1]

QUIET RESISTANCE

"Dad used to say, 'Enough is enough, and too much is plenty.' We decided the same thing this Christmas. All that commercialism was really getting to me, so our quiet resistance to it was right on. Those gifts of time and effort mean a lot more than boughten stuff would have. Like this one."

Eighteen garbage pickups. Would that be four and one half months' worth? No, it could easily be one and one half years' worth! That startles a person who has been deceived into believing that more is better.[2] But consumerism and garbage go together: the more we buy, the more we inevitably throw away. What must be resisted is this excess.

Consumerism involves both necessities and "excessities." *Necessities* are those things that can be equitably shared and that are everyone's right to possess. The way they are produced and sold—production materials and side effects, and marketing techniques and the price—do not deplete resources cause pollution, exploit people, or cause starvation.

Excessities are those things that cannot be equitably shared and that are not everyone's right to possess. They are luxuries. They are the pernicious cause and the cancerous products of misuse of resources, pollution of the environment, manipulation of people, and nondistribution of wealth.

LIFESTYLE OF PROTEST

"Remember that old New England maxim, 'Use it up, wear it out, make it do, or do without'? Why is that so hard? Why are consumer lifestyles so hard to change? I was reading in a book the other day[3] that it is very common for people to impulsively buy new things for short-term certainty (the new shoes fit, even though they may soon be outgrown, be 'out of style,' or actually be worn out). It's that need for certainty, the stability of knowing something for sure, security at any cost. The hooker is they may even have a fear of being supplanted by things—overrun by objects—but their primary meaning in life is in buying even more. Only a lifestyle of protest is going to beat that system."

What needs to be protested is building our lives around *comfort*. Tibor Scitovsky, in *The Joyless Economy*, makes the distinction between comfort and stimulation. "Comforts not only fail, typically, to carry external benefits, many of them generate external nuisances as well. This is certainly true of many of those that substitute mechanical power for human effort, because they often generate noise, chemical air pollution, or both. It is also true of many of the comforts that consist in being free from insects, from garden and house pests, since they, too, worsen the environment, and it is true, too, of those comforts provided by appliances, packaged products, and throwaway but durable (i.e., nonbiodegradable) objects whose containers and carcasses cover our beaches and countryside in ever-increasing density."[4]

Further, in our relentless pursuit of comfort, we save effort only to run the risk of dying of a heart attack, we save time and then waste it, and we save being bothered and in the process waste resources. "Inactivity promotes obesity and directly increases the incidence of heart disease, partly by allowing the heart muscle and arteries to lose their elasticity too soon with age, partly by raising, for any given diet, the serum cholesterol and serum triglyceride levels in the blood—all of which

contribute to the hardening and narrowing of blood vessels and increase the chances of heart disease and coronary attacks."[5] There is something absurd about spending one's day surrounded by power-driven equipment and escalators, riding mowers, and golf carts to help save effort as well as time on every move at work, at home, and at play, and then proceeding on doctor's orders to squander the energy and time saved on jogging around the block or riding an "exercycle" in the bedroom!

"The good life," as we all know, is care-free. "Most of us cannot be bothered to turn the lights out and the radio or TV off when we leave a room…We use food lavishly and throw away remnants rather than save them for later use in another dish or to feed to pets [or to compost]…; we sooner replace than repair our durable belongings… [And look at] the high rate at which we generate garbage"[6] rather than be bothered with recycling.

Stimulation is economic or noneconomic satisfaction that is not based on the economy of effort, of time, nor of care and bother.[7] It is not the comfort of the temporary security provided by accumulation of possessions, but the aliveness and fulfillment provided by the enjoyment of living freely, unencumbered by materialism.

Comfort displaces stimulation when we try everything once or twice, or in three easy lessons if necessary, just so we can avoid the embarassment of not knowing what is happening. We are comfortable, but we lose the sweetness of the fruits of commitment. We also lose out on real stimulation many times when we are actually seeking stimulation: the three main sources of excitement in the United States are watching television, driving for pleasure, and shopping![8] By relentlessly pursuing the hollow novelty of TV watching, spectator sports, and junk foods, we are not even aware of the stimulation we are missing from crafts, participant sports, and sensitively prepared food. We end up care-free and bored from gullibly chasing those fleeting satisfactions of the marketplace, and fatter but not happier despite the bloated *gross* national product.

A lifestyle of protest is (1) a refusal to be hoodwinked by advertising, (2) resistance of excessities in favor of necessities, and (3) protest against comfort in favor of stimulation. Specifically, such a lifestyle has a multitude of possibilities. Some have already been suggested:

1. Use the vote of your purchase wisely.
2. Develop diverse noneconomic satisfactions.
3. Give noncommercial gifts.
4. Buy less.
5. Buy only from those producers who meet high ecological and psychological standards of production and marketing.
6. Refrain from impulse buying to meet a need for certainty.
7. Substitute human effort for mechanical power whenever possible.

8. Replace the bored life of comfort—the carefree "good life," the surface sampling of everything, and the passive pursuit of hollow novelty—with the fulfilled life of stimulation—responsibility, commitment, and participation.

Example:
- Buy what reflects your taste.
- Garden; go on nature hikes; meet informally with others.
- Give gifts of time and effort.
- Have monthly garbage pickups.
- Demand responsible use of resources, nonpolluting side effects, nonmanipulative advertising, and a fair price.
- Use it up, wear it out, make it do, or do without.
- Put the bee outside, don't spray it; carry things in your hands, not in nonbiodegradable containers.
- Protest the economy of effort, of time, and of care and bother; turn off unused lights; use leftovers; compost; repair rather than replace if at all possible; recycle; develop a craft skill; play games; cook creatively.

Arthur Gish, in his chapter "How to Spend Less and Enjoy it More,"[9] gives several more specifics for a lifestyle of protest, as does John Taylor, in his chapter "The Cheerful Revolution."[10] Among Taylor's suggestions are: "Let's blacklist any brand we see advertised more than once in a week, and switch not to a different brand but a different product altogether....Let's take the trouble and expense of searching for natural foods produced naturally—free-range poultry and their eggs, stone-ground wholemeal flour, etc., of which a little does more good. Let's go for quality in other things as well, and make them last even if we have fewer of them. And if something we've liked a lot is broken, let's bear the whole pain of that and not try alleviating it with a quick replacement."[11]

As a final suggestion for a lifestyle of protest, the following *buying guide* might by useful:

I first ask myself what my smallest need is: what is a necessity? I then ask if the satisfaction of that need is dependent upon buying something. If it is not, I satisfy without buying. If it is, I find out the names of several producers of what I need. Then I look into each company's production and marketing methods for comparison with what I consider to be appropriate standards. If I thereby eliminate all but one producer, I buy from the remaining one. If none of the producers meet my standards, I can either make the thing myself (preferably utilizing intermediate technology[12] or by restoring or modifying a "throw-away") or do without.

Want to join that little family's resolution?

Kirk Farnsworth is a professor at Trinity College in Deerfield, Illinois

---

THE PROTEST PRE-TEST

Questions

1. What is my minimal NEED?
2. Is the SATISFACTION of my need dependent upon a marketable product?
3. Who are the PRODUCERS of the product I need?
4. Which producers can I eliminate because of the acceptable LIMITS I have set on their use of resources, production side effects, advertising techniques, and/or price?

Responses

yes   no

1._____

2._____

3._____

1._____

2._____

3._____

Actions

HAVE A NATURAL HIGH
BUY IT.
MAKE IT.
or
DO WITHOUT!

[1]*Thomas Merton*, Raids on the Unspeakable. *New York: New Directions, 1964. p. 9.*

[2]*See (and use!) Doris Janzen Longacre*, More-with-Less Cookbook: Suggestions by Mennonites on How to Eat Better and Consume Less of the World's Limited Resources. *Scottsdale, Pennsylvania: Herald, 1976.*

[3]*Jacques Ellul*, Hope in Time of Abandonment, *New York: Seabury, 1973.*

[4]*Tibor Scitovsky*, The Joyless Economy: An Inquiry into Human Satisfaction and Consumer Dissatisfaction. *New York: Oxford University, 1976. p. 144.*

[5]*Ibid., p. 158.*

[6]*Ibid., p. 171.*

[7]*Ibid.*

[8]*Ibid.*

[9]*Arthur G. Gish*, Beyond the Rat Race. *Scottsdale, Pennsylvania: Herald, 1973.*

[10]*John V. Taylor*, Enough is Enough: A Biblical Call for Moderation in a Consumer-Oriented Society. *Minneapolis: Augsburg, 1975.*

[11]*Ibid., p. 78.*

[12]*See E.F. Schumacher*, Small is Beautiful: Economics as if People Mattered. *New York: Harper & Row, 1973.*

4.

Family Transition:
HALF THE BATTLE

The idea of celebrating an alternate Thanksgiving, birthday, or Christmas, of remembering family and friends with love instead of with wasteful, expensive, here-today-gone-tomorrow gifts seems

Getting Started

very contemporary—an answer perhaps to the problems of an overcrowded, underfed planet. But it is not really new. In 1513 Fra Giovanni was expressing similar sentiments in a Letter to a Friend:

"I salute you. I am your friend and my love for you goes deep. There is nothing I can give you which you have not got; but there is much, very much, that, while I cannot give it, you can take.

"No heaven can come to us unless our hearts find rest in it today. Take Heaven! No peace lies in the future which is not hidden in this present little instance. Take Peace! The gloom of the world is but a shadow. Behind it, yet within our reach, is Joy. Take Joy!...

"And so, at this Christmas time, I greet you. Not quite as the world sends greetings, but with profound esteem and with the prayer that for you, now and forever, the day breaks and the shadows flee away."

For those of us already convinced of the rightness of an alternate Christmas, however, the question often is not Why? but How? None of us finds it easy to resist the lure of the marketplace at this time of year. (And no wonder—every possible attraction from gaily wrapped packages and carols to the scent of evergreens and the ho-ho-ho of Santa has been arrayed against us.) *But it is possible.* Families who have already made the transition are most encouraging. Here are some of their suggestions as well as some of my own; all are based on practical experience.

START EARLY

Last year was our first try at an alternate kind of holiday and we started to talk about it in October. It was none too early. Other families, who plan to make all their gifts, start in the summer when there is still time to stitch, carve, preserve, gather herbs, or whatever.

The Advent Wreath tradition, which is again enjoying a renaissance, focuses attention on the coming of Christ instead of Santa. The lighting of candles—one during each of the four weeks preceding Christmas—is such a beautiful yet simple ceremony that even young children can participate and understand.

DISCUSS

Tell the children what you're thinking, why you'd like to change and ask for their opinions. Expect them to understand and be enthusiastic. But be open to their ideas and honor any of their objections.

One woman, a widow with two children, aged 13 and 14, wrote me, "The thing that convinced them to go along with me and try the alternate Christmas was the fact that it was so ecologically right and, too, because we decided that the money we saved would go to help others less fortunate than ourselves."

Some parents call a special meeting of a family council. The Keip family from Pacific Grove, California, went out to dinner together— "a very special treat for us—to talk about and plan for our Christmas celebration."

When you and the children have agreed, tell grandparents, aunts and uncles, cousins, friends— anyone with whom you normally exchange gifts— so they'll know what to expect, too.

Last year we decided that instead of exchanging lots of expensive presents, we would "adopt" a family in our own country who would not be likely to have any Christmas at all without somebody's help. We sent long letters to our families, telling them what we were going to do and explaining that even though we would not be buying gifts as usual, we still loved them. "As we make our attempt at a new kind of Christmas we want you to know that we will be doing it with all of you very much in our minds and hearts..."

SUBSTITUTE NEW TRADITIONS FOR OLD BUYING HABITS

One family with three boys spent a weekend cross-country skiing. That worked out so well that at Easter they planned a theater trip instead of giving in to the Easter basket ritual. That was not so much of a success, however. The key, they told me, lies in selecting something everybody will enjoy. No mean feat for most families, but perhaps the choosing can in itself become a festive event.

You can make a tradition of the alternative gifts

themselves. At their planning dinner the Keip family discussed "coupon books," tickets "for things we will do for each other." After Christmas I learned from Mrs. Keip that the coupons had been a big success on the day itself and continued to be long afterward. "I think this will become an increasingly important family tradition with us in the Christmases ahead," she wrote.

Our adopted family turned out to be six fatherless children whose mother was gravely ill in the hospital. So we still had to fight the Christmas crowds to buy food and necessary clothing for them. But we tried to turn the chore into a special day and we must have succeeded because we enjoyed it more than any other Christmas shopping we've ever done.

MAKE THE TRANSITION GRADUALLY

The friend in Connecticut, who took her family cross-country skiing, compromised last year by putting a few things under the tree. "They were all lost or broken within 30 days; we're still talking about the skiing. So I think next year we'll just forego presents entirely."

It's part of the commercial mystique that surrounds Christmas that says it must always be a perfect day. Don't be pressured and don't be rigid. Families who have established their alternative traditions say they had to be flexible, willing to change and adapt. If something doesn't work this year, try something else next year. Eventually you'll evolve an alternate Christmas that is truly life-supporting and also truly yours.

When you first begin you may wonder if the idea will work for you at all. Have you really ruined Christmas forever? No, say the families that have persevered. Jane Mall, from Hinsdale, Illinois, wrote me that her family had many doubts last year. "It wasn't until after Christmas that we realized what we had done. It was when we received the thank-you notes. The home-made things were so much appreciated; the idea of an alternate Christmas was new to the recipients and they wanted to know more about it...Then we felt very good about what we'd done and vowed to do the same for other celebrations. It really is worth it! In fact, we can never again go back to the

wasteful, selfish way of celebrating Christmas again."

Last year was our first attempt, too, and I had the same doubts. Our children are still very young, our families loving and openminded even if they do sometimes think we're a little crazy. So change seemed possible—even necessary—at this time in our lives. But for us, too, the insights and rewards didn't come until after Christmas. For me personally there was a feeling of freedom, of having truly enjoyed a day that had always been marred by last-minute trips for that elusive perfect gift. And then there was the enthusiasm of others. One teenage nephew sent us money he'd earned to buy "something" for our adopted family. A cousin sent a donation to a favorite charity in our name.

We still don't know how our future Christmases will turn out, but we'll never go back to our old buying habits to celebrate it.

Carole G. Rogers

One Family's Program for Change

My children used to complain to me that they were the only ones in the school lunch room who had sandwiches made of whole wheat bread. I understood their concern to be like their peers, and I didn't want them to feel like "oddballs" or outcasts. Yet, sometimes it surprised me that they are not *more* different than their friends because I know that my values and my perspective of the world are quite different from that of my neighbors. Then I realized that my values were not yet those of my children. Perhaps you have noticed a similar gap in your family. Why is that? How can we change it?

I have two sets of values which conflict. On one hand I value good nutrition, elimination of heedless consumption, and life in harmony with the earth and its people. On the other hand, I value the freedom of children to choose and to make mistakes. I value their autonomy. I do not believe that we have the right to impose our values. In fact, while my way may be right. I find that I'm not very effective when I endeavor to impose my value system. It usually backfires and they work long and hard at rejecting my values!

If we wish to give our children their right to individuality and yet wish to live out our own values with the hope that they will someday adopt these same values for their own, we have to deal with the question: "How can we most effectively influence the values of our children?"

I have found that my values will be accepted by my children only when the atmosphere in our home is conducive to teaching and learning—only when there is an atmosphere of trust and respect for the children's individuality.

In Paul Tournier's book, *The Meaning of Gifts*,[1] he cautions us to avoid projecting our own taste into our gifts. "It is hard," he acknowledges, "to accept the fact that our children's taste may be altogether different from ours, but," he says

The true meaning of love is understanding the other, attempting to know him and to recognize him…even if he be one's own child…as a person…The child needs to feel that his own particular identity is respected; otherwise, either he will withdraw and become a stranger to his own parents or else he will cease to recognize his personal tastes and will remain a dependent child.

To unilaterally choose gifts which reflect only our values or to unilaterally eliminate gifts because we believe them wasteful and unnecessary is to lack the very values of respect and consideration for others which we are endeavoring to teach.

TRUST AND RESPECT

Listening, and letting our children know that we hear them, has been the first step in our home in establishing an environment of trust and respect. Listening to them when they complain about lunch or when they plead for the latest toy advertised on TV, we need to hear their claims, their needs, their feelings, their frustrations, their wants, and their joys. It is only within an open and respecting relationship that our values can be taught and "caught."

DISCLOSING OURSELVES

Next to listening, however, the next most important component in building a respecting relationship is the giving of ourselves. We must speak up, too, and disclose our feelings, wants, needs, joys, frustrations. We must tell them how we feel about using white Wonder Bread—and why. We must tell them if we feel cheated when we buy cheap plastic toys which break soon after opened. We must tell them if we feel concern for a poor worker in Asia or Mexico who has worked long difficult hours so that we can enjoy an inexpensive consumer item. We must tell them if we do not have enough money to buy all the things on their lists because there are other priorities where we wish to put our money—like food, clothing, and charitable contributions.

We have found that what's crucial in the teaching/learning that takes place when we disclose ourselves is *when* we choose to share ourselves. To lecture about the poor Asian women in direct response to their eager request for a gadget or toy means to them that we have not listened, and they certainly do not hear our story about the low-paid Asian worker. (Do you remember how much empathy you acquired for the poor starving Chinese children when you were little and your parents lectured to you about their needs while you sat alone in tears staring at your peas after everyone had left the dinner table?) At such a time we are wasting our breath; we probably induce hostility rather than a feeling of concern and sympathy.

DISCUSSION STARTERS

Our family has made use of "no problem" times, when tempers are even and tummies are full, to address ourselves to value-laden topics, particularly our materialistic lifestyle and our commercialized celebrations.

One of the teaching strategies we have used at the dinner table is called "Unfinished Sentences." On 3 x 5 cards I write a "sentence stub" which each person at the table must complete. Some that we've used are:

The best thing that happened to me today was…
The nicest thing about Christmas is …
What I remember most about last Easter is …
My best friend is …
The thing that worries me the most is …
Birthdays mean …

Another strategy we use to provoke discussion is "Fantasy." Some of the Fantasy situations we've proposed are:

- If you won the $1 million lottery, what would you do with the money?
- If you could live any place in the world except where you live, where would you want to live?
- If you could spend a day with anyone except a family member, whom would you choose?
- If you could not spend any money at Christmas time, what kind of gifts could you give?
- If you had all the toys and clothes you could possibly want, what then would you want for your birthday?

Another strategy we use involves "Ranking"—prioritizing our needs and wants and desires:

List in order the five things you want most to happen at Christmas.

Which of these would be the worst for you?
- to have to go to church on Christmas eve
- to do without new toys on Christmas
- to make Christmas gifts instead of buying them

What is the most important thing about Christmas?
- remembering Jesus's birthday
- giving and receiving gifts
- family and friends getting together

What would be the most meaningful wedding gift?
- a silver place setting
- a tuition gift for a marriage enrichment course
- a live plant to symbolize the life and growth in a relationship

The strategies are intended to give family members a structured opportunity to share their view and to discuss the topic. If each person's view can be heard and discussed nonjudgmentally, then there is also a lot of relationship building as family members get to talk about themselves and as we become more intimately acquainted with each other.

By using a variety of value clarification strategies such as those in *Helping Your Children Learn Right From Wrong*[2] we have accustomed the children to talk openly about value-laden topics. Then when it comes to holidays and celebrations it is not so strange to discuss the values inherent in our styles of celebration.

While there exists a gap between our values and those of our children there are, in the words of Sidney Simon, two things children need before there is a possibility of their changing their values: (1) nourishment, (2) alternatives.

Nourishment is what we are providing when we listen to and relate to our children as well as when we provide them with nourishing meals. The emotional nourishment comes about as we build a relationship—as we care about one another, listen, and share. The alternatives comes as we disclose where we're coming from, as we discuss different ways of doing things, as we read the *Alternative Celebrations Catalogue* together, and as we try alternative ways of celebrating.

ALTERNATIVES

At Halloween we have tried to adapt the traditional candy giveaway in a variety of ways. Instead of candy, we have baked nutritional goodies and handed out raisins, nuts, apples, and homemade popcorn. We have talked about UNICEF and tried to focus on Halloween as a time to give to and collect for UNICEF. The Gerhards of Walla Walla, Washington, inspired us; they pass out a copy of this note:

Dear Trick-or-treater:
We are giving 5 cents to UNICEF for every child who comes trick-or-treating at our home. Because you have come other children around the world will receive a gift of food and medicine to help them have the joys of life which you have. Thank you for coming to our home and helping us to help other children like yourself all around the world.

Another alternative was suggested by a friend in Eden, New York. She was disgusted with the tradition of the birthday child handing out candy to classmates, so she arranged with the teacher to give, instead, a *real* celebration. She invited a guitarist to visit the classroom and lead the children in singing. Following the singing each child was given a donut carefully set on a circle of cardboard. In the middle of each was a birthday candle. Following the singing of "Happy Birthday" and the eating of the "cake" the children were able to appreciate the picture on the cardboard circle. My friend had covered the circles with wrapping paper decorated with butterflies. To carry out the butterfly theme 25 butterflies were drawn on a large sheet of shelf paper. Each child was invited to write his or her name in one of the butterflies as a birthday wish. The mural has hung for the duration of the day and then taken home by the birthday child as a permanent memento of the class's good wishes.

At Eastertime we have sought alternatives to the needless chocolates in the Easter basket. The solution has been gradually to cut down in number and ultimately eliminate the candy by replacement with other items which focus more on the meaning of Easter. One year it was a large button-pin with a picture of bunnies and the phrase "Love is the answer." Another year it was a 69¢ ARCH book entitled *Kiri and the First Easter*[3] purchased at the local religious supply store. Another year it was a poster that read "Sharing is Caring."

Our Christmas celebration changes began by adding things more meaningful and eliminating that which was least threatening to do without. As we could talk more about the meaning of Christmas and the effect of our consumption-oriented celebration we were able gradually to substitute homemade gifts. One of the early nonthreatening changes we made was a shift from the use of Christmas wrapping paper to the use of the colored weekend comic page of the newspaper for wrapping. The change made sense to our children because they had been involved weekly in recycling newspapers as well as old school papers and mail. They had observed all year the piles of wasted paper and recalled our saying many times that it takes 17 trees to make a ton of paper.

House decorations were also an area where early changes were made. We ceased buying the expensive plastic commercial items and instead surrounded ourselves with homemade decorations and those which reminded us of the religious meaning of Christmas. The cutback on gifts was accompanied by discussions about our family budget and priorities and the addition of an Alternative Gift Certificate to all of our relatives and to our own family. The presence of such a certificate under our own tree gave our children an opportunity to discuss which life-supporting group they would like to see receive our gift. The shock of less toys and things under the tree was reduced by inviting family and friends for Christmas dinner at our house on Christmas day. It made the Christmas day very busy, but the hustle and bustle was centered on preparing for company instead of the hurried tearing open of boxes. An after-Christmas trip also involved us in the joy of reuniting with friends rather than our children counting their presents and comparing their "loot" with that of their neighbor friends. By now they are becoming accustomed to nonmaterial gifts. Last Christmas we designed and mimeographed this certificate for use by others in our church:

To_____
name
This Certificate entitles the above named bearer to receive
_____
_____
from me with warm Christmas Greetings.
_____
Signed

I heard that the gifts given by way of the certificate ranged from everything from backrubs to promises to cook or clean!

On our last wedding anniversary our daughter, in great need to give us something, went to the garage, sawed a piece of scrap wood, added two clay sculptured faces, and "engraved" the plaque with gold paint to read "The Great Parents' AWARD." We like to think that her creativity was a result of our introducing alternatives throughout the year to the traditional "buy-a-gift" syndrome.

We like to think that what we believe and what we do has an effect on the lives of our children. If we can relate to our children in a trusting and respectful manner and provide them with alternative ways to view the world and relate to it through our celebrations, our children will be open to our values. It is even possible that they will one day apply these same values more vigorously and with more commitment than we now have the courage to. Perhaps they will ultimately lead us!

Carolyn C. Shadle   is an education consultant in
Eden, New York

[1]Paul Tournier, The Meaning of Gifts (Richmond, Virginia: John Knox Press, 1963), p. 18.
[2]Sidney B. Simon and Sally Wendkos Olds, Helping Your Child Learn Right From Wrong (New York: Simon and Schuster, 1976).
[3]Carol Greene, Kiri and the First Easter (St. Louis, Missouri: Concordia Publishing House, 1972).

Women and Celebrations: The Fable of Maybe-Maybe Land

This story takes place in Maybe-Maybe Land. (It couldn't have happened in Never-Never Land, as you will see.) Maybe-Maybe Land is made up of ordinary folks who try to enjoy life as much as possible because life is good. And because they love each other and enjoy life, they have lots of occasions for celebrating. These celebrations are a very important part of the fabric of life for the Maybe-Maybe Landers. The celebrations are often quite gay and frolicsome, not frivolous, but essential to the balance of life. There is something they all have in common. All seem to call for lots of fine food, dressing up, and above all, lots of gift-giving.

There is just one thing amiss in the lives of these happy people. Although these celebrations are very important to everyone, and all share in the celebration, the women must do all the work! And after the parties are over, they must clean up the mess.

But perhaps the worst problem for the women of Maybe-Maybe Land is their culture and its influence on them. You see, Maybe-Maybe Land culture is afflicted with something known as the "Supermom Syndrome." "Supermoms" are good wives and mothers, beautiful and well dressed, even when scrubbing floors or cleaning up after birthday parties. They never become cross or short of bouncing energy. Kitchen floors always shine like mirrors, and even while putting on spectacular celebrations single-handedly, "Supermom" keeps up with the prophylactic qualities of toothpaste, mouthwash, and laundry detergent.

How did the "Supermom Syndrome" become a part of Maybe-Maybe Land culture? Some of it certainly filtered down from the ancestors who

worshipped hard work and independent effort. But there is something else. Maybe-Maybe Landers' homes all have little moving-picture sets telling stories about families *supposedly* just like their own—all with "Supermoms." To make things worse, companies pay to make the stories possible, and broadcast their own "mini-stories" to sell products to mothers and children.

Now the women in our stories are intelligent, and know the stories are not true. But they still are influenced by the "Supermom" image that is pushed upon them. They often feel frustrated because they cannot keep up with the image that surrounds them. They want their families to be happy and well cared for, and they really want every holiday and celebration to be a special occasion. They keep trying, but the harder they work, the more separated they become from their families at those important moments for loving and sharing. Their frustrations make them feel cheated and "guilty" because they can't enjoy the festivities.

But that isn't the end of the story. It's just the beginning. One day the women of Maybe-Maybe Land got fed up with the "Supermom Syndrome." (You remember they are all very intelligent—so it stands to reason that they would not put up with the nonsense forever!) And better still, their husbands and children got fed up with the exploitation too. Being bright, creative people, they got together to change the situation.

Some wanted to throw out celebrations altogether, feeling women could handle things if there weren't extra burdens. Their view was not popular. Others wanted to rotate all jobs concerning family living and celebrating. But this sometimes became very complicated.

After much thought and discussion, the Maybe-Maybe Landers realized that it was all right to want celebrations to be special occasions. What had

been wrong was their assumption that you had to be a "Supermom" for it to happen. With family sharing, they could all help Mom, and have more fun to boot!

They had come up with an idea for alternative celebrations and there was no stopping them! The possibilities were fantastic! They noticed that "community" and "whole family" celebrations discouraged competitive cooking and decorating. They also discovered that they saved a great deal of money, and were more creative and original as they shared the joy of making gifts and sharing chores and ideas. They also found that their religious celebrations became more meaningful, and they felt much closer to God and their neighbors.

In a nutshell, they discovered through their alternative celebrations that in truly authentic and joyful celebrating, the preparations and the occasion itself cannot really be separated! When everyone shared equally in the planning, preparation and "work" of celebrating—just as they had always shared in the fun—there was no way to distinguish between the preparation and the fun!

Eugenia Smith-Durland   is involved in peace and prison projects in Philadelphia, Pennsylvania

Celebrations in Extended and Blended Families

How do you make significant progress toward changed and less consumptive celebrations in the extended family, or in the extra parties in a blended family? ("Extended" = nuclear family plus grandparents, aunts, etc. "Blended" = combined families with stepparents and stepchildren.) Many of the letters we receive at Alternatives refer to the difficulties of dealing with extended-family members who do not share the same concerns about celebrations and may feel rejected as old traditions are laid aside.

On a recent Phil Donahue show which focused on the problems of blended families, one stepparent said that if celebrations could be done away with, many problems relating to her stepchildren would be solved. With thirty-five million children living in blended families in the U.S. today, there is no way to avoid the issue.

Celebrations are not always steps to reaffirming and strengthening ties in the extended family. Conflicts about how to spend limited time, whose traditions to follow—in addition to the issue of quite new patterns of celebration—are commonplace, but not easy, issues with which to deal. Making this more complicated are blended families in which children's time must be shared between former spouses, and perhaps four sets of grandparents. Tension between former spouses, and often differing values, can make celebrations times of extreme anxiety.

There are no easy answers! It does little good to rail out at the high divorce rate, or the fragmentation of the nuclear family. If celebrations are to be occasions for nurture and fun, sensitivity and acknowledgment of these problems are essential. The following suggestions may help in avoiding potential problems:

1. Before you talk with the extended family members or ex-spouses, have a clear idea of your own about the significance of the event.
2. Let extended family members and ex-spouses know about your ideas well in advance of the event.
3. Sensitively discuss with your children the different perspectives and practices they may encounter in their celebrations at Grandma's or at their other parent's home.
4. Eliminate a tone of self-righteousness about your new way of celebrating.
5. Be flexible in the dates of your celebration. Alternatives can also apply to the day of celebrating.
6. Finally, even though your immediate family unit may be in the minority, hold fast to your own plans for alternative celebrations!

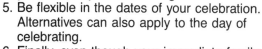

5.

Holidays

January and February

NEW YEAR'S DAY

An excellent occasion for a gathering of family and friends for fellowship and brainstorming about plans for alternative celebrations during the coming year. Making a covenant with family and friends to work together for change will begin building the support you will need during the year. Doing a cost analysis for the Christmas just celebrated may be a good way to start.

New Year
Record your commitments for changing this year's celebrations (be specific!):

1._____

2._____

3._____

4._____

EMANCIPATION DAY

The day in 1863 when President Lincoln signed the Emancipation Proclamation, is an excellent opportunity to begin studies and activities on the history of Black people in this country which can culminate in a special observance of the birth of Martin Luther King, Jr., on January 15.

MARTIN LUTHER KING'S BIRTHDAY

Not yet authorized by Congress, the birthday of Dr. King, January 15, is emerging as a national holiday to commemorate the life of this leader of the Civil Rights Movement, who was assassinated in Memphis, Tennessee, on April 4, 1968. The day is generally observed in ways to remind Americans of the goal of equal rights for all Americans.

- Read a biography of Martin Luther King, Jr. or a book of his sermons.
- Initiate a special observance of the day in your church, community, or school.
- Check out a record from the library and listen to his "I Have A Dream" speech.
- Join with others in your community who are observing the day.

VALENTINE'S DAY

Not much is known about the real St. Valentine, but it is believed he was martyred in Rome about A.D. 270. Some say he was a Christian priest or bishop and that his crime was that of performing illegal marriages. Marriages had been outlawed by Claudius II in the interests of "national security" because it was believed that family ties made soldiers less willing ro fight. Whatever his crime, the story goes that while held in prison, Valentine became friends with his jailer's daughter. On the eve of his execution, he thanked her for her care and kindness in a note which he signed "Your Valentine." And so was born our tradition for exchanging such notes.

An alternative celebration of Valentine's Day can be a time of remembering and celebrating personal relationships between lovers, wives and husbands, children and parents, and friends in noncommercial ways.

If you do decide to keep the tradition of giving valentines, keep the spirit of the celebration, too. Making your own usually costs less, encourages kids to enjoy working creatively with family members or friends, and also reduces increased commercial consumption. And the personal effort involved will surely mean a lot to those who receive a homemade Valentine.

We celebrate Valentine's Day by having ice-cream and cake for breakfast. It's dumb, but it reminds us of the crazy days of courtship when we took time out to do things like that, and the whole tradition is still young enough to freshen up our lives for days afterward.

Paul and Linda Hartman   La Mesa, California

The nicest gift that I ever received for Valentine's Day was a plant instead of flowers, a living Valentine that really brightens up the room. ♥

Phyllis Drury

My children came up with a good idea for Valentine's Day. They had decided to decorate the family bulletin board with pictures of things they love, but as they worked, the theme developed into pictures of "loving." So we had snapshots of best friends on graduation day; new baby in great-grandmother's arms, grandparents on fortieth wedding anniversary; big brother smothering little sister in a bear hug, and so on. Best of all, there was a picture of my husband and me, kissing outside the church door on our wedding day. Directly under that one, they pinned up a picture of our seven children, and explained, "From this loving came all this loving".

Joan Coogan   Olympia Fields, Il.

In keeping with the spirit of kindness shown by the jailer's daughter, it seems most appropriate to include in our Valentine's day celebration consciousness-raising and meaningful activities on behalf of those in prison.

So where do we begin? By reading, talking, looking, questioning—finding out what the penal system is really like. Start by contacting some of those groups which are working for prison reform and asking for their literature: Offender Aid and Restoration (OAR), 414 Fourth St., Charlottesville, Virginia 22901; Southern Coalition on Jails and Prisons, Box 12044, Nashville, Tennessee 37212; American Civil Liberties Union, 1346 Connecticut Ave., N.W., Suite 1031, Washington, D.C. 20036. Then, on Valentine's Day, invite a group of good friends over for potluck supper and a discussion on prison problems and what you can do about them.

Or work in the classroom, a school, a church group, a civic club, to create a Prison Awareness Fair. You can make as much or as little of it as you want: literature table; speakers from local jails—both prisoners and prison officials, if you can arrange it; inviting a group of parolees to celebrate with you and share their stories of what it's like inside and what they'd change about the system; a play, choral readings, songs that depict prison life—as in the trails and tribulations of the blues or more thought-provoking problem plays.

If you're really ambitious, create a task force and work toward a community-wide Valentine's Day learn-in—using radio talk shows, newspaper columns, speakers at a festival rally or at club meetings to provide a forum for discussion of the pros and cons of various solutions to "prison problems." Plan a community meal of typical prison fare and sell it at the cost-per-meal in your local jail or nearby prison—or sell it at a profit and use the proceeds to help fund a continuing task force to follow up on what you've learned during the fair.

A simpler celebration would be to plan Valentine's Day parties for your group and invite several parolees to join you for discussion. Perhaps you could help them form a speaker's bureau or, if your arbitration skills are really good, you could develop panels of speakers—composed of two or more "sides" in prison issues, such as the prisoner, the prison guard, the superintendent, Joe Citizen, the prisoner's family, the judge.

While you're planning parties, you might want to extend your reach to include other kinds of prisoners: those who are imprisoned in drug abuse, for instance, or mental institutions. Invite people who have begun to find their way out—ex-offenders who are trying to reconstruct their lives, recent releasees from mental institutions, participants in a halfway house program. Explore the possibility of sponsoring one of them (or the family of one of the inmates) over a period of a year or so—to help them get back on their feet (and to help you learn more about your own abilities and inabilities). Some jails and prisons have a similar sponsorship for inmates—allowing them to be released a day at a time for leisure activities both of you could enjoy together.

In the third edition of the *Catalogue*, we described the success of a schoolroom Valentine's Day in which elementary students were encouraged to give money they would have spent on valentines to groups working for prison reform and to make their own valentines, in the form of notes to each of their classmates beginning. "I like you because..." That idea could be expanded to include writing valentines and periodic follow-up letters to prisoners. There is no better way to find out what the life of a prisoner is like than by talking to him/her, and few jails allow community groups to fraternize. Some will, however, supervise a "pen pal" program. If your local officials won't, two national organizations can help: Prison Pen Pals, Box 1217, Cincinnati, Ohio 45202, which will send a list of names and backgrounds for you to choose from; or Prisoners' Dialog, c/o Rolling Stone, 625 Third St., San Francisco, California 94107.

Another Valentine's Day celebration could involve preparing some sort of musical or dramatic presentation and carrying it to a jail or mental institution. Any kind of entertainment officials will let you import will be appreciated. If your interest and skills go beyond presenting outside materials, perhaps you could start a drama group, writing class, or band among the inmates themselves. Or offer to teach any other skills you have in the educational program at a jail, work camp, or drug halfway house in your area.

Or if you're more passive than active, donate books and magazines, used but working radio or television sets, sports equipment—anything to pass the time, as one of the major corrosive effects of incarceration is boredom.

We make all these suggestions advisedly, of course. Each community differs, rules vary from institution to institution (and some are reasonable, some aren't). We expect you to discuss fully what you're planning to do with others who have been involved in prison projects and to find out whether inmates or ex-offenders need or want your schemes, what kinds of legitimate problems officials and social workers have and what kinds they've fabricated, how the system works in your community and what you can do about it.

If you're uneasy about how you will get along with each other, approach prisoners as you would anyone else—expect it to be difficult to communicate, but possible (though occasionally it turns out to be impossible). Remember that prisoners are human beings and no matter what crimes they have committed, their human dignity is not affected by it—nor are their human needs. Just as we ask others to accept us—faults and all—so they ask us to accept them and affirm those things which are lovable in them in spite of their failings.

Adapted from Alternatives' Wedding Packet.

March and April

ST. PATRICK'S DAY

St. Patrick's Day is the celebration of the life of the missionary who brought Christianity to Ireland in the fifth century. The day has little of the religious significance it does in Ireland, and has become a day to celebrate Irish ethnicity in this country.

An alternative to present custom might be a reflection on the contributions St. Patrick made to Ireland, while at the same time reflecting on the ways that religious divisions can be exploited to serve other interests.

APRIL FOOL'S DAY

On the first day of April most folks have had the more or less humorous experience of discovering their coffee sweetened with salt. Traditionally April first is the day for such practical jokes. But if you're tired of the same stunts each year, why not plan something radically different for April Fool's Day this year?

The origins of April Fool's Day are obscure; it is variously attributed to the fruitless mission of the dove from Noah's Ark, the adoption of the Gregorian calendar, agricultural festivals, and the uncertainty of the weather. It has been confused with the medieval Feast of Fools, a mock religious holiday celebrated during Epiphany in which lower clergy and lay people were "elected" by their peers to serve as a bishop or archbishop for a day. The purpose of this fun was to unmask the pretensions of the power elite in order to make their power less irresistible.

The festivities often went beyond simple charade and became occasions for all sorts of sacrilegious and bawdy carryings-on. The Feast of Fools was suppressed by both the Catholic and Protestant Churches during the Reformation, while April Fool's Day was widely practiced without censure by the Church.

These celebrations pointed out two very important things. First, life was not intended to be humorless—play is a necessary part of full humanity. Second, it was rarely in their control that some of them were clergy, some bishops, some rich and others poor, some powerful and others oppressed. Not only was it not in their control but their station and circumstance had no relationship to the value of their personhood. The Feast of Fools celebrations were intended to bring this reality to consciousness, not simply by satirizing the elite but by pointing out the arbitrariness of fate. (The theological jargon for this is "the inscrutability of divine providence.") It is not clear whether the two Church bodies suppressed the celebrations because of the debauchery or the fact that it represented a threat to the establishment.

Holidays are days set apart; the normal is interrupted momentarily so that something extraordinary can be seen more clearly. April

Fool's Day can be a day in which the normal is suspended—even overturned, when the Yin becomes Yang. We can know ourselves more fully by temporarily turning the tables and playing practical jokes with our own lives. To emphasize the suspension of ordinary routines, one could change jobs with somebody for the day. Wife and husband could change jobs or roles. Children and parents might switch or teachers and their students might find some way for the students to teach the teacher the things they value. Another way of approaching it would be to select something you don't normally do, but think you would have fun doing. If, for instance, your life-routine doesn't usually have a place for dancing or singing or painting or *anything* you'd really like to do, then declare April first the day for doing that. You might even discover a hidden talent. The point is not however to be a good artist or a good musician. The point is to do something just for the fun of doing something you want to do.

PURIM

Purim, the Feast of Lots, based on the story of Esther in the Old Testament, is a Jewish festival celebrating their miraculous deliverance and power to survive, despite being subjected to violent persecutions. This is a good occasion for non-Jews to read and reflect on the history of anti-Semitism.

PASSOVER

Pesach (Passover), observed for seven or eight days, commemorates the Israelites' redemption from slavery in Egypt. The original directions for the celebration are found in the twelfth chapter of Exodus. One of its most important elements is the obligation to retell the story of the exodus from Egypt and the meaning of the Passover meal. "...when your children say to you: what do you mean by this service? Then you shall say...."

Through the ceremony of the Seder ("order" or "procedure" of questions and answers) the different generations at the table recount the story and the meaning of the celebration.

LENT

Lent, the forty days prior to Easter beginning with Ash Wednesday, was originally a period of fasting and penance for new converts preparing for baptism on Easter Eve. When Christianity became the state religion of Rome in the fourth century, the church was endangered by throngs of new members. As a counter measure, the Lenten fast and practices of self-renunciation became requirements of all Christians. It became a time of recommitment against the threat of being assimilated into the popular culture.

With popular culture so much a part of Christian practice in America, the serious observance of Lent can be an important means to gain a new perspective about the tension between loyalty to God and loyalty to Caesar.

The six-week period before Easter is a time to look at life and assess how to personally implement the values of peace, community, and equality of all before God. Historically, it has been a time for fasting and abstinence because it came at a time when the winter food supplies were low. The traditional Lenten fast consists of two very light meals and one full meal per day, with meat served once, and nothing between meals. Friday was a meatless day and Ash Wednesday and Good Friday fast days.

The fasting and abstinence of Lent have been tradition—a way of indicating the need to sacrifice for the Lord. While many who fast find it difficult, the signing of a covenant or contract may make the obligation a little firmer and the task easier.

Lent is a time for taking stock, both of ourself and our society. This generally somber season can be one of growth and celebration if one focuses on the celebration of the resurrection that culminates the Lenten period. Lenten traditions can be serious, and bring home such issues as world hunger and poverty, and yet still celebrations, as the following article describes.

Stone Soup

"Stone Soup," the story, has long been a favorite with many children we know. It is about a wandering minstrel who taught people how to share during a famine. Now through a fairly recently established "tradition," that story has become a wonderful reality in our church.

Each year, during the early part of Lent, we have a time of hunger awareness when church members have at least one meatless meal a week, or cut back on normal eating habits in some other way. The money that is saved by this frugality is set aside for our Hunger Fund. (At some time during this period, the young people also have a 24-hour "starvathon" at the church, during which they eat nothing and spend their time discussing books and filmstrips about the causes and implications of hunger—and for which they get pledges for the Fund.)

This all culminates the week before Palm

Sunday on what we call ComPassion Sunday with a moving service during which all these gifts are brought forward and put into a large papier-mâché loaf of bread. Following this service we always have our famous "stone soup" lunch.

That morning, early, the soup pot is started and as people come to church they bring "fixings" for the soup—vegetables, spices, maybe a soup bone. Children in some of the elementary Church School classes cut up the vegetables and everything simmers while we are in church. After the service we all enjoy this delicious soup along with some homemade bread prepared by a group in the church—and those attending contribute what they would have paid for a Sunday dinner at home to the Hunger Fund.

This special occasion concludes with a filmstrip or a retelling of the story and the happy singing of songs in celebration of our sharing. Because of this, the story "Stone Soup" has taken on added significance for our children.

Khuki Woolever   Oneonta, New York

PALM SUNDAY

Palm Sunday begins Easter Week, celebrating Christ's arrival into Jerusalem. Maundy Thursday commemorates the Passover supper of Christ and the disciples. One old custom had the sovereign of a country wash the feet of paupers of his or her age, in memory of Christ washing his disciples' feet. Then the king or queen would distribute money, clothing, and food to the poor to be reminded of humility.

I have developed a twenty-first-century tradition that seems fitting for "preparing the way of the Lord." We always spend Palm Sunday afternoon in a big trash pick-up on our section of the county road. Usually the snow has melted and fishing season has opened, so the beer bottles alone fill several bags.

Marion Ellis   Dover, New Hampshire

Peace Cakes

Palm Sunday has been a time of sharing peace cakes. A homemade bun or sweet bread is given to others with whom communication has ceased and as a preparation for Good Friday's message of forgiveness and Easter, in order to reestablish respect and peace. These could be shared in a group, or with another group, between men and women, young and old, white and black to personally commit oneself to establishing peace among people.

EASTER

Easter, the most important festival of the Christian Church, celebrates the resurrection of Jesus Christ from the dead. The Feast of Easter had been well established by the second century but there was a controversy between the Eastern and Western Churches over which day it should be observed. The Council of Nicaea in 325 ruled that Easter should be on the Sunday following the first full moon after the vernal equinox (March 21).

While much emphasis is given to Jesus's resurrection as assurance for a general resurrection, its real significance lies in its being the sign of God's validation of the ministry of Jesus on earth. That ministry of healing, teaching, preaching, and suffering on behalf of the poor and outcast did not end on the cross. In the

resurrection that ministry has become the universal ministry for all who would follow Jesus. Jesus spoke to his disciples after the resurrection: "As the Father has sent me, so I send you."

Under the onslaught of attempts to make Easter a "Second Christmas" by the commercial interests, it is difficult to keep the real purpose of the celebration in perspective. Easter is *big business*: In 1980 Americans spent

- $90 million on Easter cards
- $550 million on Easter candy
- Almost $1 billion on Easter clothes
- An undisclosed amount on Easter toys

There is another level of concern with our Easter celebrations. Although many attemps have been made to link the Easter bunny and Easter egg

And on the Third Day . . .

T.R. Peterson '81

traditions to the resurrection, those traditions actually divert attention away from celebrating the resurrection. They may also plant the seeds of doubt concerning the resurrection in children's minds. As children grow and learn that there is no Easter bunny—that it is a myth we have passed on to them as truth—they have less reason to believe what we teach them about the resurrection.

An alternative Easter will avoid its commercial trappings, and focus on the victory of Christ over death and the forces of evil (and not what we can enjoy now that Lent is over, or what the Easter bunny has brought). It will include renewed commitment to the ministry of Jesus, a ministry to which all Christians are called.

This Easter we couldn't even get excited—after

12 years in a row of the big ham dinner routine, and none of the children were willing to go to church. Besides, all our closest friends were vegetarian. I didn't want Easter Day to just slip by unnoticed.

Taking a big chance on northwest Montana weather, I began to organize a potluck vegetarian picnic in an area by Flathead Lake. Easter noon was balmy and sunny with an endless view of snowy mountain peaks. We gathered nearly 30 people from age one to fifty—hunted eggs, skipped rocks on the lake, played softball and badminton and ate a delicious meal of chowder, salads, homemade breads and cake (not to mention rosé wine). Friends played the harmonica and banjo.

It was a perfect celebration for our family.
Pam Jeffcoat   Kalispell, Montana

No New Clothes

Reducing clothing purchases frees up extra income. Consider what might happen in a congregation liberated from this consumer practice. If 100 families diverted $200 this Easter from clothing purchases to a human welfare cause of their choice, the total would amount to $20,000. Making this kind of breakthrough is not easy, for we have been conditioned by advertising and social pressure to feel uncomfortable wearing clothes that are out of style. For the sake of humanity and our own liberation we must overcome this.

Eggs

Blow out eggs by making pinholes in each side and forcefully blowing. Use the eggs for scrambled eggs for breakfast. Dye the shells in dyes made of the outer onion skins for yellow, coffee grounds for brown. (Cover the skins with water, boil) Inside the eggs you could insert a slip of paper that describes a gift of yourself—time, a day spent with someone, a pledge to volunteer time to an organization needing your skills.

Or inside could be a statement of what the person has felt in the time of Lent, or the vigil, or what spring means to the life of all. These could be commented on by another person who breaks the shell to talk of new life.

Children's traditional excitement for a rather meaningless Easter Egg Hunt can be captured in a Search for Seeds. Seed packets are hidden instead of eggs, and finders are encouraged to plant and care for their treasures themselves. In this way, the concern for life is carried beyond the one celebration to everyday living—and kids learn (perhaps even unconsciously) an appreciation for the growing cycle of living plants.

Easter Season

Easter and Spring

The word Easter is derived from the Anglo-Saxon name for the Teutonic goddess of spring, Eostre (Ostera). A day was traditionally set aside for a pagan observance of the Earth's awakening. Primitive Christians built on this festival, adding to it the celebration of Christian values and beliefs. Easter, with its message of new life and resurrection, is the central holiday in the Christian tradition. For many, Easter Eve vigils and sunrise services have been part of the Easter celebration. This dates back to a time when the sun was thought to dance as it rose on this day, and people would gather, especially near water, to watch the sun "dance" on the waves.

Many Easter symbols come from ancient myths and legends. Egyptians saw eggs as sacred emblems of the renovation of humankind after the Deluge, and Jews adopted the symbol as part of their celebration of the Exodus. The egg became for Christians a symbolism of a chick being "entombed" in an egg is clear. The hare was an ancient symbol of the moon, and because traditional spring feasts were set by the moon's phase, the hare became entwined with the celebrations. As Easter became a Christian festival of spring and new life, the hare maintained a central position as the Easter bunny.

Sharing

Spring is a time of newness. What better way to commemorate the coming of spring than by introducing people to something new? Perhaps it might be taking someone caving who has never gone. Show someone how to sprout seeds for eating. Loan some of your favorite books. Plant some vegetables or flowers for a friend who can't get to it.

Easter cards comprise a good bit of revenue for card corporations. School and community groups can get together to make them out of scraps or cheap paper, writing their own thoughts and exercising their own creativity. Although it takes a bit longer, the new ideas of expression are reward for the time. Older people and young people could share this task. The money diverted from the commercial cards could be put into an action project.

Group Things

Give a show for Easter. Include everyone that would like to participate. Stage a processional. Fill balloons with helium and release them at a set time. Wear costumes of flowers, of spring, of eggs. Sing. Paint a mural that day. Celebrate around a tree. Encourage people to share their different memories, their differences as well as their similarities. Have spontaneous or more well-planned scenario enactments. "You six are all flower bulbs under the ground. You are a bird flying North from the South. You are a sun rising;

a tree realizing it's time to bud again." Build a sculpture out of people.

Sponsor an environmental fair followed by a massive cleanup of a stream, park, or section of a city.

Make a people tree—a special tree that blooms with people on one special day of the year. Everyone who can climbs into it and perhaps hangs banners from its limbs. Or a rock/boulder that comes alive with people on one special day.

May and June

SHAVUOT

Shavuot, or the Feast of Weeks, is observed fifty days after Passover. According to tradition, it was on this day that Israel received the ten commandments and the covenant with God was sealed. In Reform Judaism, Shavuot is an occasion for confirming young girls and boys, bringing them into full adult membership in the congregation.

PENTECOST

Pentecost, observed fifty days after Easter and ten days following the Ascension, celebrates the descent of the Holy Spirit on the disciples (Acts 2:1-6). The name was taken from the Jewish Pentecost (Shavuot) which is fifty days after Passover.

Even after the resurrection, the disiples were still fearful. It was the coming of the spirit that enabled them to continue the ministry of Jesus. An alternative Pentecost for Christians should be a celebration of the power of the spirit which enables them to participate in that ministry which, if faithfully followed in identification with the poor and outcast people, will lead to suffering and a cross.

MEMORIAL DAY

Memorial Day, first observed in 1866, was to honor the war dead of the Civil War, both North and South. In time it came to include commemorating the lives lost in all wars.

An alternative Memorial Day celebration will recall not only the tragedy of lives lost in war, but will also confess the futility of war itself as a means to resolve conflict.

Let us suggest Memorial Day as a day of joyful celebration of the living rather than a brooding over death, or at least consider the real meaning of Memorial Day. It was begun to remember victims of our wars, so let it be broadened into public services of mourning for the victims, military and civilian, of all wars. If the local patriotic service cannot be refocused, then gather your friends who care deeply for world peace and design and conduct your own public service. Gather an offering for some local peace organization.

Richard Rodes   Columbia, Maryland

PARENT'S DAY

Our celebration of Mother's and Father's Days has one thing in common with the intentions of their founders—we say we are honoring our parents. But Anna Jarvis's efforts to call attention to adult children's neglect of their parents haven't had much effect, and very seldom is a father honored in the spirit Mrs. John Dowd honored hers for rearing his family alone after their mother's death. On Mother's and Father's Days, unfortunately, we honor the almighty dollar more often than we do our parents.

As adults, and also as children, we often neglect our parents. We take them for granted and fail to show appreciation for their nurturing, or we consider them nuisances rather than people like us with a need to give and receive love. As a result, we are ready targets for advertisers who appeal to our guilt feelings to fill their pocketbooks. "Remember Mom" and "For Dad on His Day" send millions rushing out to buy gifts that will prove affection or pay Mom and Dad back for all their sacrifices.

The sales thrust extends to grandparents, aunts and uncles, sometimes even sisters and brothers. Anyone who remotely qualifies as a mother or father figure, especially anyone who has been ignored during the months preceding the holiday, is likely to receive some type of acknowledgment. Restaurants, clothing merchants, florists, and candy stores do a bonanza business.

We could suggest doing away with Parents' Days and making every day a people's day, on which we honored them and thought of ways to help them and bring them joy. In fact, making every day a People's Day is what we do suggest. But it's also fun to have special days for Mom and Dad. The trick is celebrating them appropriately, given the influences on us to buy and be done with it.

The original celebrations focused on the parents of adult children—their need to be cared for in old age or illness, and the child's desire to show appreciation for the parent's own years of caring. Our focus could encompass all the needs of our parents or the needs of all the aging and ill in our society.

What do your parents need that you can give them on their day? Or what do they need that you can promise on their day and do another? Pick something that will satisfy them, not something that will make you feel less guilty. Breakfast in bed on a rainy Saturday or a school day may mean more to Mom than one on Mother's Day, and a weekly game of chess may mean more to Dad than dinner out. The point is: don't get entrapped by the occasion, but make the holiday one which shows your sensitivity to their needs.

Sometimes Parents' Days can be complicated by too many parents. When there are two grandfathers and a father involved, a family can get wrought up over sharing time with each person. If you need to divide your attention, talk

about it with the people involved and plan ahead. Maybe you can celebrate Mother's and Father's Days, two Grandfather's Days and a Grandmother's Day.

Or maybe you can share your celebration with aging friends outside your family. Holidays, especially those which are highly commercialized, have a very negative effect on those who don't feel a part of them—like many of our senior citizens in homes for the aged, nursing homes, and hospitals. Use Mother's or Father's Day to focus attention on them, to visit them or to begin a self-education program on their needs. You might enlist your family or a community group in the project as well.

See if your community has resources available for its senior citizens, and if it doesn't, see what your group can do to get something started. Make sure your local government is taking advantage of available programs and resources. Check into local employment practices and see if there is discrimination against those who are "too old" to get jobs while they have the mental and physical stamina to work.

You can also use the day to share your talents and skills with older people. You might help an older friend plant a garden or, if the work is too taxing for your friend, offer the time and tools to start it yourself. Let the older person do the easier tasks, and plan future time for heavier follow-up work. Your mutual harvest of goodwill will be plentiful.

If you'd rather focus on showing appreciation for your parents, don't rely on a greeting card to convey the message. Try a family or group discussion about what you appreciate in each other. Or if talking is difficult, write a letter. Try to share what you feel today, for tomorrow one of you may be gone. You might also ask children from an orphanage or foster home to join you and your parents for a holiday outing, or pledge to start a regular program for sharing with parentless children the experiences your parents have given you.

Other Thoughts

A lot of mothers really are uncomfortable about Mother's Day because it's mandatory. As an alternative, we suggest sending a gift or letter to your mother on your *own* birthday. She thinks about you that day; in fact, it probably means more to her than it does to you. The people we know who tried it said their mothers were touched and pleased. One woman saved her money all year and on her own 35th birthday sent her mother money—the mother needed money more than she needed anything else except the love involved. *(Editor's Note: Ditto for Father's Day.)*

The Gray Panthers, a national action group of all different ages, works with a score of contemporary problems facing old persons—representing age realistically, housing, fighting mandatory retirement, transportation, health, schools for all ages, legislation, employment. Each affiliate in the Gray Panthers network is independent and determines its own needs and priorities. A gift to parents could be helping to set up a local chapter. Judy Gross in the national office, 3700 Chestnut Street, Philadelphia, Pennsylvania 19104, will be delighted to hear from you. Her phone is 215-EV2-6644.

For Mother's Day, why not give a contribution to local women's centers, libraries, or some organization that your mother has shown an interest in or given her own time to?

Aviva Cantor Zuckoff   New York, New York

Organize a workshop on "Keeping a Journal." Suggest it to parents as a way of recording their thoughts and feelings as they grow older.

Ask parents to write about their childhood. Give them a notebook and a pen and lots of support. Stress how valuable a written record of their memories is for them, for their families and friends. This could evolve into a group workshop, "Celebrating Childhood." A lot of grandchildren would be happy to receive a story from their grandparents about growing up.

Mother's Day need not be limited to celebrations of mother, but can be a time to celebrate women. Many mothers bear a heavy load of family responsibility because they work and still continue to keep the lion's share of the family duties. Mother's Day is a good time to start a "working mother's awareness" program. If your family is one of these, think about how the family runs. Is there work sharing by all family members, or does mother still do the organizing? Just because she can do jobs with ease when other members of the family cannot doesn't mean she wants to. Families tend to give up on helping because "it's so much easier for her." That is an excuse. Why not sit down with the family on Mother's Day and discuss sharing tasks and readjusting the work load more fairly?

Or start a project on women's rights. Many states have discriminatory laws against women in jobs, getting credit or owning property. Mother's Day might be a good day to start a women's rights study/action program—either in your own family or in a community group.

Ellen Dittmer   Jackson, Mississippi

Can They Celebrate With You?

July and August

INDEPENDENT DAY

Independence Day, first observed in 1777, celebrates the day of the signing of the Declaration of Independence.

John Adams: "It ought to be solemnized with pomp and parades, with shows, games, sports, guns, bells, bonfires, and illumination from one end of this continent to the other, from this time forward forevermore."

Samuel West: "Unlimited submission and obedience is due to none but God alone....To suppose that he has given a set of men power to require obedience to that which is unreasonable, cruel and unjust is robbing the Diety of his justice and goodness...."

Independence Day July 4

"Give me your tired, your poor,
your huddled masses yearning to breathe free,
the wretched refuse of your teeming shore.
Send these, the homeless, tempest-tost to me,
I lift my lamp beside the golden door."

Frederick Douglass: "What to the American slave is your Fourth of July? I answer, a day that reveals to him more than all other days of the year the gross injustice to which he is the constant victim. To him your celebration is a sham; your boasted liberty an unholy license...."

In celebrating the birthday of our nation we are celebrating a very human and imperfect creation— one we may love and cherish, but one in need of our constant efforts for discipline and change.

Let us not forget that we, as a nation, have invited and cried out for the strangers we find among us. In the words of Emma Lazarus, inscribed on the Statue of Liberty at one of our major gateways, we have asked the world for nearly 100 years to:

> Give me your tired, your poor, your huddled masses yearning to breathe free, the wretched refuse of your teeming shore, send these, the homeless, tempest-tost, to me. I lift my lamp beside the golden door!

An alternative July Fourth may be informed by these two considerations: First, that unlimited loyalty is due only to our Sovereign God, and not to our nation. Second, that our legitimate patriotism requires us continually to call our nation back to those human and life-supporting reasons for which it was founded, not the least of which is to welcome the strangers found both inside and outside our borders, whether migrant farmworkers or Haitian refugees.

- At your family or group gathering, read the Declaration of Independence and talk about its relevance for other subject peoples.
- In planning your Fourth of July discuss the statements of Adams, West and Douglass.
- Memorialize some of the "tired and poor" who have come to these shores.
- Plan an activity in which you compare why your ancestors came to America with why people are coming now.
- Work with others in your congregation or community to help resettle refugees.
- Plan activities for children without fireworks.

WOMEN'S EQUALITY DAY

Women's Equality Day commemorates the victory of Women's Suffrage Movement when, on August 26, 1920, women's voting rights were secured by the ratification of the Nineteenth Amendment. The struggle had been long and often bitter. The unjust status of women had been an issue early in U.S. history. Abigail Adams once wrote.

> If particular care and attention are not paid to the ladies, we are determined to foment a revolution and will not hold ourselves bound to obey any laws in which we have no voice or representation.

There have been many changes in the status of women since that time, but equality with men is still unrecognized. Women's Equality Day provides an occasion to recall the history of women's struggles for status and rights.

- Study the unique contribution of women in American history.
- Support the ratification of the Equal Rights Amendment.
- Support development efforts that provide significant roles for women.
- Investigate your school and community programs to see that equal access is provided for girls as well as boys.
- Evaluate the distribution of responsibilities in your household.

HIROSHIMA DAY

Now that we know what nuclear weapons (and waste) can do to people and the earth, will we wait around like sheep until it happens? Or will we get as aroused as we would if a strangler were loose in our neighborhood?

One way to get a handle on this horror is to commemorate Hiroshima Day, August 6, with rituals and educational events in churches and communities. Nuclear weapons, power plants, and waste may be "out of sight" but we can't let them be out of mind unless we have lost ours.

In planning a Hiroshima Day commemoration you may wish to write to the following groups for ideas and materials:

Mobilization for Survival 1213 Race St. Philadelphia, Pennsylvania 19107 215-563-1512

World Peacemakers 2025 Mass. Ave. NW Washington, D.C. 20036

SANE 318 Mass. Ave. NW Washington, D.C. 20002

Union of Concerned Scientists 1208 Mass. Ave. Cambridge, Massachusetts 02138

September and October

LABOR DAY

With the Industrial Revolution came the unprecedented concentration of laborers, working and living in deplorable conditions, and grossly underpaid. They organized to get better wages and working conditions and to enhance their status in society.

In 1882, Peter J. McGuire, president and founder of the United Brotherhood of Carpenters and Joiners of America, called for a day to honor labor and acknowledge the contributions of labor

to American life. McGuire suggested the first Monday of September because it would come at a pleasant season and halfway between the Fourth of July and Thanksgiving, thus filling a wide gap in the chronology of legal holidays.

In the midst of the last summer outings and getting the kids ready to start back to school, Labor Day offers a good opportunity to study and reflect on the role of labor in this country, the ways workers are treated, and what organized labor has done. The result of such study and reflection may be to participate in boycotts or shareholder resolutions against corporations who continue to exploit labor at home and abroad.

- Plan activities that will help you and your children better understand the history of the labor movement.
- In a family or group gathering, arrange for a viewing of a filmstrip or film like *Guess Who's Coming to Breakfast* (filmstrip) or *Day Without Sunshine* (film).
- Support efforts of poor workers (e.g., farmworkers, woodcutters, and textile workers) to organize.
- Talk to people with different ideas about the power and role of labor unions today.

ROSH HASHANAH

Rosh Hashanah (Jewish New Year), a one- or two-day celebration beginning on the first day of the lunar month of Tishri, marks the beginning of ten days of penitence before the Day of Atonement (Yom Kippur). The special theme of the occasion is remembrance—remembering God's creation, the special witness of Israel, and their successes and failures in bearing that witness.

YOM KIPPUR

Yom Kippur, the Day of Atonement, is the most solemn holiday in the Jewish Year. It falls on the tenth day after Rosh Hashanah and is the culmination of ten days of repentance and preparation. On the day, all but the sick and children observe a rigid fast. The old rituals of sacrifice and scapegoat were replaced with prayer and penitence after the destruction of the Temple in A.D. 70 and services in the synagogue are central on this day, focusing on repentance and atonement.

SUCCOTH

Succoth, the Feast of Booths or Tabernacles, is the Jewish autumn harvest festival. The unique activity of this eight-day celebration is the dwelling in booths of branches and boughs decorated with fruit. The booths are to remind the people of how God had the children of Israel dwell in booths when they were delivered from Egypt (Leviticus 23:42-43).

HALLOWEEN

Halloween is a night of spirits, and has a history rich in religious traditions. It is historically All Hallow's Eve, the night before All Soul's Day, decreed by Pope Gregory to honor all saints who had died. In the Middle Ages it was known as a time favored by witches and sorcerers.

Halloween costumes started in medieval times when churches displayed relics of saints. Those parishes too poor to have relics let parishioners dress up to imitate the saints.

Tricks on Halloween stem from the belief that ghosts roamed the countryside that night making mischief.

Many Halloween traditions come from the Irish and Scottish. Bobbing for apples is one of these. The jack-o'-lantern supposedly comes from an Irish legend about an old sot, Jack, who made a deal with the devil for his soup. The angered devil supposedly threw a live coal at Jack, and it landed in a half-eaten turnip in Jack's hand. The resulting coal in the turnip became a jack-o'-lantern.

Halloween was not widely observed here until the 1840s, when there was a great Irish immigration due to the potato famine.

The blend of legend, religion, and mischief has

combined to make Halloween a unique celebration. Commercialism has had its effect on the festivities, as children beg for costumes like their favorite television characters and treats which are hopelessly lacking in nourishment. Trick-or-treating has been on the decline in the past few years. Parents are reluctant to send their children out into any but the closest neighborhoods, and children are discouraged from accepting any treats that are not commercially packaged.

The Halloween costume party for family and friends is the most positive way to create an alternative Halloween, especially if you follow the suggestion in *Voluntary Simplicity's* Chapter VIII and return the event to the celebration of the saints. Children could come dressed up like the saintly people of history. In keeping with the spirit of saintliness, help the children make treats for others rather than begging candy door to door. Visit pediatric wards, homes for the aged, or shut-ins. Turn Halloween around: take the treats to *give*.

Another alternative Halloween party would have

the guests create their own costumes, rather than buying them. Or have a party to *make* costumes. Provide guests with old clothing and other materials so that they can create their own dress. Let them make up their faces using various old cosmetics, grease paint, or any other harmless coloring items you might have. Note: have plenty of baby oil or cold cream around for the clean-up.

Refreshments: cider and donuts are always favorite treats. Homemade donuts are very popular with children, easy to make, and delicious and cheap. Take packages of biscuit dough, punch out holes, and fry in deep fat for just a minute or two, until brown. Glaze with honey. Or make cookies from wholesome ingredients.

Entertainment: A scavenger hunt is fun. Or a blindfolded walk. All the guests wear blindfolds, and hold hands in a line. The leader takes them on a walk, usually outside, giving them directions on where to step, duck, or touch whenever necessary. Groups should be small (no more than five) for the most fun.

Why not sit down with children at some point before the trick-or-treat hour and talk about things we *ought* to fear: famine, world hunger, hatred, war, racism, and injustice. Perhaps these concerns can become the real spooks and goblins as the child forms opinions about what is important in life.

Another alternate idea for celebrating Halloween has already caught on well: on Halloween, suggest to the children that they collect money for UNICEF instead of collecting candy for themselves. Literature and the UNICEF cans can be requested through your local UNICEF information office, or by writing to:

U.S. Committee for UNICEF   331 E. 38th Street
New York, New York 10016   attn: Ms. Muriel Brady

We were inspired by some of the ideas in your Catalogue and came up with a new way of celebrating Halloween—for us, at least. The general greed for "goodies" of most trick-or-treaters has bothered us for a number of years, but we didn't know what to do about it. This year we decided that in our own small way we would like to turn their greed into something that helped to meet the needs of others, and that would also try to get the youngsters to begin thinking about other persons' needs.

We printed copies of this statement and put them in each child's goodie bag:

Dear Trick-or-treater:

We are giving 5 cents to UNICEF for every child who comes trick-or-treating at our home. Because you have come other children around the world will receive a gift of food and medicine to help them have the joys of life which you have. Thank you for coming to our home and helping us to help other children like yourself all around the world.

This was a small beginning for us this year, but we hope it may get some parents to do some rethinking when their children ask them to explain what our "treat" is all about.

Dan and Jonnie Gerhard   Walla Walla, Washington

A lot of people think that there should be more depth to Halloween than the usual excitement of "trick or treat." Halloween means "the eve of all hallows," and it gives the opportunity to commemorate the most unlikely list of saints you can imagine. Try this blessing for the Unlikely Saints:

For those whom we remember best as our teachers, for giving us values and goals,
We give thanks,
For those who have lived with us, loved us, shared our trials and still allowed us to become who we are,
We give thanks,
For those who led us out of our own personal slaveries and taught us the meaning of being free,
We give thanks,
For those who were sensitive enough to offer us words of comfort when we were anxious,
We give thanks,
For those who visit the lonely and clothe the naked and feed the hungry not because it's an injunction from above but because it's the joy of their own being,
We give thanks,

For those who taught us to love mostly by loving us, expecting nothing in return,
We give thanks,
For all who are martyrs without labels and those who offer good words because the act is reward enough,
We give thanks,
For those who allow us freedom to have more than a second-hand faith and who thereby provide us with our own real struggles without interference,
We give thanks,
For those who are gracious in old age and who are saints not so much because of their accumulated wisdom but because they invite us into the depth of long life without fear,
We give thanks,
For those who are genuinely funny and give cheer to life and good humor to day by day perceptions,
We give thanks,
And finally, for those who now surround us, family, friends; for those who share our secrets, for those who wish to know us better and for those who—by being a part of the community of the saints, give us courage and hope to live,
We give thanks.

Jack Lundin   Lombard, Illinois

November

THANKSGIVING

Ever since humans began to harvest food, there was a period of time set aside to celebrate the harvest. This usually came at the end, just before the hard winter months. Ancient cultures held festivals in honor of the Earth Mother; the Greeks honored Demeter, and the Romans Ceres. Jews celebrate harvest in several periods throughout the year. Passover marks the harvesting of the barley grain; Shavuot marks the harvest of wheat and ushers in the fruit harvest, and Succoth celebrates the end of the harvesting year. In medieval times many Europeans observed the Feast of St. Martin of Tours on November 11, and "Harvest Home" celebrations began with the reign of James I.

The "first" Thanksgiving in America is subject to debate. Some credit the Jamestown settlers, others a later group captained by John Smith. William B. Newell, a Penobscott Indian and former chairman of the anthropology department at the University of Connecticut, says that the first official Thanksgiving Day was proclaimed by the Governor of Massachusetts Bay Colony in 1637 to celebrate the massacre of 700 Indian men, women, and children who were celebrating their annual Green Corn Dance (their Thanksgiving). For the next 100 years, says Newell, "every Thanksgiving day ordained by a governor was to honor a bloody victory thanking God the battle was won."[1]

Most people, however, associate, the first Thanksgiving with the Pilgrims. These people

THE GREAT THANKSGIVING MYTH

once fled to Holland to escape religious persecution, but found religious difficulties there, too. They sought out the Virginia colony in North American—a small band of forty-one. This sixty-seven-day voyage landed them in Provincetown Harbor, rather than Virginia, where they found a recently vacated Indian settlement. There they discovered corn left by the natives for spring planting, and took about ten bushels, more grateful for the food than concerned about anyone's future crop.

The Pilgrims eventually chose Plymouth as the colony site—this was once territory of the Patuxet Indians, but they had been annihilated by plague. So the Pilgrims were able to use the vacant fields and abandoned shelter. The Pilgrims were not agricultural people—they were generally townsfolk, whose choice to settle land stemmed from their desire to serve God rather than an urge to till land. Fortunately, they had the help of one Patuxet, Squanto. He had been captured by an Englishman, sold into slavery, escaped, and managed to return to his deserted village six months before the Pilgrims. He helped the colonists during that first winter, which took a severe toll from scurvy and pneumonia. The spring brought new hope, and the Pilgrims prepared their fields, aided by Squanto, who had not only served as their first agricultural agent, but also as a go-between with other tribes, helping arrange the pact that allowed the Pilgrims and Indians to live in peace.

After the months of suffering, the colonists had good reason to celebrate the harvest. They had built some homes, and harvested corn. The woods were full of game. A feast was decided upon. Chief Massasoit was invited to share the celebration, and share he did. Ninety braves came with him—probably to celebrate their traditional harvest feast. They brought with them five deer to add to the provisions, and a gigantic feast was served up of wild geese, ducks, lobsters, eels, clams, oysters, fish, berries, biscuits, and breads, corn cooked in a variety of ways, and puddings of cornmeal and molasses. Sweet strong wine from wild grapes added to the occasion.

While the women in the group of fifty colonists cooked the meal, the men and children played games, which were generally considered by this austere group a waste of time. The settlers showed off their marksmanship with firearms, while the Indians showed off theirs with bows and arrows.

These were days of celebration. The festival lasted for days, with little attention to religious services. It is thought that the Pilgrims chose to keep their harvest festival secular because they disapproved of the mingling of religious and secular celebrations. It seems to have been a one-time occasion, with no thought to future celebrations.

There was little to celebrate when the Pilgrims first arrived. The next year's crop was sparse, and there was no festival. That following spring brought drought. But when the rain finally fell and provisions arrived from England, the governor proclaimed July 30, 1683, as one of Thanksgiving. There were several other Thanksgiving holidays proclaimed, but not until 1789 did it become a national holiday, declared by George Washington. He did not declare another for six years. Not until Abraham Lincoln became President did Thanksgiving become an annual occasion, marked by presidential proclamation.

[1]*Akwesasne Notes*, by Mohawk Nation. Vol. 12-Aug. 1980. p.3

Images and Myths

If you were to direct your imagination toward Thanksgiving, that national event which we celebrate both as a cultural holiday and a religious observance, what images would you find surfacing? Since many like ourselves were at least raised in a fairly traditional environment, we can most likely recall a whole host of pleasant memories: entire families and old friends coming together, possibly for the only time in a year; having a houseful of guests with all the extra couches and even floor space used for bedding; the preparation of food going on days in advance; a feast of those special foods—turkey, dressing, cranberry sauce, pumpkin pie; feeling less guilty (in regard to your own weight problem) about eating "too much" than at any other time; enjoying a listless afternoon catching up on conversation or watching some of the best football games of the year with loved ones. You can doubtless continue the imagery, adding any number of your own particularities.

Increasingly, however, sensitive Americans are finding these memories and contemporary realities ambiguous at best and oppressive at worst. To begin with, women are now revealing to us all a most embarrassing fact—the fact that such images, such a myth (to use a more precise term) is a predominantly male projection. Thanksgiving has been far from relaxing for women. For them, even after a sumptuous meal, the reality of dishpan hands, mounds of leftovers to be put away, and tired feet, bears much truer than the myth of a cold beer, a comfortable chair, and television entertainment. Even being *able* to watch the game would be consolation to only a few.

Even so, this iconoclasm is but one of the counter-myths that we find blossoming around this occasion. At least two others are beginning to bear down upon us with relentless force. Of the two the first has been more thoroughly called to our attention by the media, but the second is no less real, though less sensational. They are: the world food shortage and the oppression under which our native peoples, the American Indians, live.

History tells us that the initial occasion which we now commemorate as Thanksgiving was a rather generous event. The then landholders sacrificed their exclusive rights to the land, realizing that the bounty of their homeland was plentiful and sufficient to easily support these newcomers. Actually, even to think of the Indians as "landowners" would do violence to their own understanding of their relationship to the earth and its property, a notion we moderns find near impossible to imagine. The new tenants, after several years of severe hardships, were finally able to stabilize themselves after a particularly good harvest. And, as a kind of symbolic covenant, the European settlers invited the Indians to share in a feast to celebrate their newfound prosperity. With increasing scandal, however, we are discovering that this myth too was one told by only a few and by only the dominant. European greed seemed to know no end. Maybe the Indians were just too optimistic about human nature. They have since learned better.

Little need be said concerning our other Thanksgiving focus. The extremity of the world food shortage now begins to pervade our consciousness. Both the personal and the social myths, the myths of what constitutes "necessary" consumption and the "compassion" of American aid at home and abroad, are exploding before our eyes. We are shocked at the discoveries (1) that the "normal" American diet is highly extravagant by global standards, and (2) that America has acted more often than not as a slumlord both for its native peoples and for the Third World rather than as a generous big brother.

As this shock is internalized, our first reaction will doubtlessly be that Thanksgiving as a holiday should be done away with, that we should no longer be party to the perpetuation of this hoax.

We think, however, that such an attempt would be as foolish as it would be futile. Thanksgiving as a cultural and religious celebration, even as a false and destructive myth, is deeply ingrained into the American psyche. Myths seem to have a resiliency with a strong resistance to dissolution. But it is the very fact of their resiliency that gives them elasticity as well. They can stretch and conform to new shapes, new realities. Alternative Thanksgiving celebrations can transform the old myths so that old illusions are exposed and new directions are discovered.

Ken and Nancy Sehested   Atlanta, Georgia

American History: A Native American View

This teaching was given to us by Sakokwenonkwas, who has been a spiritual inspiration to the many people who have heard him speak as he has traveled with White Roots of Peace and on his own missions. He is a Mohawk, Bear Clan, and now sits in the council of the People of the Flint at Akwesasne.

A long time ago, before the arrival of the white man to our country, here lived our grandfathers and grandmothers. At that time, life was hard, but our people were happy and healthy and some say they lived to be over a hundred years old.

Well, those ancestors never really died because the life they possessed still lives in you and me,

their grandchildren. It is also said that our ancestors were a holy people, and were so sacred in their day-to-day life that the Creator spoke to them and guided them in various ways. Today, we are the evidence of those very lives and the words God spoke can still be recalled, though those words are but a whisper nowadays.

One of these warnings I will attempt to write in story form as I recall it and translate its symbols.

A long time ago, before the white man came, our people lived in several villages and these villages were established by clans. The means of providing a living in those times were agriculture, hunting, and fishing.

One early morning, two men set out on a hunting trip. They paddled their canoe on the river for a long distance when suddenly a brilliant flash of light struck them in their eyes. The two men couldn't figure out what that light was. It appeared to be coming from up-river, so they hurriedly paddled their canoe to the source of the flashing bright light. There they saw lily pads floating on the water. On top of the lily pads were two small snakes about one inch long.

One of these tiny snakes was the color of silver, and the other the color of gold.

Every time these tiny snakes moved a certain way, the sun's rays would hit upon the bodies of the gold and silver snakes, causing a reflection.

The two men were just amazed at their discovery, and never had either of them seen anything so beautiful in their entire lives. Now the two men began to think about the small snakes. They thought that if the wind were to come up, it would cause the waves upon the river to become very big and the snakes could drown. Also, they thought if some birds flew over, they might spot the beautiful snakes and swallow them. Then they thought because the river was so wide, the snakes might not find any food and they surely would starve to death.

So it was the two men finally decided to discontinue their hunting trip and take the two beautiful snakes back home to their village. When they arrived at their village, the word was soon out that the two hunters had caught something never seen by any people of North America before. Everyone from that village gathered to see the small snakes. All the people sure thought that these snakes were the prettiest sight imaginable. The two men then built a small stockade for the small snakes. This stockade was for the snakes' protection against the wilderness.

By this time, people from neighboring villages heard the news and came to see. As days went on by, the people observed that no matter what time of day or night they looked at the two small snakes in the stockade, they never slept, but were always moving, and as the light hit upon their bodies, it would throw a sparkling light that was most beautiful. The people also observed that no matter how many insects they fed them, the snakes never had enough. Their hunger was unbelievable.

The snakes had grown to a foot or so in length by this short time. In the days following, the people would hunt larger game such as squirrels, frogs, chipmunks, but they could never catch enough to satisfy the hunger of the two snakes, which by now were several yards long, and just as silver and gold as they could be.

Again, the people had to hunt even larger game—rabbits, muskrat, and beavers, but even these could not satisfy the hunger of the gold and silver snakes. By this time, the snakes had grown about thirty feet long, and another stockade had to be built for them.

Now the people of the village had to hunt deer every day in order to feed these two huge serpents. The serpents ate so much that the

people of the village began to notice that they didn't have enough deer to feed their people.

Although the serpents grew more beautiful with their size, the people were becoming alarmed as they didn't know how much longer they could continue to feed the serpents and their people too.

One night, all the people of the village were asleep. The dawning of a new day came. The elders were busy sweeping and cleaning in and around their longhouses. The small children were already up and playing all sorts of games. The fragrance of the morning meal could be smelled in the brisk morning air. Everything was normal, until suddenly, a great noise was heard. The serpents had broken the stockade.

The screaming of small children was heard coming from the area where the serpents were kept. As the elders rushed toward the commotion to find out what was happening, they saw the serpents swallowing their children. They saw their children's legs kicking from the serpents' mouths, and then completely swallowed.

The elders rushed to save their children. They grabbed stones, poles, and whatever they could get their hands on. Then they began to beat upon the serpents, hoping the serpents might vomit the children up still alive. But instead, the serpents grew more angry and devoured some of the elders. The entire village was in an uproar. All the people were so scared they didn't know what to do.

After many lives were lost, the serpents apparently decided to eat something else and they left the village and headed south into the wilderness.

Now that the serpents were gone, the people began living a routine life again, but their lives were never to be the same. In the minds of the people, they knew that somewhere those serpents were roaming free and the fear was always there that they could return to the village any time.

A month or so went by when some runners returned to the village. The runners reported that they had seen the gold and silver serpents toward the south. They said the serpents now were several miles long, and had attacked many of the villages to the south. The runners told the people that the deer and other such animals were becoming scarce as the serpents' hunger never ceased.

Months again went by when more runners excitedly entered the village. Again the report was that they also had seen the gold and silver serpents. The serpents had destroyed many villages, and eaten many animals. The reflection from their gold and silver bodies glowed even in the darkest of nights. They had grown so that they were bigger than the highest mountain. They were so long you could not see from one end of them to the other. They were always moving and never slept. As they moved, they crushed entire forests beneath them. When they crossed a river, they

indented the earth with their weight, causing the river to flow in a different direction. As they passed over these rivers, they caused the rivers to become so muddy that no one could drink from them—if you were to bathe in a river where the serpents had been, you would be dirtier than before you started.

The runners went on to say that even if a mountain were in their path, the serpents would go right through the mountain and even knock it down. They said the heads of the serpents were big, and they breathed flames of fire. They said if you got too close to their heads, you would die as the breath of the serpents was too hot.

Time again passed on by. The day all the villages knew would come to pass was now encroaching steadily. From the north came the brilliant silver light—from the south came the brilliant gold light. The whole sky seemed to light up. Immediately, the people became frightened. It was the serpents coming toward the village. One man said, "Let us do this." Another man said, "No, let us do this, for it will destroy the monsters."

Just as quickly, another man stood and said, "No, I have a better idea to do away with these serpents." So now it was that the people's leaders began quarreling with one another about the best way to handle the problem. Then the people began yelling at each other, even fighting one another.

... But the two huge serpents got closer to the people of the village. The fighting and yelling of the people grew more fierce. There were people killed because of the fighting, and blood stained the mother earth. As the serpents moved in closer, the people panicked, and everyone seemed to lose hope—it appeared close to the end.

It was at this moment that the clouds darkened in the west. The whole sky soon became hazy and the day almost turned to night, but the people continued to argue and fight and it seemed they would have no end to their frustrations.

Suddenly, our Grandfathers shot a giant bolt of lightning from the west. It struck right in the midst of the confused people. It was this big lightning arrow that shocked the people back to their senses. Soon following the lightning, the Grandfather Wind blew his strong breath, causing things to be knocked over as the wind traveled in and around the longhouses and trees.

The Grandfather Wind then spoke. He spoke the words sent by the Creator and this is what the Wind said:

"My children, you have not much time to save

yourselves, so you must listen carefully to what I tell you. There will be a little boy who will lead you to safety. He will tell you to prepare an arrow—and on this arrow you must have a white arrowhead. He will then tell you to make a strong bow, and only from a certain kind of tree. He will then tell you to take a hair from a pure woman, and string the bow with the hair. When these things have been prepared, the little boy will lead you to the wooded area on top of a big hill. On the top of this hill, you people will wait with your bow and arrow. When the serpents find you there on top of the hill, they will raise their bodies on the north and south of the hill. As the serpents raise their bodies high over the hill and come down over the people with their mouths wide open, the little boy and the people will point the arrow directly at the serpents' heads and wait until..."

This is the end of the prophecy as far as we know up to this date. That's where it ends.

Now we ask, what does this story mean? I asked the elders, and this is what they said.

The gold serpent represents the United States of America.

The silver serpent represents Great Britain and Canada.

The white arrowhead represents our chiefs and medicine people. They will lead and direct us.

The hair from the pure woman which is to string the bow represents our clan mothers. They are to be real mothers again.

The bow to be made from a special tree is representative of the people. Our people are special, and the people are the power.

The serpents swallowing the children represents that our children will be inside the serpents' bellies. Now let us think about it—most of our children speak the language of the serpent and no longer Mohawk, the language intended by the Creator. Even our children no longer know our ceremonies, or act according to our ways.

The serpents swallowing the elders represents that our elders will not identify with our own ceremonies, but in fact, identify themselves with the ceremonies and life of the serpents.

The serpents' constant threat represents how the countries of Canada and the United States try to make us all citizens of their countries so there will be no more Onkwehonwe (Indian nations).

Pointing the arrow at the heads of the serpents and waiting represents the people who must get ready and prepare themselves by purifying spiritually and then the Creator will instruct those of us who do this what we must do in the future. They say Senkwaiatison (God) the Creator will talk again to us, perhaps as the Grandfather Wind did back then.

They said the people will see the tracks of the serpents, and they will become frightened and will begin to understand what is meant. This is all...

They said, "Sometime in the future, the children will raise up the sacred Indian ways again."

Now I would like to make some comments, as I have traveled since 1965 all over North America. As I traveled, I can surely say I have seen the tracks the serpents left behind. They are still making new tracks every day.

I have seen the rivers made dirty and undrinkable and I know the serpents have been there.

I have followed the serpents' tracks from the eastern seaboard and I have seen grasslands, forests, and even mountains knocked down—I know the serpents have been there.

Clear to the Rocky Mountains and further beyond. I have seen strip mining where now nothing will grow—I know the serpents have been there.

I have felt the hot poisonous breath from the serpents' heads in New York City, Chicago, and Los Angeles—I know the serpents have been there.

I have been to the countries of the Sioux, Cheyenne, Pomo, and Hopi, all of whom were great nations, but today are only reservations—and I know the serpents have been there.

Brethren, I ask you to listen to the whispering words of our grandfathers and think.

This is all.

Sakokwenonkwas
(©Copyright 1974 by Sakokwenonkwas. Reprinted with permission from Akwesasne Notes, *Mohawk Nation, via Rooseveltown, New York 13683.)*

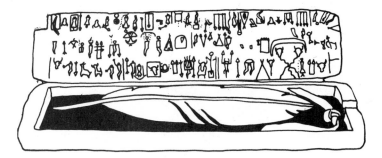

Native Americans—Action Suggestions

- Become as well acquainted as possible with the conditions of Native Americans.
- Get acquainted with the Indian tribes in your area and in your state. Are there reservations nearby? Are there Indians off the reservation now living in your community? What are their particular needs? their concerns? their place in society? Are there cases of injustice that need to be dealt with?
- If you are a church or synagogue member, how does your congregation relate to the Indian? Is there any local involvement in Indian affairs? Does your religious community have any national program? Is there a social action committee dealing with Indian concerns?
- Have you corresponded with your Congressional Representative and Senators? With state officials where they are involved?
- What is your local newspaper doing? Does it continue stereotypes about Native Americans, with references to scalping, savages, drunkenness, etc.? Have you talked with anyone about this? Have you written any letters to the editor?
- Does your TV station carry programs that further the dehumanizing stereotypes about Native Americans? What can you do to change this?
- What do the children learn in the local schools? Are they still studying "How the West Was Won"? or have they heard the Indian's case for "How the West Was Lost"? Do they get an uncritical presentation of the white people's belief in "manifest destiny" or do they learn what this meant to the original "Americans"?
- Make a study of the textbooks used in your local schools using *Textbooks and the American Indian* as a guide.
- Examine the resources in your local libraries. Help them become aware of the problem. Suggest books written by Native Americans and publications such as *Akwesasne Notes*.
- Consider the possibility of forming a study and support committee to involve local and regional people in the Indian struggle. In many places there are local and regional issues to relate to; in other places national issues may be the focus.

Fellowship of Reconciliation   Nyack, New York

Native American Periodicals

Akwesasne Notes
Mohawk Nation
via Rooseveltown, New York 13683
   Published five times annually, this tabloid is a healthy 50-pages-or-so, with feature articles, news and comment, and some fiction and poetry. It is free, but contributions are encouraged to cover costs. They also publish a variety of books and pamphlets, two of which are: "B.I.A. I'm Not Your Indian Any More," an account of the famous Trail of Broken Treaties of 1972, with "Twenty Points," the well-thought-out demands for historic change in the relationship between Native Americans and the U.S.A. ($1.95). "A Hard Look at American Catholic Folklore: Mohawks, Martyrs, and Myths." Two articles by Richard L. Lunstrom (25¢).

American Indians Crafts and Culture
Box 3538
Tulsa, Oklahoma 74101
   Published monthly except July and August ($5 per year).

Wassaja
1451 Masonic Avenue
San Francisco, California 94117
   A national newspaper of Indian America with special sections on education and art ($10 per year).

78

Bibliographic Resources

National Indian Education Association
Project Media
3036 University Ave., SE, Suite 3
Minneapolis, Minnesota 55414
"An Index to Bibliographies and Resource Materials"
Table of Contents:
other, more specific bibliographies
resource materials
commercial film catalogs
periodicals
Native American periodic publications in print
Native American radio programming
Native American tape services
radio stations interested in beginning Native American programming
films, filmstrips, filmloops (with critical recommendations)
records, cassettes, and reel-to-reel tapes (complete with addresses and costs of materials)
Cost: $2.50

ERIC Document Reproduction Service
Computer Microfilm International Corp.
P.O. Box 190
Arlington, Virginia 22210
This is an extensive bibliography on American Indian affairs put together by the Minnesota State Department of Education.
Table of Contents:
Elementary, junior and senior high school library books (synopsis provided)
pamphlets
newspapers and periodicals
picture, photographs and reproductions of paintings
maps
films, filmstrips, slides, records (with critical recommendations)
professional materials for teachers and administrators
arts and crafts
speakers bureau
Indian organizations and services in Minnesota
out of print books
Cost: $8.14 (includes tax)

Both these resources are excellent; both are about the same length.

Native-American Organizations

American Indian Historical Society works to correct textbooks, and sponsors conventions at which Indian scholars discuss important issues of Indian life. 1451 Masonic Ave., San Francisco, California 94117.

American Indian Movement. Although they are mostly known for their "confrontations" like Wounded Knee, they also carry on activities in four other areas:
1) a research and technical assistance service to meet the needs and requests of Indians everywhere in a variety of ways;
2) they maintain a Native American Speakers' Bureau;
3) they carry a bibliography for "American History" courses, available on request;

4) they operate their own "Survival School System." "A Survival School stresses Indian participation and control. Self-confidence and Indian pride are built in the students…These are qualities they need to have to survive in a white-dominated world. Too, the Indian culture—a way of life, a history and a heritage—can survive only through our children…Cooperation, traditional in Indian life, is stressed in learning…Most public schools are operated on principles of competition and individualism which are foreign to the traditional Indian values" (from their material). "Something you should probably note in your guide is that AIM works for justice for Indians in a variety of ways at many different levels, as may be appropriate to a particular case or situation. But ultimately, AIM is a movement of national liberation, seeking a return of sovereignty to Indian nations, meaning control of land, natural resources and Indian people by Indian people" (from their letter). AIM, P.O. Box 3677, St. Paul, Minnesota 55101.

Americans for Indian Opportunity has a variety of information pieces, with some particularly fine recent reports on native peoples and natural resources. 1816 Jefferson Pl., NW, Washington, D.C. 20036.

American Indian National Bank was established under federal banking laws and is subject to normal regulatory requirements of the Comptroller of Currency and fully accredited and insured by the FDIC. Old Coyote, president of the bank and a Crow Indian, stated: "The new bank is the keystone of an envisioned national Indian financial structure that will eventually encompass banking operation, venture capital, industrial capital and insurance services to Indians throughout the U.S."

Only Indians may purchase stock in the bank. Tribes, organizations, and individuals have been invited to buy shares, and to put their money into their own Indian-controlled banking situation. Their efforts are aimed at putting Indian monies to work for Indians.

Association on American Indian Affairs, Inc. publishes *Indian Affairs Newsletter* ($3.50 a year subscription). 432 Park Ave. South, New York, New York 10016.

Canadian Association in Support of Native Peoples. 277 Victoria St., Toronto, MSV 1W2, Ontario, Canada.

Indian Press Association is an excellent bibliographic source for news coverage. 408 Zook Bldg., 431 Kolfax, Denver, Colorado 80204.

Indian Rights Association "...is a nonsectarian, nonpartisan organization supported by the contributions of its members and friends. It strives to keep acquainted with American Indians and informed about their problems and desires, so as to assist them as best we can, and to inform our members and the public generally about contemporary Indians." They publish *Indian Truth*, a monthly newsletter ($5 students and Indian, $10 regular). 1505 Race St., Philadelphia, Pennsylvania 19102.

Institute for Development of Indian Law is "a nonprofit, private, educational corporation founded by Indian attorneys in 1971. It is a research organization with litigation potential and is developing a philosophy with regard to Indian law with a special emphasis on the three areas: treaty rights, taxation of Indians, and recognition of Indians with respect to federal rights." They publish an Education Journal issued 10 times a year (no price listed). They also have a chronological list of Broken Treaties in a series of books for $30.00. 927 15th St., NW, Washington, D.C. 20005.

Hunger and the Lifestyle Connection

Into the consciousness of a nation already troubled by the repercussions of political intrigue, the war in southeast Asia, poverty and urban unrest, the mid-1970s brought reports of a scourge which was ravaging the world. Hunger hit the headlines with compelling intensity: Famine in Bangladesh! Drought in the Sahel! Most Americans learned about the existence of hunger through televised pictures of dying babies and starving people waiting in line for food rations. They listened to the statistics of the food crisis affecting over 450 million of the world's poor as national leaders gathered in Rome in 1974 for the World Food Conference.

Other Americans did not learn of hunger in the last decade: they have lived their lives in a food crisis. These are America's hungry. Tucked away on Indian reservations, in migrant worker camps, in former plantation regions and the hollows of Appalachia, in urban ghettos and sharecropper shacks, are the very old and the very young, the men and women whose stomachs are rarely full and whose bodies are never properly nourished. In 1978 it was estimated that at least 26 million persons in our country lacked the resources to provide adequate diets for themselves. According to a study conducted in 1975, 1.1 million infants and children in the U.S. were suffering from undernourishment severe enough to handicap their brain development.

What is not so generally known by Americans is that all of this has been happening in a world which, from a global perspective, has enough food to meet the basic nutritional needs of all its people. In their provocative book, *Food First*, Lappe and Collins report that farmers of the world are producing about 2 pounds of grain, or more than 3,000 calories a day, for every child, woman, and man on earth. More than the nutritional minimum, 3,000 calories is what the average American consumes daily. Such an estimate of worldwide plenty is conservative for it does not include the many protein-rich staples such as beans, potatoes, cassava, and range-fed beef, not to mention fruits and vegetables.

We live on a planet with food resources more than adequate for its population, and yet malnutrition continues as the world's most widespread cause of physical and mental debility, disease and death.

Why?
- Because some countries allow corporations to use their best farm land to produce crops (coffee, sugar, cocoa, beef, etc.) for export to wealthy nations rather than food for their own people;

- Because some companies entice women to relinquish their own natural food resource for their infants—breast milk—in favor of a commercial product which, in unsanitary conditions of poverty, is too expensive, inappropriate, and even lethal;
- Because "aid" from wealthy countries is most often designed to develop and protect their markets, not to eradicate poverty in the poor countries;
- Because federal programs to alleviate malnutrition in this country have all too often been motivated by corporate and political self-interest rather than genuine attempts to eliminate hunger;
- Because lack of employment opportunities prevents many from gaining the economic resources necessary to purchase the food which is available;
- Because some nations spend so much money for arms that they can't afford to develop their agricultural potential;
- Because a legacy of colonialism has left the control of international trade and intercourse between nations in the hands of the wealthy nations;
- Because the potential contribution of women to development in the Third World has been virtually ignored and their traditional status undermined;
- Because systematic discrimination against some ethnic/racial minorities has been so institutionalized as to effectively cut them off from the means of self-development;

- Because the fruits of the Green Revolution for the most part aided only wealthy farmers and widened the gap between the rich and poor;
- Because the breakdown of the larger family has resulted in many old persons being left alone, poverty-stricken and unable to care for themselves;
- Because those who *know* enough do not seem to *care* enough to end hunger.

What Must Be Done?

If the causes of this scourge are so many, so complex and so interrelated, is there anything that can be done? .

Or are we doomed to see a world in which the haves build ever-higher walls to protect themselves from the ever-growing numbers of the have-nots and pay ever-increasing amounts of money for arms to keep the have-nots from storming the walls of plenty?

To know *what* must be done if malnutrition is to be eradicated is not as difficult as knowing *how* to do it, and neither are as difficult as actually *doing* it. But to have an idea of what must be done is the starting point without which there is no knowing how or in fact doing. So, what must be done?

(1) *Each nation has to decide that providing adequate nutrition for all its people is among its highest national priorities.* A 1978 article in the *New York Times* entitled: "Malnutrition Taking Bigger Toll Among Mexican Children," pointed out that in many developing countries agricultural priorities are first, food for export; second, food for

industrial processing; and only third, food for the population at large. That is a formula for malnutrition. The agricultural priorities must be reversed if all people are to be adequately fed.

The determination to provide adequate nutrition for all its people involves more than a nation's agricultural priorities. Other priorities must include making possible employment for all who can work so that they will have the money to buy food that will be available when the agricultural priorities are changed. If the opportunity for employment for all people is realized in the society, the cancerous core of the cause of malnutrition will have been eliminated. Employment opportunity, however, will not solve the problems of those who cannot work: the young, the old, the sick, and the disabled. A society that can decide to change its agricultural priorities and provide full employment opportunities is also a society that can provide for the "welfare" of its helpless in ways beyond the imagination of those who have experienced the impersonal and dehumanizing welfare system in the United States.

(2) *The international community of nations must decide to accept a more equitable basis for mutual intercourse than presently exists.* With justification the poor nations of the world cry out that "the rules of the game are unfair." It is not too difficult to understand why those countries, with 70 percent of the world's population, reject a system which awards 70 percent of the world's income to the other 30 percent of its inhabitants. That inequity is due less to ignorance, laziness, and lack of resources than it is to the fact that the "rules" of the world economic "game" —as applied to trade, the international monetary system, the operation of large multinational corporations—are "fixed" in favor of the industrialized nations of the world. Those rules are the legacy of Western colonialism.

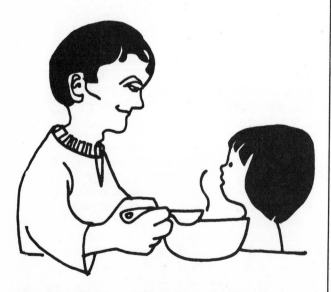

What the developing nations of the world are calling for is a new international economic order (NIEO), in which the poor countries get a fair price for the goods they produce for the industrialized countries and in which poor countries are not forced by wealthy countries to produce goods for them at the expense of providing food for their own people.

There should be no illusions about the difficulties in getting the community of nations to play by a new set of rules. And as Geoffrey Barraclough, one of the best known analysts of the world economic crisis, has reminded us, if one looks at present indications, the prospects for a new world economic order look slim and those for new world economic disorder look alarmingly large. However, just as it was possible for slavery to be ended in this country, as it was possible for Western political colonialism to be ended in most of the Third World, so it is also possible to end economic colonialism.

While there are many other decisions that need to be made if hunger and malnutrition are to be

eliminated, there can be no substitutes for the decision at the international level providing for more equitable dealing among nations, nor for the decision at national levels to provide adequate nutrition for all their people. The implications of these two decisions are far-reaching. How the decisions will get made may not yet be clear, but that must not detract from the necessity of seeing that they are made.

What Can I Do?

Specifically, what can I do to ensure that the decisions at national and international levels are made and implemented? Commensurate with the seriousness of the problem and the difficulties in getting the important decisions made is the seriousness with which we approach the problem personally. What is required of us is nothing less than a lifestyle focused on the problem and its solution. We suggest that there are five vocations in this responsible lifestyle:

1. We must be *students* so that we can see beyond the headlines and political and corporate rhetoric to understand the fundamental issues. Both study and reflection can lead us to a recognition that employment, welfare, and the New International Economic Order are hunger issues.

2. We must be *activists* in our local community.

The integrity of our commitment to the hunger concern is reflected in our ability to recognize the dimensions of hunger at home and in our willingness to be involved with the poor in its elimination. There is no substitute for direct personal involvement.

3. We must be *advocates* at local/state/national levels on government and corporate policies and practices. We must stand in those arenas where the poor are not present, whether at a company stockholder meeting or at a Senate hearing; our voices must echo those of the poor whose access to the decision-making process at both government and business levels has traditionally been blocked. Several excellent organizations are available to assist you in this effort: Bread for the World, the Interreligious Taskforce on U.S. Food Policy, and the Interfaith Center on Corporate Responsibility.

4. We must be *responsible stewards* of our financial resources, committing them to church and other voluntary efforts to combat hunger and monitoring their use in our individual and corporate lives. Through both our charitable contributions and our financial investments we can make strong statements about our stand for equality and justice. As churches develop programs which are more controversial, your informed support may well be critical.

5. We must be *pioneers* in finding new ways of living characterized by using only that which is absolutely required. This means developing a lifestyle that will be a microcosm of the kind of world order which must come to be. It means developing immunity to that disease which is endemic to our society: consumerism, or consumption for its own sake, which might be called the "Madison Avenue Syndrome." The life of voluntary simplicity is a luxury which we receive in exchange for rejecting our bondage to consumerism. It becomes a sign of our personal liberation as well as a symbol of our solidarity with sisters and brothers for whom simplicity is a "given," not a choice.

For the past seven years many of us have worked to mobilize people in our churches into the kind of lifestyle just described. We have sought through this mobilization to build a broad-based consensus of concern among our church constituencies. In doing this we have adopted a style which sought to be inoffensive and low key and an approach which, while straightforward regarding facts, sought to be moderate regarding actions.

That mobilization must continue to be strengthened through individual commitments. Moreover, it must be strengthened through *deepened* commitments which carry with them a sense of urgency about implementing solutions to hunger. We must end the complacency with which we deal with the "statistics" of hunger by making it our own struggle, by joining hands with its victims and working toward their victory.

Colleen Shannon-Thornberry   Staff Associate, Presbyterian Hunger Program, Atlanta, Georgia/New York, New York
Milo Shannon-Thornberry   Former Coordinator for Hunger Concerns of the National Council of Churches, Currently Director of Alternatives

Action Ideas

In terms of specific Thanksgiving events, we have done basically the same thing each year. The night before we have a liturgy in the soup kitchen, after which we prepare the food for the following day. On Thanksgiving itself, we also serve a regular dinner: turkey, potatoes, dressing, green vegetable, juice, and desserts to about 300 people (not quite a small family gathering!). We get an excellent response from all kinds of people, and we really do feel on that day an abundance of food (as do the people in

the kitchen). That evening at the hospitality/prandial house there is again a large dinner (for about 50 or so) for the people who live with us, as well as for members of the community.

I know that some people have begun a tradition of fasting on Thanksgiving, especially because of the situation of world hunger. I believe it is an admirable response, but because of the work we do, and the kind of people we deal with, we feel that we should feast on that one day, and that the poor deserve the best kinds of food. Individuals in the community have taken part in fasts of different kinds, vigils, etc., for people who wish to share their food with the poor. One thing of importance that I would like you to emphasize is that while Thanksgiving is a day when we do think of food, it is important that food once again become the *basic* thing that it is; that we have to regain a whole theology of food, about the kinds of food we eat, and why we eat them. Thanksgiving should just be a beginning for that kind of reflection, not a one-shot deal.

Rachelle Linner   Community for Creative Non-Violence
Washington, D.C.

Earlier this spring, we sent requests to some of our panelists for suggestions on alternative ways to celebrate the Thanksgiving holidays. I would like to forward some comments from an American Indian member of the Panel of American Women. Briefly, she suggests holding a congregational dinner featuring native Indian dishes where recognition would be given to the contributions the Indians made to the beginning of the Thanksgiving tradition. Such a program of course would be faithful to the truth in historical facts.

Shirley Morantz   Executive Secretary
Panel of American Women, Kansas City, Missouri

Consider using the Thanksgiving season as a time to start a voluntary simplicity study-action project which would end with an alternative Christmas campaign.

We had a number of people who were new to the community and without ties to family and friends here. So several men in the church volunteered to cook turkey for Thanksgiving for these people. One woman made up a list of things to bring and filled in names of persons willing to bake a pie or bring a vegetable. Many of us were skeptical about how well it would come off, but about two weeks before the holiday, something like 35 people had signed up. We ended up with 60. One of the former ministers of the church came back with his family so this became a way that they could share in the giving of thanks. While many single people showed up, a surprising number of families did too. Mothers escaped the labors of slaving all day in the kitchen for one big orgy, followed by endless dishwashing while the men watched football.

Before and after the meal there were puzzles, games, and discussion starters lined up. Someone was going to bring a TV, but fortunately it was broken so all of us escaped the trappings of the "boob-tube." After the dinner the price of the meal was announced and people were asked to donate about a dollar if they could.

It was a real success. Another event was planned for New Year's Day and people are thinking about it for this year again. While the idea is simple, it provided a real opportunity for people without a place to celebrate Thanksgiving and an alternative for those traditionally trapped by "family."

Rev. Jerry Haas   Pacific Beach Methodist Church
San Diego, California

Last year we began a cooperative congregational garden. We started in the spring...and even had church school pupils starting seeds inside. We also used John Denver's record of "Whose Garden Was This?" Our garden proved very productive and we distributed much produce from the narthex.

For Thanksgiving Sunday we pulled it all together with a large display of our harvest... we also used the following litany...

A Thanksgiving Litany for a Garden

Leader: Whose Garden was this?
People: It was Frank's and Ruth's and God's and ours.
Whence came the seed?
It came from those rooted in the faith and from some whose faith had not yet taken root.
How were the seeds planted?
With loving care and the knowledge that seeds can move mountains.
How were the seeds cared for?
Lovingly and according to the instructions that the tares were to be cast aside.
What was the harvest?

*Tomatoes and corn and beans and concern and
involvement; the fellowship of sauerkraut
suppers, and the knowledge that as we do
God's will, we learn God's love.*

Whose garden is this?

*It is the Lord's and the fullness thereof, and we
are the sheep of his pasture, the inhabitants of
his garden of Eden. Let us give thanks to the
Lord; for his bounty is great.*

ALL: Amen.

*Vern Campbell   Peoples Presbyterian Church, Milan,
Michigan*

Plan Your Offering of Letters

Bread for the World's Offering of Letters is a way
for Christians to express their faith in an act of love
on behalf of our hungry brothers and sisters in the
world.

The Offering of Letters is an invitation to
Christians across the country to place in the
Sunday collection basket, as an offering of our
citizenship alongside our regular offering of money,
letters to public officials—the President,
Congresspersons, Senators—on a carefully
selected public policy issue or piece of legislation
which affects the lives of hungry people.

Bread for the World selects a single timely and
appropriate focus each year, and encourages local
churches to participate.

In 1975-76, Bread for the World launched a
successful nationwide Offering of Letters
campaign which brought about a far-reaching
declaration of intent from our public policymakers:
The right to food, declared the U.S. Congress,
"shall be a fundamental point of reference in the
formulation and implementation of U.S. policy in all
areas which bear on hunger."

More than a quarter of a million letters were
received in Congress, and this demonstration of
public concern and support resulted in the
passage of the Right-to-Food Resolutions in both
Houses of Congress.

In 1976-77, as a natural follow-up to the Right-
to-Food victory and to the 1974 World Food
Conference, individuals in churches across the
land engaged in another successful Offering of
Letters campaign—this time around the need for a
U.S. grain reserve to aid as a buffer against
famine. Again, sufficient support was
demonstrated so that legislation was passed in
both Houses of Congress, and in November 1977
the Administration announced a grain reserve
program based on a formula and guidelines
almost identical to those recommended by Bread
for the World.

In 1977-78, the focus of the Offering of Letters
was to encourage President Carter to take major
leadership in the fight against hunger at home and
abroad.

The Thanksgiving Season provides an ideal
time for the Offering of Letters in the churches,
though many churches, for one reason or another,
opt to have their Offering of Letters at other times
of the year. Any Sunday is appropriate between
the time the offering topic is announced by the
national office of Bread for the World and the time
when appropriate action is taken in Washington.

Each year, Bread for the World produces a flyer
suitable for use as church bulletin inserts which
introduces the Offering of Letters and its public
policy focus for the year. The flyers may be
ordered in bulk from Bread for the World at cost
($1.00 per hundred) or reproduced locally. They
should be introduced on the Sunday prior to the
date selected for the offering. People may write
their letters at home or at church on the Sunday of
the offering—depending on local preferences. A
special offering basket may be provided or
worshippers may bring the letters forward in a
procession. In one parish a procession outside to
the mailbox was incorporated into the service.

*Write to Bread for the World and inquire about
this year's Offering of Letters.* Ask for information
and a sample copy of the flyer. Also ask about
suggestions for incorporating the offering into the
Sunday worship service.

*Bread for the World   207 E. 16th St. New York, New
York 10003*

Hunger Action Resources

Most denominations have various programs
dealing with hunger and poverty. Find out what
your denomination is doing and how you can be a
part of it. Most denominations also have printed
resources available with suggestions about what
you can do.

You may also want to contact the World Hunger
Education Service, a nonprofit organization with

programs of public education, networking, and
leadership development for hunger education and
action. Dr. Patricia L. Kutzner is Director. Among
their resources are the following:

- *Hunger Notes*, produced monthly by the staff.
  Subscription $10 a year. Bulk rates.
- *Who's Involved with Hunger*, a 36-page
  organization guide. $2.50.

- *Audio-Visual Resources on the Politics of Hunger,* annotates films with ordering information. Includes a few titles on each of the following topics: multinational corporations; international economic order; poverty and power in the Third World; rural and urban poverty in the U.S.; Native American issues; and citizen action strategies. The guide costs $1.00.
World Hunger Education Service
2000 P Street, NW (Suite 205)
Washington, D.C. 20036
202/223-2995

Selected Readings

Food First: Beyond the Myth of Scarcity, Francis Moore Lappe and Joseph Collins. An encyclopedic compendium of facts, this question and answer book is a basic reference tool about food, food policy, self-reliance, and popular myths about the food crisis. Perhaps the most important book about food printed to date. $3.25.
Bread and Justice: Toward a New International Economic Order, James B. McGinnis. In a world beset by complex problems where people are starving and unjust social structures thwart the poor and the hungry in their attempt to change these conditions, McGinnis explains some of the national and international policies that have brought us to our present crisis. He tells about the real effects of hunger and poverty. He examines what the Gospel and the Christian religious tradition tell us about justice among people. Paulist Press. $4.95

DECEMBER

CHRISTMAS and HANUKKAH

For many who want to celebrate the birth of Jesus Christ, instead of being a time of joy and peace, Christmas may be a time of frustration, disappointment, and embarrassment:

frustration at finding that it is the advent of Santa Claus, rather than Jesus, that claims most attention and energy;

disappointment at being so hurried and harried that the wish for it just to be over becomes paramount;

embarrassment at being so pressured into buying *things* for family and friends who may have little need of them while so little attention is given to those whose needs are great.

These experiences are not new. The history of the celebration of the birth of Christ has been a history of struggle to separate the commemoration of Jesus's birth from pagan influence. The selection of December 25 as the date coincided with the feast in honor of the Sun God in the cult of Mithras, the official Roman religion in the late third century. December 25 also came at the end of the Feast of Saturnalia (December 17-23) which commemorated the Golden Age of Saturn.

It is likely that December 25 was set to provide Christians with an alternative to these popular festivals. Christian celebrations of Christmas, then and throughout subsequent history, have often taken on the character of the surrounding pagan festivals, whether in Rome, Northern Europe, or in America. In our case, the issue of accommodation to the worship of consumption, comes closer than anything else to being the "state religion" in North America.

One need not be a Christian to experience a profound ambivalence toward Christmas. With the encroachment of some popular elements of commercialized Christmas into Hanukkah, many Jewish people are experiencing an obscuring of that festival's religious significance.

Celebrated at about the same time as Christmas, Hanukkah, the Feast of Dedication, is an eight-day festival begun in the second century, B.C., celebrating the driving out of the Syrians and the restoration of traditional worship during the Maccabean Revolt. The festival is also called the Feast of Lights because of the traditional practice of burning candles in the Menorah (nine-branched candelabrum). It is ironic that with the significance of this celebration lying in the struggle of Jews to preserve their integrity against social pressure for assimilation, its popular celebration in Jewish homes is often an example of cultural assimilation, thanks to the tremendous cultural and economic forces swirling around Christmas.

Many other people, while not concerned about observing a religious holiday, experience anger and frustration at having their emotions manipulated by the "hard sell" to buy at

Christmas. Few there are, religious or nonreligious, who will not experience disappointment at unfulfilled expectations at Christmas, expectations magnified all out of proportion because of its commercial value.

How we celebrate Christmas has been one of the primary concerns in each of our Catalogues:

In the *first edition* we tried to isolate some of the crassly materialistic expressions of how the business community exploits the birthday of Jesus:

- from a *Time* article: "to seduce the shoppers, stores across the U.S. are resorting to unprecedented gimmicks and highly unusual pre-Christmas sales."
- from a *Business Week* story: "the merry selling season" and "the lusty aroma of fresh money."
- from *Christian Century:* the Bad Taste Award for the toilet which plays the Ohio State fight song when the lid is lifted.
- from the Neiman-Marcus Christmas Book: Crown Russian sable cape for $42,000; elephant-hide kit for $100; champagne bucket for $170; full-dimensional life-size dummy of your favorite person programmed to laugh at your jokes or say yes in any language you choose at the touch of a remote control button—for $3000.

The connection between our wastefully consumptive patterns and the world's underdevelopment and poverty was made and we stated: "The will to be fair, to share, to live on less, to *practice* justice in our lifestyle and celebrations…this is where we can begin to incarnate our convinction that people can change the world."

In the *second edition* we said if we truly believe Christmas is the celebration of new life, then let us support *life* in the ways we practice the day. Let us be aware of the waste of the earth's resources and put an end to it. Let us be aware of the exploitation of ourselves and our children, through loud, obnoxious advertising schemes, and boycott nonsensical gifts that no one needs.

We pointed out the contradictions between the theoretical Christmas of peace on earth, good will to all—and the Christmas of reality. We quoted

Mason Williams' thoughtful statement: "People used to buy things because they needed the things to survive, not because the things needed people to survive."

The Christmas section of the *third edition* began like this: As I sit here during the middle of July pulling together these ideas for celebrating an alternate Christmas, department stores are ordering tons of plastic and metal decorations. Buyers are stretching their brains for new sources for unusual gifts, for the products they pray will become the fad and rage of Christmastime. BankAmericard is contracting with its advertising agency to create a new Christmas television spot as smooth and clever as last year's. Ad agency writers and artists are climbing the wall for a new twist, a novel approach, some catchy idea to get you and me to buy lots more things.

We went on to say we believe this insanity is contrary to the national (and personal) self-interest. And not good for the rest of the world. Those who place profit above all else co-opt Silent Night, Peace on Earth, and the star of Bethlehem, not from religious motivation but to sell soap, electric trains, and food processors. We pointed

out that was analogous to kidnapping the baby Jesus and holding him for $10 billion ransom each Christmas!

In fairness, two things should be said: there are a few merchants who sensitively try to avoid commercializing Christmas; and each of us shares responsibility with the merchants by choosing to buy the $10 billion in extra purchases. (By Christmas 1982 that figure is to rise to about $20 billion.)

What was there to say new in the *fourth edition* about reducing the prostitution of Christmas? In the first three editions of the Catalogue we encouraged individuals to take personal action and many did. We realized, however, that more than personal actions were needed. We needed to organize and act in concert with others. The creative energy and combined imagination and action of concerned people working together will produce the desired goals much faster than the same number of people going through the same process as isolated individuals. That's why the fourth edition sought to provide incentive and resources for persons to organize: study action groups, alternative Christmas festivals, and general community organization.

Our focus continues to be on organizing. In addition to making available the resources for organizing through the fourth edition (and now in this special edition) and the Newsletter, we now sponsor and provide resources for:

- An Alternative Christmas Congregational Campaign
- A National Best and Worst Christmas Gift Contest
- Alternative Christmas Community Festivals

In this special edition we have included both the personal experiences and ideas of people in the earlier editions, as well as the resources for organizing in the fourth edition and those developed since that edition. Although you will find suggestions about alternative giving and gifts in this chapter, these are dealt with in more detail in chapter 6, "Giving and Gifts."

Looking at Some Alternatives

The challenge of Christmas may simply be to cope with it, but there are many who find themselves doing more than brashly plowing through a list of gifts to be delivered and expressions of friendship communicated. Those who are Christian seek ways to rediscover the significance of Christ's birth. Those who are not Christian must surely find it necessary to scrutinize what is going on around them and either avoid, tolerate, or enjoy the festivities.

Gifts

Somewhat ahead of time, review what is hoped for in the Christmas season, and what the family expects. It may not be the year for a radical breaking away from gift-giving, but try for spending limitations. By planning early, there is the chance to give more careful thought to each gift decision.

Considering one person at a time, giving careful thought to personal interest, is not only good practice in caring, but also in deciding what's really appropriate for each individual. It can also prevent the exasperated store-to-store trek, hoping for an inspiration and usually ending up with something impulsive instead of something important.

It's better to think about gifts away from stores, away from catalogues. Think about the person! Only *after* contemplating the type of gift to be given, should one selectively shop for that gift.

As for giving to a cause instead of to a person, this must be done with the person in mind. A young person who has always received something tangible may not be ready for a shift to money given for social purposes. But relatives with well-stocked homes and larders are often quite pleased *not* to receive some peculiar item they didn't want anyway. It all depends on the person. The purpose is giving that makes sense to the recipient as well as to the giver.

Another part of the gift-planning is to determine what help children need, encouraging them toward the meaningful rather than the wasteful gift. Give guidance on gift-giving to children who don't have money. All (adults and children) can have skills and talents which might create handmade gifts. Most people place special value on those things in which someone has invested time and care, be they pictures, poems, homemade chore coupons, or clever, hand-crafted projects. It is well to ask, "Will the person for whom I'm making this want a homemade gift?" Some people don't find any meaning in them, and that must be considered. Or, if the homemade projects will make one so tired and tied down as to become unhappy, then they shouldn't be attempted. Most of us can't knit three sweaters in the last weeks before Christmas, or sew or carpenter or anything else, if there is time pressure. So, there must be a decision about what personally made gifts can appropriately be done.

The "alternative" idea became a part of our family's thinking about 25 years ago, at which time we decided to stop exchanging Christmas gifts in our family and instead use the money we would have spent on gifts to help at some point in the world. In the early years we used to sit around the table after our dinner on Thanksgiving Day and discuss how we would

use our Christmas Fund, to which everyone (even the little ones) contributed. In recent years the family has scattered and the collection of the Fund is by mail, solicited by a mimeographed letter. There are twenty-eight in our family group now. Participation is voluntary, and there is not 100 percent participation, but we think it is wise to continue it. This past Christmas we collected $235.

Carolyn Miller   Columbus, Ohio

One of the finest Christmas presents you could give your city is to set up an Alternatives Fund like the one in Richmond, Virginia. A small group meets regularly to pool their surplus income resulting from simple living practices. Periodically the money is sent to local, national, and international projects which have been carefully checked out. For a whole city the Fund would work something like a mutual stock fund in reverse. The portfolio of projects would be researched for maximum benefit from contributions and low overhead. As money was deposited to the Fund, gifts would be made to different groups based on urgency and long-range goals.

Write to Al Watts, 3127 Cofer Rd., Richmond, Virginia 23224 for more information.

Give a gift of transportation to help friends carry things and go places with less dependence on the smogmobile.
shopping carts   bus tokens   bicycles
bike repair books   backpacks   baby carriers
bike touring club memberships   bike baskets
cloth or net shopping bags

Ecology Center   Berkeley, California

Last Christmas, our family and some others (who normally spend a small fortune on gifts for one another), decided to put an end to the absurdity of it all. We weren't able to end it all together, but we did manage to divert $300 to life-supporting celebrations of our own. There were 4 adult couples who participated. We met together to decide where the money normally spent on gifts would go. In this case, 3 different areas were touched: the fund for the family whose policeman father was shot, money to help a boy that we knew who was in prison, and money to help some one who was very ill.

Also last Christmas, we got together and gave a party for all of our children. The party was devised around the plan to have the children wrap their own toys to give to other children. We read to them from the Bible about what Jesus said about love and giving, and we saw some beautiful responses on their faces. The children had brought a trememdous amount of gifts that they wanted to give away; toys, books, clothing. When all the things were wrapped, we took the children and the gifts to the home of a family, fatherless, with 16 children. They understood that they were not taking these gifts to show that they were good boys and girls, but rather because Christ could show love through them. They were humble, and I don't think that they will ever forget the experience.

Paula Sevier   Birmingham, Alabama

Decorations

What is meaningful is what should be done. The sentimental trimmings should take priority over the elegant, the expensive, the extensive. The question to ask is, "What look do we want?" Ask kids how they feel, and proceed from there, sometimes negotiating over a change or over how to put up the decorations.

Certainly, decorating is an area for cautious spending. Not all families like the arts/crafts homemade masterpieces, but neither is it necessary to spend $10 or $25 more on classy gadgets that catch attention in the store and embarrass the budget later, especially since their use is so limited.

If decorating is a problem, the deciding should be done in consultation with one's own values and tastes. What looks good at the neighbors, in the store, or in a magazine, may be worth adapting, and then again, it may be a mistake.

For those in doubt, try the pleasant simplicity of decorating with greens. They can adorn shelves, tables, mantels, be tied with thread or wire into swags, or put in vases. Highlights can be a red bow, a shiny ornament, candles (reasonably distant from flammables), fruits, nuts. It's possible to create a very desirable holiday effect and spend next to nothing.

Christmas Ornaments

Make either for yourself or for small gifts. Surely everyone can find scraps of colorful material around their house. Use these to make ornaments, by cutting 2 pieces the same (in any number of interesting designs: stars, circles, diamond-shaped), turn inside-out, and stuff with cotton from asprin bottles, etc. You'll find that they will have interesting family associations as the years go on.

J. Loerke   Eagle, Wisconsin

Paper Ornaments from Circles

Materials: 1. bright poster board; dinner plate or a gallon plastic ice cream container for a circle form, or anything about that size in diameter; scissors; string.

Methods: 2. Cut 7 round disks out of poster board (lightweight), using medium-size plate or ice cream container for form. Fold all but one disk in half. On the fold cut with scissors, about halfway in from each end. Slip cut disks into edge of single flat disk. String and hang.

2. For a single swirl use a round disk made of lightweight paper. Cut into the disk, spiraling inward until you reach the center. For garlands, cut spirals in brightly colored tissue paper disks in layers. Turn the paper as you cut. The result is a bouncy twist that can be hung sideways in garlands around the room.

3. Fold circle into fours; manila folder paper is good for these. Follow the curved side, cut into folded paper leaving about one inch at inner edge. Open it and pull strips opposite ways from each other. Decorate with magic markers.

Dough Ornaments

For flat, permanent, cutout ornaments mix:
4 cups flour
1 cup salt
1 ½ cups water
Food coloring or paint (optional)
Roll with rolling pin, cut out with knife, cookie cutter, lids. Use different objects for texture. Make hair by forcing clay through a piece of window screen, or squeezing through a garlic press. Screw a small hook or press a loop of string into dough for hanging. Bake at 150 degrees in home oven until hard.

Ornaments from Recycled Materials

1. Paint a shallow can. Punch holes in center of top rim for hanging. Fill with 3 dimensional panorama and hang.
2. Decorate tin can lids with seeds, beans, tiny pine cones, seed pods, or bits of yarn. Punch a hole for hanging.
3. Cut cardboard from cereal boxes, cracker boxes, shoe boxes into shapes. Cover with tin foil and "tool" with magic markers.
4. Cut angels out of aluminum pie plates.
5. With a felt tip pen, draw a design on a large juice or coffee can. Fill with water and put in freezer until solid. With an ice pick, punch holes in can following lines of the design. Add candle or low-watt light bulb and you have a lantern.

Socializing

Much emphasis is placed on holiday parties, and often they result in unnecessary exhaustion, even sadness. On the other hand, Christmas has become a celebrational season, a time for getting together with special friends. So, ask:

"Is my party one more of many, which bring the same people together, or is it for a certain number of friends who otherwise won't see one another?"

"Is my party to repay invitations which could as easily be done another month, or is it people I especially want to be with at this time?"

"Can I afford the time and energy right now; will the entertaining be a pleasure for me as well as my guests?"

"Is there an innovative approach, such as taking the party to an older adult's home or a hospital, singing and celebrating there? Such as making sure the invitation list includes some persons who might otherwise be forgotten?"

If the decision is to entertain, then it should be done in one's own style, be that carefully organized or last-minute-spontaneous. A way to avoid tension is to be honest about doing things personally. Just because there's an imagery of elegant decorating and serving or of having dozens of family members together on Christmas, it doesn't mean that's the only way or the best way. Try for integrity and enjoy it more.

Make a piñata with the children, fill it with sugar-free candy, nuts, little bags of popcorn, toasted soybeans, fancy crackers, etc. Invite the neighborhood children in on Christmas Eve to break the piñata. The use of the piñata as a Spanish custom could be explained to the children. A library would have instructions to make it; basically, it's just a decorated shape of paper-mâché with the goodies inside.

Bob and Kathleen Keating   San Antonio, Texas

Cards

How clear it has become that holiday card lists can be a burden or a pleasure. There is no need to belabor the point that if December is the *only* communication of the entire year, it *may* be a very important point of contact with a distant friend or it *may* be a meaningless formality, better retired. Ideas:

• skip a few years and then review the list
• only send cards to those to whom a letter is also sent
• do it Valentine's Day or Thanksgiving instead of Christmas
• make the cards so they, in themselves, are personalized gifts
• spend some caring about the message and the price. Very expensive, large cards that say "peace on earth" over a white velvet dove might better be replaced by a $15 gift to a peace organization or a hunger program
• don't send cards to people seen often; greet them personally
• display the cards uniquely according to your own preference

Personal
~~Alternative~~
Gift Card

We wanted to give you something important and meaningful for this occasion— but...

Front

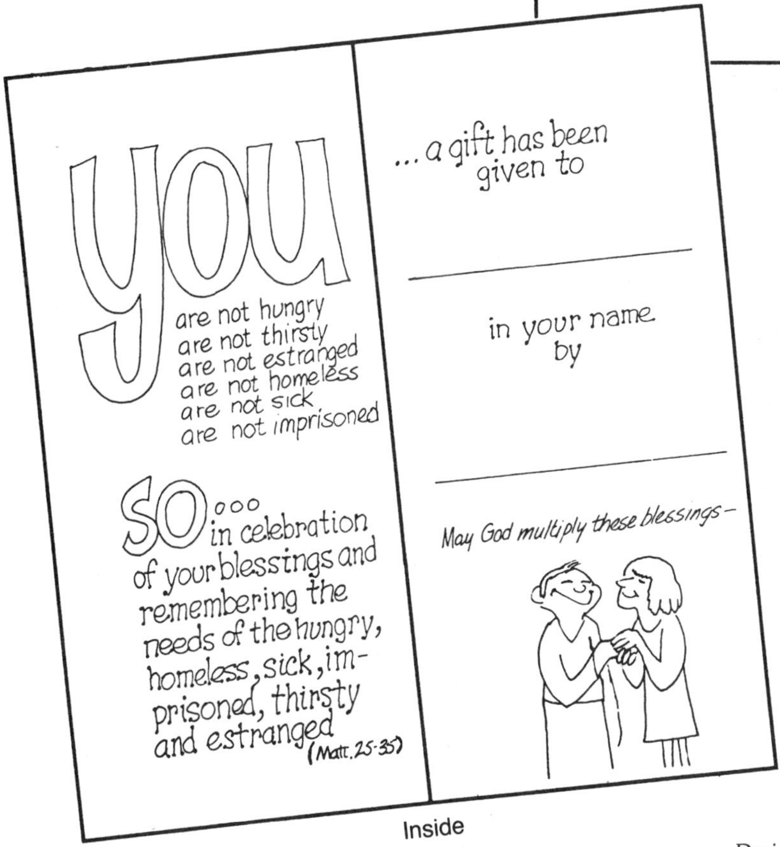

you
are not hungry
are not thirsty
are not estranged
are not homeless
are not sick
are not imprisoned

SO...
in celebration of your blessings and remembering the needs of the hungry, homeless, sick, imprisoned, thirsty and estranged (Matt. 25:35)

...a gift has been given to

_____

in your name by

_____

May God multiply these blessings—

Inside

Designed, conceived and developed by June Barneson and Marilyn Adams of Chico, California.

Frustrated by the rapidity in which they arrive, we abandon display efforts and collect cards in a dish. Then, after the season, one card at a time is taken out and put on the dinner table. The sender is remembered in that day's prayer and often a letter is sent. This extends the pleasure of the friendship.

I was sick and tired of receiving Christmas cards from people I see all the time. It's wasteful and ecologically unsound. I asked the people at the *Montclair Times*, our local paper, if they would print a "Community Season's Greetings Card" in the form of a full-page ad at Christmastime, listing all the people who made a contribution to charity that year instead of sending cards to their friends in town. They agreed, leaving me to select the charity, stipulating only that it be local. After researching, I chose the Salvation Army because of their reputation for delivering the goods where they most need delivering with a minimum of nonsense.

Over two hundred and seventy families responded. We collected about twenty-three hundred dollars, all of which went for food allowances, clothing, and small gifts for deprived families, nursing home residents, and the homeless people who rely on the Army for shelter. Because regular advertisers in the *Times* contributed the space, our total overhead was seventeen dollars, the price of the fliers.

Paula Krongard   Upper Montclair, New Jersey

Tonight I knocked out an improved version of what I think I'll call my June Christmas Card. I hope I won't chicken out of sending it to about 20 people—good friends all—with whom I *exchange gifts*. Either they or I started it, eons back (I am over 60) and, of course, I (or they) felt they had to reciprocate. This is an attempt to substitute *Reciprocate* with *Alternate*. I may lose a few friends along the way, but it's worth a try. The substance of the letter is this:

GREETINGS

The annual rite of gift-giving (except where children are concerned) becomes an increasing burden which tends to smother the simple beauty and humility that emanated from the manger in Bethlehem.

If you understand and share my concern, let us resolve to break the habit this coming holiday season. That others have already taken this position is evidenced by a three-year-old organization known as Alternatives.

Frank H. Teague, Jr.   Woodstock, Vermont

Programs

Even religious activities of Christmas are only as important as their contribution to positive love actions. The church community, as much as the family or the individual, needs to review the purpose of each event. It's highly significant that we put something extra special into the worship events, but just as five Christmas trees would distort a small house, an uncoordinated clamor of church programs can tire people and detract from Christmas meaning, whereas careful planning can heighten everyone's sensitivity to the Word of God made flesh in the world—today.

A brief mention of Santa Claus is essential here. While this whole culture has a noble and delightful origin, apparently quite innocent, in the man who gave dowries to the poor women and later a sleigh of toys to some children, he has been co-opted by the commercials and idolized as the one who gives gifts to those who are "good," so that families have been reported to take great pains to convince their children of his very reality. How is it expected that they are going to believe in a real Jesus whom they cannot see, when such concerted effort is made to help them see an unreal gift-giver, who appears at every affair?

When developing the church calendar, as in planning worship, we've learned to begin with God, for indeed, this dialogue is with God, to bring before ourselves the image, the message, the practice of truth. Today, when the church has broken free of some constraints, it's essential to remember that it is still God-the-creator, not man-the-clever, who is the focus of every worship, including Christmas.

Charity

Hopefully, if care is taken to review values, customs and lifestyles, there will be both an extension of meaning which exceeds the December celebration, and there will also be love and charity in all activities. There's no point in ignoring the value of extra giving for worthwhile causes as the year ends, nor denying that this season is one of extreme loneliness for many people to whom we can reach out. But neither loneliness nor giving are limited to December.

As one of the goals of the Alternatives Movement is to stress the giving of oneself, it is important to take time away from the material aspects of what we do and to focus on allowing the time to simply be, for the sake of loved ones, for the sake of unloved people of whom we could be more aware, and for the sake of our own spiritual need.

Let that which we are going to do for the holidays be done thoughtfully and meaningfully. Let us change what takes away from personhood and from the well-being of humanity. We can stretch our imaginations so that the celebration of God's birth does honor to the Lord and strives for the peace on earth He came to proclaim.

Grace Braley   Pearl River, New York

Alternative Christmas Celebrations

Christ's Birthday—December 25 has been chosen as the date to celebrate Christ's birth (no one knows the correct date). Thus, all that we do in connection with "Christmas" should give that message— "Christ has come to bring love and peace and to show us a better way." In our customs and celebrations, what message comes through?

Does it say, "Christ has come!" Does it say, "God sends his love to you!" Or does it say, "More for me and mine!"

Creativity—We should encourage the wealth of creativity displayed during the season—art, crafts, music, drama, literature, etc.—both to participate in and to enjoy that of others. Take advantage of the many religious Christmas musical and drama events.

Joy—We should express joy and happiness, but not the revelry brought on by expensive gift exchanges, alcohol, wild parties, etc.

Family togetherness and customs should be encouraged. Remembering family and friends everywhere is good.

Gifts—Ideally, Christmas gifts are given to "Christ," by giving to "even the least of these," who cannot repay or from whom we expect no gifts.

Gift giving should be token expressions of love, not displays of extravagance—and preferably they should be homemade. A gift should be a sharing of something one is, rather than giving what the other needs or wants.

If it is not possible to make the gifts, second best is to buy gifts from some organization which is seeking to uplift the poor, such as Koinonia, Chruch World Service, F.O.R. books—or give gift checks in their honor to life-supporting groups.

Santa Claus—He must be excluded from a Christian Christmas, for he has become the God of Materialism—parents take their children to worship at his feet. He brings extravagant gifts to the rich—and makes unfulfillable promises to poor children, which further demoralizes their parents in their eyes. *Christ* is the spirit of loving and giving! Let's not confuse the message for our children.

Christmas cards—Make your own or buy from some organization whose funds go to help people, like F.O.R. or UNICEF. Be sure that their message reflects Christ's message. Send them early to avoid the rush—or consider the European custom of sending New Year's greetings. Instead of just cards, write newsletters, giving all of the latest news from your family. Many churches encourage their members to sign a common, large "Christmas Card" at the church and enclose the money that they would have spent on individual cards for church friends, to be used for sharing with others in need through their church.

Christmas trees—What do they say to you? If they say, "Santa is coming," reject them. If they say "Rejoice, God sends His love and beauty!" enjoy them.

If you do have a Christmas tree, consider:

Live trees signify life, but are wasteful of money and lumber. You might buy a tree with roots, that can be planted outside later.

Be sure that the decorations carry the desired message. Consider a "Chrismon" tree (Christian monograms) which carries white symbols of Christianity—stars, crosses, shepherd staffs, flowers, crowns.

Home—Have Advent celebrations; play carols; bake Christmas cookies; decorate; plan family ways of sharing with the poor and lonely.

Adult celebration—Leave the "baby in the manger" in the background, and concentrate on the *adult* Jesus, who lived a new life and taught a new way of relating to others. What other great person in

history is honored by talking about the circumstances of his birth only? Emphasize Christ's contributions. Remember that without Easter, there would be no Christmas!

Winter—Although it is difficult to disassociate winter from Christmas, they are not synonymous. Let's save "Frosty the Snowman" and "Jingle Bells" for after Christmas—most of the winter weather comes later, and we need something to cheer us then!

We realize that these suggestions are quite different from traditional observances, but so was the Christ, whose birth we seek to celebrate. We are called to, "Be not conformed to this world, but be transformed by the renewal of your mind, that you may prove what is the will of God, what is good and acceptable and perfect" (Romans 12:2). Let's face it—if we are faithful in seeking to follow in our Master's footsteps, then we are bound to be out of step with much of the world.

Simplicity—Keep your celebrating simple enough that you will not end up saying such things as, "I'll be glad when Christmas is over!" Plan ahead; don't tackle more than you can accomplish; schedule free times to meditate and wonder; spread your sharing with others over the entire year at their birthdays, etc. Be faithful in sharing with the hungry throughout the year, not just in December. (One church has a "365 fund" which is obtained from their church Christmas card mentioned above. This money provides food, gas, etc. for the many needy that come to the church for help throughout the year.) Make every day a celebration of Christ's love.

The above thoughts are not meant to dictate practices to anyone, but rather to encourage creative, intentional thinking and celebration. At least these are some guidelines that we follow on our "journey." Perhaps it will help our friends to understand us better.

A.C. and V.G. Cuppy   4019 Hillbrook Drive Louisville, Kentucky 40220

Gift Giving

Dear Friends:

This year we would like to do our Christmas gift-giving a little differently than in the past. As you know, through the last few years we have become more and more concerned about America's patterns of excessive consumption of the world's resources, while so many must do without.

About 3 years ago, a gift we shared with many of you was the *Alternate Christmas Catalogue,* plus a gift certificate for you to choose one of the life-supporting projects or products listed in the catalogue. It gave us satisfaction to know that the money we spent on "your" gift that year was actually going to help projects and people who are not as well off as you or we, instead of to large companies, and corporations which produce the many plastic gadgets and gifts that are sold every Christmas at a profit of more than $10 billion total,

and in the process use up more and more of the diminishing resources of the earth.

However, since that year, we find ourselves having lapsed back into the old habit of rush-rush, buy-buy, spend-spend on commercial gifts for Christmas. (We too seem to be tightly bound by tradition and years of habit.) This year we want to again make the effort to change that trend in ourselves, and to ask you, if you would like, to join us in it.

Most likely the gift we choose for you this year will be selected from the *Alternative Catalogue* and will be in the form of a donation and/or membership for you in a people or earth-oriented organization, a subscription to a magazine we think meaningful, a book we have found helpful, or a product which helps support struggling peoples. We hope to be able to choose an appropriate and meaningful gift for you and that through it you will be reassured of our love for you.

We also hope you will want to join us in this effort by reciprocating in kind. If you plan to give us a gift this year (please don't feel obligated—a long letter will make us about as happy as anything), we'd like to suggest that it be done in one of the following ways:

1. Redirecting your gift money by making a donation to a worthy cause of your choice. If you would like suggestions from us, some of those we are interested in are as follows:

World Peace Tax Fund   National Council for a WPTF 2111 Florida Ave. NE   Washington, D.C. 20008
UNICEF   U.S. Committee for UNICEF P.O. Box 5050 Grand Central Station   New York, New York 10017
Fund for Humanity   Koinonia Partners Inc.—Fund for Humanity Route 2   Americus, Georgia 31709
Bread for the World   207 East 16th St.   New York, New York 10003
Environmental Action   Suite 731 1346 Connecticut Ave. NW   Washington, D.C. 20036
Friends Committee on National Legislation Box C. 245 Second St. NE   Washington, D.C. 20002
United Farm Workers   P.O. Box 62   Keene, California 93531
Gray Panthers.   Gray Panthers National Headquarters 3700 Chestnut St.   Philadelphia, Pennsylvania 19104
Public Action Coalition on Toys 800 4th St. SW, Suite N 125   Washington, D.C. 20024
Action for Children's Television 46 Austin St.   Newtonville, Massachusetts 02160
Fellowship of Reconciliation Box 271   Nyack, New York 10960

2. Handmade gifts or "gifts of self" (sharing of a talent, your time, a tape or letter, etc.).

3. Books, articles, or magazine subscriptions which you find meaningful and would like to share. (In the case of books or subscription, please check first to see if we already have them.)

4. Commitment to a simpler lifestyle. We don't mean this is just a general sense, but in specific, concrete ways. Some things that come to mind in this area are:

- Cut down on meat consumption (one, two, three or more (?) meatless days a week.
- Make your own bread with whole wheat flour and other natural grains.
- Cut back on junk food: sugar-laden cereals, cold drinks, pastries, potato chips, and their relatives, and substitute more healthful items (such as those offered in *Diet for a Small*

companies which sponsor programs of violence on TV.
- Arrange car pools whenever possible, instead of traveling alone. Saves gas and air pollution.
- Use public transportation, bicycle, or *walk* as often as possible.
- Spend more time with your family or loved ones, relating to each other, playing, talking, loving. Don't let your time together be dominated by outside things that "entertain" (TV, movies, spectator sports,) and keep you from interacting with each other.
- Spend some time every day, or take off an occasional weekend, for quiet meditation/comtemplation/prayer/devotion. Don't let the ratrace of schedules and duties deprive you of that time we all need to revive our spirits, to keep in touch with ourselves and God.

Planet by Frances Moore Lappe).
- Refrain from buying any new clothes, shoes, or accessories for 6 months to 1 year.
- Gladly accept *used* clothes for yourself and used clothes, toys, and books for your children.
- Think twice before you buy a new consumer item (i.e., a new gadget to clutter up your kitchen or house). And even if you think you "have to have it," put off the purchase for another month.
- Borrow and share tools and appliances that you need only occasionally, such as lawn mowers, crockpots, sewing machines, bicycles, blenders, clothes for special occasions, slide or movie projectors. Joint purchase of such items with several others might be a possibility too.
- Be selective about television—avoid crime dramas and other shows of violence. Cut down the number of hours of "just watching" (1 hour per evening?). Turn off the sound during commercials (you'll get plenty of exercise!). Don't buy products from those

The list could go on and on—please feel free to modify the ones suggested and to add your own original ones. But we would like to know (since it's a gift to us as well as to yourself) what you have chosen to do. Knowing that you are making an effort will help us in *our* efforts and we can be more responsible to each other in our commitments. And whenever you or we run across pertinent materials or articles related to the chosen area(s), let's share that kind of thing with each other too throughout the year.

Well, those are some of our plans and ideas for this Christmas. Let us know what you think. If you feel especially positive or negative about this kind of effort, do let us know. We want to be in dialogue about it. And please don't feel you *have* to join us, or "cooperate" with us if you don't want to, but we do hope you will understand why we want to change our personal habits in gift-giving, and that it certainly doesn't mean that we don't love you anymore. On the contrary, we feel it is a broadening of our love for you—on to others!

Louise and Walter Durst

Alternative Christmas Rituals

as tried and contributed by many families …

ALTERNATIVES?

1. *Travel.* We leave the familiar environment. Sturbridge, Massachusetts, celebrates Christmas as the settlers celebrated it—simply, noncommercially. A trip at Christmas can be helpful to change a routine and gain perspective.

2. *Cards.* No one is allowed to give a storebought card. Each must make his or her own and compose a verse.

3. *Eating tree.* Holiday cookies are made and decorated and used for tree decorations. On the afternoon of Christmas or some other holiday, Open House is held for neighbors and friends to drop in and enjoy the fruits of the eating tree.

4. *Visits.* During supper on some particular day during the holiday season (such as Christmas Eve) we think about older people who have no families or whose families are away, or who might be a little happier at just the sight of us. (At this point we can't stand the sight of each other.) We let the dishes go, wrap up a few packages of cookies, and go!

5. *Christmas diorama.* A kind of diorama which replaces the creche has been developed. It includes the panorama of Jesus's life story and tries to convey the basic impression of Jesus as a teacher with some of his teaching evident.

6. *Drama.* Christmas can be celebrated with father (or mother) and children planning a drama of the birth of Jesus while mother (or father) prepares Christmas breakfast or Christmas dinner.

7. *Memory tree.* A tiny permanent tree, originally started by husband and wife on first Christmas, is decorated with mementos, hobbies, and interests, and added to each year. Each Christmas Eve, lights are extinguished except for two candles beside the little tree and the events represented by the "ornaments" are recalled.

8. *Good to the last …* When the tree is taken down, it is cut up into lengths and used for a special wiener roast in the fireplace or it may be chipped for spring compost.

9. *12 Days of Christmas.*

a. In order not to swamp children with gifts all at once, the custom of receiving one gift on each of the 12 days before Christmas.

b. We have 12 candles on the fireplace mantle. We start lighting them on December 12 until all are lit on December 24. We sing carols and read Christmas poems and stories for the 10 to 15 minutes the candles burn.

10. *Advent candles and wreath.* Light one of the four advent candles on each Sunday before Christmas—accompany with carols, poems, and stories.

11. *A gift for someone in need of a gift.* Family (or two families) gathers to make a gift for someone who might not have one at this season.

12. *Holiday blessings.* On Christmas night all branches of the family get together for a covered-dish supper and a little service. Everyone tells what they feel was their special blessings of the year.

13. *Doctor's prescription.* "Take one every four hours" is the prescription one doctor's family receives on Christmas. Beginning on the day before Christmas each member of the family opens a gift every four hours. This is done so that every gift may be cherished.

14. *Gift hunt.* Gifts are hidden; persons must follow a treasure map to find them. Pictures of where to look for the next clue are used for those too young to read.

15. *Preparing dinner.*

a. Everyone (including children) prepares their favorite dish—regardless of overall plan!

b. Dad (or Mom) and the kids take a hike while Mom (or Dad) prepares the dinner. They bring treasures home to share.

c. Invite a foreign student from a nearby school to spend the day. Share insights into that person's own customs.

d. Invite guests whose work takes them away from home on that day (truck drivers, for instance).

16. *Festive breakfast.* Instead of dinner.

17. *Piñata,* Make a piñata with the children. Fill it with sugarfree candy, nuts, fruits, little bags of popcorn, toasted soybeans, fancy crackers. Invite the neighborhood (children) in on Christmas Eve

to break the piñata. (See library for instruction on creating this Spanish custom.)

18. *Christmas Day.* Plan alternative activities so that the center of the day is not gift-giving. (A skit, hike, visiting friends, having friends in, cooking.)

19. *Gift-giving party.* For children (perhaps just family—cousins, etc.)—have each child bring one of their own toys wrapped to give to another child. Or have them bring them wrapped to take (en masse) to a family without many gifts.

Intergenerational (2 to 3 families)—make or prepare a gift for someone at the party to be given to them in the presence of others during the party (i.e., a coupon book, a poem, a picture, a massage, piano lessons, a hair styling, a simple creation).

20. *Send New Year's letter* (instead of holiday cards) to friends out of town—more time after the hassle to write.

21. *Family worship.* Write songs, Scripture, and poems for the holiday season on 25 pieces of paper. Each day, beginning December 1, a member of the family draws a slip from a bowl and reads it as a reminder of the forthcoming holiday.

22. Read *Feast of Fools* by Harvey Cox and *Contemporary Celebration* by Rosa Snyder.

We have the kids go and pick out a new outfit of clothes to be given away. They enjoy it and realize that it's a season for giving. Maybe next year we'll be able to make the clothes instead of buy them. We also buy food to be given away—give money to several organizations instead of buying gifts. For my parents one year we all (10 children) wrote remembrances of growing up at home—presented the booklet to them. Last year also we cooked dinner for three neighbors plus another older woman who couldn't come share a meal with us.

Last year for Christmas the kids made napkins to give to their grandparents. We used the fabric crayons and ironed the kid's own drawings on the material. This way "pappa" and "nanny" could see some art work and got a really personal gift that's ecologically helpful.

Jeann Schaller   Midland, Michigan

How to make Christmas meaningful for your children

Fred Rogers

Have you ever known a Christmas in America when the stores weren't crowded with shoppers? Can you remember a December when there wasn't a kind of special "expectancy" in the air—and the heart? Why is this? What makes our investment in Christmas so strong?

Of course there are many reasons. You have some of your own. As I think about it, I wonder if it doesn't have a lot to do with the confirmation of our humanity. We often see ourselves and our children reflected in the event. Christmas is a celebration of birth of life; and Christ's birth carries with it the promise of our own continuation from generation to generation.

But what does that have to do with shoppers crowding stores and people filling stockings and rooms with as many gifts as they can manage (sometimes more than they can manage)?

When a baby is born, the parents often feel that they would like to give that child a perfect life. It's a very natural feeling, but of course not a very realistic one, especially if "perfection" to those parents means no trouble, no tears, no fights, and providing for every need, every minute. Every parent soon discovers that that kind of perfection is far from possible (even if it were desirable). Night-time feedings and diaper changes and stomach pains and growing pains and jealousies and all the rest enter the picture very early. Parents are forced to realize, often sadly that the "perfect" untroubled life is just a fantasy, that in day-to-

day life, tears and fights and doing things for ourselves are all part of our human ways of developing into adults. Even when we're babies, we get to know about so-called imperfections in our parents' care. We have to *wait* for our food—even when we're hungry. And that waiting, that normal period of waiting, helps us to develop our capacity for striving as well as for understanding that some of our comfort comes through loving people who are outside of ourselves.

Nevertheless, the fantasy persists within the hearts of many loving parents: the fantasy that says, "Certainly there's something perfect I can give to my children—even if it isn't the whole of life ... maybe just one day each year!" And many choose Christmas for that one day. They invest in Christmas what they would like to invest in the entire year; consequently their expectations are as high as their pocketbooks are empty. They fill the house with presents and then await perfection in return. Instead, at the end of Christmas day, there are still tears and fights. The parents are disappointed; they feel that the family didn't appreciate all the effort they expended to make that day special. The perfect holiday that they anticipated includes its own imperfections, as other days of the year include theirs. And yet, in practically every home, the very next year, the very same thing happens. The human heart continues to long for the perfect day.

There's an even more universal longing, one that everyone—parents

and children alike—shares, and that is the longing to have something to give that is acceptable to others. It helps me to recognize the depth of this longing when I review my feelings about Christmas. Everyone wants to feel that he or she has something to offer. The most depressing feeling in the world is that one has nothing to offer ... nothing that's acceptable.

The way a mother receives the simple touch of her infant's hand at her breast means so much to that infant's beginning feelings of having something acceptable to give. The way parents receive a child's early "productions" in the toilet gives that child beginning notions of how welcome his or her actions are. And so it goes in all of our development. We collect clues all along the way as to how acceptable to others we really are.

And that is what is important on Christmas day—accepting our children and each other for what we really are rather than trying to create an artificial perfection made of material gifts. But how do we do this? What kind of positive, intangible clues of acceptability can we express to each other?

There is a custom among Polish people, continued by many immigrants to this country, that I think captures both the spirit of Christmas and the feeling of family we try to nurture. Just before starting the holiday meal, one of the parents passes a large wafer to everyone in the family. Each person breaks off a piece of the unleavened bread and holds it in the hand. The eldest begins the ceremony of pressing his or her wafer individually against the wafers of all the others, expressing loving wishes for the holiday, leaving a fragment of his or her wafer with each of the others, and taking a fragment of theirs. By the end of the ceremony each member of the family has broken and shared his or her wafer with every other member and has been given a morsel of each other's wafer. Only then are the wafers eaten, so that the family truly shares a common bread and confirms for each

have an even deeper understanding of being essential and a greater knowledge of the confirmation of membership that participation brings.

Store-bought decorations might give the Christmas tree a "finished" look, while children's painted clay decorations may not seem so shiny; nevertheless, the children's decorations reach far deeper into the feelings of everyone who finally gathers for the holiday. Cookies cut out by the children may not turn out to be as "fragile" as the ones an experienced cook might make, but they will be edible and they'll demonstrate to the child who cut them that he or she has something to offer that others are willing to take into themselves and make a part of their special celebration.

And those sometimes crude presents that children often bring home from school; Those handprints or potato-print pictures or those pieces of

place (some teachers give suggestions as to what they might like to construct for Christmas), they'll be sensitive to the notion that it has worth or it hasn't. The way parents and children interact on such an occasion as the "giving" of such a gift is very important. To children presents are really of the "self" and they want so much for their "self" to be acceptable.

Parents also long to give something of value. The real offerings that are of important to children are first the gifts of being included in a participatory way in the plans of the holidays. Next are the gifts of the things that parents know the children really want and know that they can use. One little boy I know asked his parents for Scotch tape for Christmas. His parents were sensitive enough to know that he really meant it and they got it for him. He used that tape to make a number of things. I know another boy who wanted high-top boots for his present. His parents thought that he was kidding and so they bought him toys, as they did for the other children in the family. He was a depressed little boy on that Christmas day. All he wanted were those high-top boots. What fits a child's needs may not be the most attractive thing in the toy shop, but children usually know what will suit them best.

person that what he or she has offered is acceptable to all the rest. The youngest has just as many fragments to eat as the eldest, and has the chance of feeling as much a part of the family as anyone else.

Almost every family has some yearly tradition: Many trim the tree together or sing seasonal carols as a group. Many share a common feast at the holiday. It is a very positive action to include the children in these activities; but if they have a part in selecting the tree, choosing the songs, and cooking the feast, they

wood and rope for tree decorations have so much value. And the value is that the child put something of himself or herself into making them. Even if it wasn't their idea in the first

TO CREATIVELY DEPRIVE
A CHILD
MEANS TO KEEP HIS senses
AND MIND FREE
OF MATERIAL GOODS THAT
OVERWHELM HIM
COLMAN MCCARTHY

Children often see things on television and they are told in subtle ways that they should want such things. Children sometimes therefore ask for things that are more extravagant than parents can reasonably afford. Well, children can hear and accept a sentence like, "I'd really like to give that to you, but that's something that is more expensive that I can afford." Working through a disappointment like that can be a healthy experience for both parents and children. Even if it were possible to give someone everything he or she asks for we would be depriving that person of many ways of growing ... many ways of understanding oneself and loved ones.

A woman I know remembers how she pleaded with her parents for a pair of ice skates when she was in the sixth grade. It was an expensive gift for their budget that year, but they finally said yes—if she would wait until the day after the holiday when the sales started. Her parents knew their word was important, so first thing on the morning of December 26 they were at the store and my friend got her skates. She still thinks her parent's request was logical and the memory of that Christmas remains one of the best. It's funny, she says, but she wasn't even envious of her neighborhood playmate who also got ice skates—and other fancy gifts all brightly wrapped and waiting under the tree on Christmas morning.

Sometimes in our society, Christmas is interpreted to children in such a way as to imply that their parents (or the fantasy characterization of their parents called Santa Claus) are omnipotent. That if parents want to, they might gratify every wish that the child has. Children are therefore led to feel that on Christmas they will receive every gift they've thought about. A child surrounded by unwrapped presents may look up and ask, "Is that all?" What do parents do in such a circumstance? The child may need desperately the support of the parents' own grasp on reality, so that their telling him or her the truth of their pleasure in giving and the human limitations may really restore to the child the capacity to enjoy what he or she has. Parents need not worry about how to express such things but should feel confident in their own ways of communication with their children. Words aren't as important as meaning. No matter what you say, your children will understand your intent. And if they have been allowed and

encouraged to participate in your family's Christmas, they will know what you mean.

The candles of Christmas have traditionally symbolized light in the darkness. They can symbolize the hope that goes beyond sadness and times of great family concern. The making of a family celebration is not meant to be something created entirely by adults for children's pleasure, but is rather a time of sharing in the making of pleasure for all. I feel that the more we understand this, the more we will realize that accepting a child's helpful participation in the life of the family is the greatest gift a grown-up can offer someone who is longing to be received "exactly as I am." And, honestly, isn't that what Christmas has always been about?

Fred Rogers, born in 1928 in Latrobe, Pennsylvania, has spent the major portion of his professional life working with children and their families through the medium of television. He is also an ordained minister of the United Presbyterian Church. He has achieved recognition of his work with children through "Mister Rogers' Neighborhood," which first appeared as a 15-minute daily program in 1963 and is now seen in a half-hour format carried by more than 240 Public Broadcasting Service affiliates. Among the honors he and the program have received are a George Foster Peabody Award, three Emmy nominations, a Saturday Review Television Award, and, most recently, the Ralph Lowell Award for outstanding service to public broadcasting.

101

A Black Looks at an Alternative Christmas

Black folk, especially those who claim the Christ, need to take a hard look at their buying and eating habits. We need to take off the "lenses which our society has put on us and put on the lenses of the Biblical faith" so that we may see clearly how our wants and desires are being exploited and manipulated by outside forces. However, we are responsible for the way we spend our money and use the earth's resources.

We need to ask ourselves some real questions. Are we part of the problem and the *solution*, or just part of the problem? What are our buying and eating habits doing to our brothers and sisters in Third World nations? What if they are supporting our consumption at the expense of their development?

As a start, black folk need to develop some alternative ways of celebrating holidays and holy days. For example, at Christmas we just spend and buy without any thought as to what all this means. Many blacks today spend too much on things, booze and parties, fancy cars and fancy living.

Blacks lay down a bad rap about freedom, justice, liberation, and development, but they do not put their money where their mouths are. The total annual income of blacks is approaching 36 billion dollars. Instead of spending say $25, $50, $100, or whatever at Christmas, why not redirect some of that amount to agencies (NAACP, Poverty Law Center, PUSH, SCLC, BMCR, United Negro College Fund, just to name a few) struggling for justice, liberation, and development.

What are we doing to help alleviate hunger in a hungry world? For the sake of the hungry, we could stop eating so much meat. We do not need meat every day to live. We could skip a meal per week, put a price on it, and at the end of the month send the amount to Church World Service, Africare, UMCOR, or some other organizations working to alleviate hunger and poverty.

To get further information on alternate celebrations, reduced consumption, and voluntary simplicity, look elsewhere in this catalogue.

It was the *Alternate Christmas Catalogue* of 1973 which started my family and me on alternate celebrations, especially Christmas.

I would like to share my serendipity with you. One day in October 1973 I walked into my office and found an *Alternate Christmas Catalogue* (first edition) on my desk. I picked it up, looked at it, put it down and said, "That's a strange name for a catalogue." However, through the rest of the day I could not get it off my mind. So I decided to take it home with me that evening.

When I walked in the door and greeted my wife she said, "What's wrong?" I replied, "Nothing, why?" "Well, you don't look too happy," she replied. I responded by saying, "Oh, I'm O.K., but I would like to go up to my study and read a little while." I did just that and began reading the *Alternate Christmas Catalogue*—not really wanting to, but forcing myself to read it anyway. When I got half-way through it, I was surprised by joy of what I had discovered. This was what I had been looking for for years and now I had found it—some alternative ways to celebrate Christmas.

I knew something was missing in my celebration of Christmas, but I did not know exactly what it was. I kept trying to fool myself in the past by conducting Christmas services, singing carols, and going home to my family to watch them open their gifts on Christmas Day. But somehow there was always a strange emptiness in my heart. "Peace on Earth, and goodwill to all men" did not really mean too much for me from the gut-level of my experience.

The *Catalogue* brought me face-to-face with the terrifying realization of my personal responsibility to help, wherever I can, to improve the lives of the unhappy, unfed, unclothed, and the unloved people of the world. It helped to remind me in a very poignant way that "God's gift to his people in Christ was based on the people's real needs in their journey through life. In Christ, God was pointing to the eternal truths of love and forgiveness and justice and peace. Likewise, today our celebration of the Christ-gift should be a direct response to the conditions of people."

Well, my newfound discovery convinced me. But how was I to get the idea of an alternative Christmas over to my family? I came out of my study, called my family together (wife, and two sons, one eleven and the other less than a year old) in the family room. We sat on the floor instead of chairs.

I was apprehensive because I was looking at my loving wife, Eunice, who always expected a nice gift at Christmas. Then, there was my son, Charles, Jr. (11 years), who really wanted the toy factory, regardless. Ken, not knowing really what was going on at the time, was looking at daddy expectantly. There I was. Eunice said, "What do you want to say to us?" I replied, "I want to share with you a great moment in my life." I told them what I had discovered and how it had convinced me the way I had been celebrating Christmas was wrong.

After I had told them the whole story, I asked for comments as to how they felt about it. To my surprise my wife said, "That's funny, I have been looking for the same thing." Charles, Jr., said, "Daddy I don't really need all those toys at Christmas. I can do with much less if it means helping persons who do not have food to eat or clothes to wear." I said to my son, if he wanted one or two toys for Christmas, would it matter if they came from a co-op. His response was, "That's O.K." Then I pressed the issue a little more, "What about toys of war and violence, tanks, toy soldiers, machine guns, cap pistols, swords?"

"Daddy, I can do without those things. I don't want to grow up and hurt anybody."

At this point I really wanted to cry—I had won my family to an alternative way of celebrating Christmas.

We took the Christmas pot of $145.00 in December and the *Alternate Christmas Catalogue* and sent that entire amount to life-supporting organizations in Alabama, Mississippi, other parts of the country, and around the world. We sent gifts in honor of each other (even my son, Ken) and our friends.

The Christmas of 1973 was for us the most meaningful and joyous Christmas that we had ever experienced, especially for my wife and me, for we have seen quite a few Christmases. We have not taken consumption out of celebrations completely, but we are "in process"; that is, we have begun to alter our way of celebrating events and holidays.

Well, that's what happened five Christmases ago, and the joy continues to overflow. Christmas is at hand again. The selling and buying spree has already been set in motion. Do something unusual this Christmas—reduce your Christmas buying and redirect the money where the "need is the greatest, the situation most desperate, and the pain is the sharpest."

Rev. Charles Hutchinson is a United Methodist District Superintendent in Bloomington, Indiana

Good-bye Santa, Hello St. Nicholas

Between Thanksgiving Day and Christmas Day each year, the baby Jesus is kidnapped by the department stores and catalog houses and held for $2 billion ransom. Or so it seems.

Many complain about what Santa Claus and his "helpers" have done to Jesus's birthday, but few people have done anything about it.

We have.

We have banished Santa Claus from our Christmas, and we have given the festival back to Jesus. We have put an end to ritual gift-giving to family and relatives. We have redirected our attention to Advent and Christmas as times of God's grace and our response. We have sought out the poor and have felt them touch us.

Establishing Customs

Shortly after our firstborn arrived, we talked seriously about the kinds of customs we wanted to establish and perpetuate in our family. We decided we should and could do something about Christmas. What better time, we decided, than when our children were open and accepting of new directions.

We looked at the patterns we as parents had inherited from our own families. Our experiences and frustrations were nearly identical. The giving and receiving of gifts had somehow become transformed, over the years, from an affectionate way of symbolizing our regard for other persons to a garish, frantic, competitive scramble to "exchange" material things none of us needed.

Our families had lived in difficult times. We had known lean pantries and homemade clothes. But on both sides, as we grew older, our homes mirrored the American experience. Affluence caught up with us and we began to be caught up in it. Our Christmas customs reflected it. The gifts we gave to one another became more elaborate and more numerous. And more unnecessary.

Self-gratifying Materialism

It occured to us that we were ensnarling ourselves in a web of self-gratifying materialism. We winced at the shrill sounds from the marketplace, a crescendo that reached its climax each December. And we added to the noise too.

An "exchange mentality" grew. If we gave, we expected to receive. While many kept saying that "the true spirit of Christmas is in giving," we began to realize such rationalization did not really mask out self-serving "swapping."

We had a gnawing feeling that there were a lot of people, somewhere, who needed basic material things more than we needed to "exchange" goods.

One November, when our daughters were ages three and one, we resolved to do better. We did some research on Santa Claus and discovered that this now-almost-totally-irrelevant prop for the annual orgy of selling and buying actually had very good ancestry. We were fascinated—and delighted—to make our acquaintance with St. Nicholas, third-century bishop of Myra in Asia Minor. He was a real Christmas flesh-and-blood gentleman. He rooted his concept of giving in God's grace. His style, therefore (and one which we decided to adopt), was imitative of Jesus's: give without identifying yourself, without seeking repayment, to those truly in need.

Therefore we decided, as an alternative to Santa Claus on Jesus's birthday, to celebrate the Feast Day of St. Nicholas on the date tradition had assigned it, December 6.

Scarcity of Information

Since December 1972, it has been "Hello, St. Nicholas; Good-bye, Santa Claus!" at our house. The first year we were not sure what to do. There is a scarcity of information on how families can observe the Feast of St. Nicholas. So we developed our own ritual.

This is what we did:

- Well in advance of the season we wrote letters to all our relatives to whom we had previously given, and from whom we had received, gifts at Christmas time. We let them know that our girls were old enough now to begin to understand the meaning of things and that we would like to let them grow up with a new perspective on giving. Hence, we explained, we would confine future gift-giving within the relationship to birthdays. We invited our relatives to reciprocate. There was some misunderstanding and some anger, but by and large we succeeded in making the transition. (After five years some still give "St. Nicholas Gifts," which we receive with thanks but open without ceremony.)

Special Generosity

- We talked about Bishop Nicholas of Myra, about his special brand of generosity, and about what we can learn from him. We composed a simple song we could learn and sing in our family, to the tune of "Jolly Old St. Nicholas," deciding that if Nicholas deserved a song title he also deserved some decent

words to go with it. Here is one stanza of it:

Thankful Bishop Nicholas,
friendly, good and wise;
When he could he helped the
poor always by surprise.
Rich men came to Nicholas,
bringing wealth to share,
So it could be sent to those
living in despair.

• The second year of our observance we made stocking puppets and a cardboard-box theater. Our characters were: St. Nicholas (red robe, clergy shirt, collar, and bishop's miter), a poor woman, the woman's hungry son, and a wealthy benefactor (a member of Nicholas's congregation). Our girls are now old enough to present the story themselves, each speaking for two puppets. The dialogue changes every year.

• We have tried to set a festive atmosphere at our dinner table on this night. The menu is special. We light candles and switch off the overhead lights. One year the girls created special placemats for everybody.

• Each year we have designated 5 percent of our December income for a needy person or family. Recently our check has gone to Lutheran Social Services. We ask not to be identified to the recipient, nor to learn who receives the gift. Our girls design the greeting card to accompany the gift check when it is mailed.

What Results?

What has been the result of all of this?

1. We are no longer involved in a "Christmas rush." There is no pressure in our family to "get the shopping done." We don't do any. December has become a delightful month in which to remember God's Advent promises, particularly when we light the candles on the wreath for evening devotions.

2. We have discovered a totally different and far richer spirit and rationale for giving. We have found that giving "in secret," without the possibility of receiving repayment, can be tremendously satisfying. We finally have made a good beginning toward focusing our giving on "the least" of God's family.

3. For us, Christmas has been given back to Jesus. We celebrate it as his time. We still cut a tree. (Usually we tag one at a tree farm and cut it only days before Christmas, so it is still green by Epiphany, January 6, when we take it down.)

There are no presents under our tree. Now we cover the floor all around it with books about Christmas. Our girls use the display as a kind of festive library all through the season. (The books interest them especially because we put them all away with the tree decorations until the next December, giving them a year's rest and making them seem somehow "new" each Advent.)

More Satisfaction

We now find more satifaction than ever in the Christmas Eve candlelight service and Christmas Day Holy Communion. Without the "unwrapping ritual," our festival time finds us looking forward to these special worship times with added anticipation.

Our daughters have accepted this shift in our practice of giving and celebrating, and they have interpreted it to others. One of them came home from school last December and reported this conversation:

"What are you going to get for Christmas?"

"Nothing. Christmas is Jesus's birthday, not ours."

"Oh, I sure feel sorry for you! You're not getting *anything* for Christmas!"

"Well, I feel sorry for *you* if that's all you think Christmas is about!"

Santa Claus hasn't come to our house for five years. We haven't missed him one bit!

Kathe Sherer is a registered nurse,
and
Michael Sherer is a pastor in the
American Lutheran Church, now
working for the Augsburg
Publishing House in Minneapolis.

This article is reprinted with permission from Lutheran Standard.

Alternative Christmas Congregational Campaign

This campaign encourages denominations to provide their congregations with resources to take leadership roles in challenging their members to a more appropriate celebration of the birth of Christ.

Is It Any of the Church's Business?

Although individuals and families can and must make their own decisions about changing the ways they celebrate, the church has a critical role in encouraging them. **Indeed, if it is not the church's business to call for more responsible celebrations of Christmas, whose business is it?**

What Can the Local Church Do?

1. Challenge commercialized celebrations and call for ways to observe Christmas which focus on the needs of others:

- Set aside a Sunday in October or early November to call the congregation to a new seriousness in the celebration of Christmas.
- Ask members to covenant to set aside 25 percent of what they spent on last year's Christmas and give it as a Christmas gift to denominational programs which minister to those in need.
- Consider initiating a community-wide alternative Christmas festival in which these concerns can extend beyond the local church into the community at large.

2. Encourage members who want to change by providing supportive programs and resources:

- Consider a mailing to members (or a special issue of the church newsletter) including the reasons for and ideas about an alternative Christmas.
- Offer study opportunities for all age groups on "Preparing to Celebrate the Birth of Christ."
- Provide guidelines for alternative giving, e.g., buying from church-supported craft groups; giving of one's time and skills; making contributions in recipients name.

3. Shape the worship life of the congregation to reflect the concerns about Christmas:

- Give particular attention to the worship service on the chosen Sunday in October or November.
- Use the "Whose Birthday Is It, Anyway?" bulletin inserts that reflect those concerns.
- Plan the Christmas worship service (on Christmas or Christmas Eve) to include a time when individuals and families can offer birthday gifts to the Christ child.

What Gifts Shall We Bring?

1. Remember whose birthday it is. Christmas gift-giving begins with a recognition that Christmas is the day we celebrate the birth of Jesus Christ. He should be first, not last, on our Christmas list!

2. Give to those he came to serve! the poor, the homeless, the prisoner, the hungry, the oppressed, and the outcast. Is there a better way to honor him than to give of ourselves to these?

- TIME: Commit time to participate in a group working with society's "devalued" persons: a senior citizen's lunch program; prison visitation; help with the resettlement of a refugee family.
- SKILLS: Volunteer to cook, repair, do bookkeeping, for example, or teach those skills to disadvantaged persons. Neither dollars nor bright wrapping paper can improve on these gifts.
- MONEY: Financial gifts to support ministries among society's "forgotten" people can make a difference. If 10,000 families divert only $100 each this Christmas, that will be *one million* dollars.

3. Plan your gift giving! Make your gift list early. Discuss with your family your willingness to spend in time, skills, and money at least 25 percent of what you spent on last year's Christmas. Warning: You probably do not have enough time or money to do everything you have done before and **add** this one: this must **replace** some of what you've done and spent before.

What Resources Are Available?

In cooperation with a number of denominations, Alternatives prepares a packet of materials specifically designed to assist congregations in this undertaking. These include posters, sample bulletin inserts, worship aids, study/action resources for all age groups, suggestions for organizing community festivals. For more information about the Christmas Congregational Campaign, write to Alternatives.

Organizing a Festival

Imagine how it would be to share and celebrate the true spirit of Christmas with your community in a well-planned and popular festival! If your congregation joined with other congregations and other community groups think how many, many more people might become involved in an alternative Christmas!

Festival Goals

A Community Christmas Festival will contribute to:
1. *Building* a community base of understanding and support for alternative celebrations;
2. *Learning* how our celebrations can be both considerate of the needs of people and kind to the earth;
3. *Diverting* "Christmas" money to community groups seeking to serve society's disenfranchised people and to self-help groups;
4. *Encouraging* persons to adopt more meaningful, humane and personal gift-giving practices;
5. *Challenging* publicly the assumption that the birth of Christ is honored in commercialized Christmas celebrations;
6. *Building* a community base of understanding and support for other cooperative people- and earth-oriented endeavors.

Planning the Festival

1. *Plan early:* Plan your festival to be very early in the Christmas season: September and October are ideal. This way you can expose the idea to many people who are unfamiliar with the Alternative Christmas idea and leave time for them to participate this Christmas. This means getting the organizing and planning process under way much earlier.

If it is October when you first read this and begin to think about a festival, *don't despair!* Adjust the scale of the festival to what you have time to organize, or use this as the time to begin organizing for next year.

2. *Planning committee:* An Alternative Christmas festival will involve many members of the community. Therefore, you should form a committee that represents all of the non-commercial interests of your community, such as people from other churches, schools, clubs, social change groups and workers. People from all of these groups will have different and interesting ideas for the festival.

3. *Where to begin:* There is no one formula about where to begin organizing a festival. Since there are so few precedents for this kind of activity, you are really on your own! As you begin thinking about where to start, consider the following ideas:

- Enlist the support of your own local church for the effort first.
- You may find it useful to approach other churches of your denomination in the community through presbytery, district, etc.
- Approach the local council of churches or ministerial association for their support and endorsement.
- Campus ministers often have the most interest, skills and contacts for this kind of organizing. Don't hesitate to contact them.
- There are many ways to organize. What is needed most are a few persons willing to commit themseves to finding the best way, and then organizing!

4. *Logistics:* Once you have a planning committee together, set up the logistics of the festival with great care: where and when to have it, how to spread the word about it, what facilities and special skills you will need, who will be in charge of what, etc. Attention to detail will pay off in a more smoothly run event and a greater sense of community self-confidence.

5. *Publicity committee*: Charged with obtaining widespread attention for this important event, this committee should be led by persons who believe in the festival and who are not timid in dealing with the media. (See the section on "Dealing with the Media" below.)

Ideas for the Festival

1. Invite as many community social change groups (hunger coalitions, senior citizens groups, environmental protection groups) as possible to put up *displays and information* tables; ask them to make signs and posters relating their issue to a need for people to reorient themselves to more socially responsible lifestyles.

2. Invite all *self-help crafts* groups in your area to come and share their creations with the community. They can have crafts available for sale as alternative Christmas gifts. And, if possible, have representatives from the craft groups present to demonstrate their skill in their craft. See Charline Watts' article, "Alternative Christmas Fair" in the *Alternative Celebrations Catalogue,* (fourth edition, pp. 212-213) for detailed information on how to put together this part of the festival. You may want to contact some of the craft groups listed in the *Catalogue* if you do not know of any in your area. Some of the groups will send a quantity of their goods on consignment for the festival.

3. You can also include booths with appropriate *food* items for sale (e.g., home-baked breads, nuts, fruits) alongside booths that educate about nutrition, food systems, hunger, and world food distribution. The hunger task forces or lifestyle committees in local churches will probably be glad to work on these booths. Also contact local food co-ops for participation.

4. How about booths with people demonstrating *how-to make* Christmas gifts? Perhaps a list of suggestions could also be made available at these booths. Each of the four editions of the *Alternate Celebrations Catalogue* has many suggestions and directions. You might be surprised to find out how many persons in your community have skills they would be glad to demonstrate in a booth.

5. Every festival needs *music and dancing*. Arrange for local groups to play music and perhaps lead some folks to dancing. What about a singalong for Christmas carols? Someone might be able to rewrite some secular songs to fit the alternative Christmas.

6. Arrange for a table where persons can find out about and enter the national *Best and Worst Christmas Gift Contest.* You may want to conduct your own community contest in conjunction with the festival.

7. Have a place where you can have *continuous showings* of "The Celebration Revolution of Alexander Scrooge" filmstrip. (This filmstrip may be available in your local church library or in your regional denominational service center. If you can't find it locally, it is available from Alternatives: rental $6; sale $17.50.) You may also want to include the "Let's Celebrate" filmstrip from the "Living Simply" series produced by Teleketics. These filmstrips will help festival participants understand the reasons for the festival and alternative celebrations.

8. You may want to have a *book* table where many of the books written on social justice issues, responsible lifestyles and alternative celebration resources could be sold as gifts for friends and family. The *Alternate Celebrations Catalogue* and other Alternatives publications could also be made available for sale at this table. Contact Alternatives for more information.

9. You can *decorate* your festival with a live tree. The best way to obtain one is to find someone in your community who would be willing to give the tree from his or her own property. After the festival, the tree can be replanted where it came from or maybe in a public park. If you can't find someone to donate a tree, then you might have to buy one from a nursery. Either way, make sure that the tree is replanted when the event is over. You can decorate your tree with handmade decorations such as strings of popcorn, chains made of paper (perhaps each link of chain could bear the name of one of the members of the community who cannot attend the festival due to illness or disability, or maybe each link could have a special "wish" of good intention printed on it), pine cones from the ground, cut-out pictures of people helping people, or any other decoration that would make your tree a *real* symbol of life. The rest of the hall could be decorated with such things as drawings from school children or paper snow flakes made from recycled paper.
And on and on and on...

An Alternative Santa Claus

Santa Claus is a very powerful cultural image in our society. An "alternative Santa Claus" could be an exciting, interesting, and attention-grabbing mechanism to call attention to the commercial-ization of Christmas. The alternative Santa might be the highlight of your festival, especially as the culmination of other activities by this different kind of Santa.

What would an "alternative Santa" look like? Perhaps the traditional Santa outfit in a different color (say, green or blue in place of the red) would be appropriate. Or maybe just the white beard and cap with overalls or some other simple clothing. Whatever you decide, bear in mind that you want this Santa to be recognized as Santa Claus but as one who is different.

What would an Alternative Santa do? This Santa should personify the spirit of Christmas and at the same time be protesting the commercialization of Christmas. There is a lot of room for creativity. Here are some suggestions:

1. Alternative Santas could show up, when appropriate, at public meetings, church functions, college campuses, and at shopping malls handing out announcements about the upcoming Alternative Christmas Festival, or "Whose Birthday Is It, Anyway?" leaflets, and talking with persons about commercialized Christmas celebrations.

2. Draft a letter to the local newspapers (signed Santa Claus) asking why people have allowed Christmas to become so commercialized. Explain that Santa is changing his ways and so should they. You may want to arrange a press conference so that you could get coverage by local TV and radio stations as well as the press.

3. If your city or town has any official Christmas festivities such as parades, fairs and the like, request that the Alternative Santas be allowed to take part.

Warning: Unlike other activities in the alternative Christmas festival, this one is sure to arouse opposition as well as support. Listen to what happened to one Alternative Santa last year:

CHICO, Calif.—"The day after Thanksgiving a white-bearded, jolly old soul showed up at a shopping mall here to give free leaflets to passersby.

"In return, the mall manager finally ran him off the sidewalk, and no fewer than four local sheriff's department cars reprimanded him for obstructing traffic.

"Some people scorned him and refused to listen to his message or to accept anything from him, one saying:

'Accept something from a green Santa? NO WAY!'

"Uh, yes, this particular Santa Claus was dressed all in green velvet, from his head to his foot.

"United Methodist John Barneson III donned his beard and his suit to give out more than 1,000 leaflets asking 'Whose Birthday Is It, Anyway?'"

(Joyce Hopkins, "Hohoho—and Green," *United Methodist Reporter,* December 12, 1980.)

Dealing with the Media

Today's mass media play a central role in the commercialized Christmas celebration. Each November and December, billions of dollars worth of ads and commercials are bought by thousands of businesses who are each vying for a piece of the Christmas take. "Television and radio stations," notes *Broadcasting* magazine, "are singing a happy tune during the Christmas advertising season."

If we hope to reach large numbers of people with the alternative Christmas message, it will be necessary to work with, or through, the media to whatever extent possible. While understanding the built-in limitations you will face,

learn how to approach the media with your message.
learn what to do when they come to you.
learn how to monitor and challenge their role in the commercial Christmas.

Celebrations belong to the people. They are not natural resources to be strip mined each year for the sake of profit

Feature Coverage

In the fall, newspapers, TV, and radio will all be hunting for interesting Christmas stories, and especially for those with a local angle. Try to arrange an appointment with the appropriate editors, producers or journalists to present them with written material and information on the alternative Christmas idea, some basic facts about the commercialization, and an outline of the local activities you are planning.

In addition to the information about your Christmas Festival, you can use information from the Christmas packet to share with them, especially information about the *Best and Worst Christmas Gift Contests.* They will be most interested in the contest if you are doing a local version. They will probably also be interested in how particular families are celebrating an alternative Christmas. If they want to know more about the Alternatives organization, do not hesitate to put them in touch with us.

Public Service Announcements

Radio, television, and newspapers generally have free announcement times or space for community events or public service announcements (PSAs). Policies on these PSAs will vary greatly from station to station, or paper to paper. Check out each media outlet in your area on policies: time, space or word limits, content guidelines, deadlines.

When writing a PSA text, be brief and end with the appropriate address or phone number. Repeat the phone number if possible.

For all publicity efforts, be sure to send copies of announcements to relevant community publications (church newsletters, college newspapers) and put posters or flyers on community and office bulletin boards.

Press Releases

A community alternative Christmas Festival is "news." You will want to prepare a press release to send to all relevant media.

A press release should be written in a particular style. In the upper lefthand corner, type in the words NEWS or PRESS RELEASE. In the upper righthand corner, put your group's name and address (if it does not appear elsewhere on the stationery). In the same corner, put the contact person's name and phone number so reporters will know who and where to call for further information. The release should include a "release date" indicating when the news item can be used or printed. In most cases, this will read "for immediate release."

A brief, interesting heading should be at the top of the release text. Remember that the person receiving your release may be reading over dozens of others that day, hunting for the most interesting item. Follow the headline with a summary of the "Who, What, Where, When, and Why" information. This should be followed by several paragraphs of background data, and possibly some quotes from relevant people. One or two pages should be the maximum length—a press release is an attention-getter, not an essay.

The releases should be mailed or hand-delivered to all TV and radio stations and newspapers in your area. A release announcing your festival should reach the media people two or three days ahead of time. If you can identify which reporters cover community news, religious affairs, and business news, send them a personal copy of the release. Then make follow-up phone calls. If the release is for the festival, ask if a reporter has been assigned to cover it. If the release was more informational in nature, call and ask if there are any more facts or figures that you can provide.

Finally, keep a file of all journalists and media contacts who cover your story or show a personal interest in the issue. Also, please send Alternatives copies of any local newspaper articles that appear on your alternative Christmas activities.

When the Media Comes

Your press release and public service announcements about the festival are successful and the media people show up at your festival. What then?

- Have press kits prepared that include copies of any relevant background materials to a journalist who will be filing the story. The press kits need not be elaborate, but they should be thoughtfully and interestingly prepared. Be sure to include any available art pieces (like the "Whose Birthday Is It, Anyway?" poster or insert) in the packet.
- Have a spokesperson chosen by your group ready to handle any questions and make statements to the press. This person should decide in advance what you want to communicate through the media. Remember that you may have all of 30 seconds in front of a camera to explain your issues.

Watch-Dogging the Media

In recent years there has been a growing movement against the barrage of TV advertising aimed at children. Until more public outcry grows against the commercial domination of our airwaves, the big corporations and the media will continue money-making at our social, psychological, and financial expense.

What you may not realize is that you can work to combat this in your community. You may want to consider forming a special committee as a part of your community alternative Christmas campaign to begin work in this critical area. Consider organizing and sending delegations to talk with the management of local media about public concern over their advertising and program policies. You might:

- Ask them for public service time on the air to let people know about resources for decommercializing Christmas.
- Ask them to do a study and exposé on Christmas marketing and advertising practices as a community service. Suggest that TV shows or newspaper articles also cover community needs that could be met by diverting money at Christmas time.
- Ask for time on talk shows to discuss Christmas commercialism.
- Express concern about TV advertising directed at children at Christmas. Since commercials promote a particular interpretation of Christmas to children, ask how the station intends to present other alternative views of Christmas for young people.

Go to any noncommercial community radio stations (college stations, stations run on public donations, PBS affiliates) and ask them to do a program on the commercial media's role in the yearly Christmas buy-a-thon.

MAYBE IN THE PROCESS
OF CHANGING OUR
WAY OF CELEBRATING, ALL OF US
CAN BECOME MORE HUMANE,
MORE SENSITIVE
TO THE WHOLE HUMAN FAMILY,
AND MORE CARING
OF OUR MOTHER EARTH.

ALTERNATE CHRISTMAS
CATALOGUE 1973

6.

Philosophy of Giving

"Giving" is as much a part of our culture as apple pie. We grow up surrounded by personal gift-giving and receiving and contributions to organizations. The religious heritage of America is filled with exhortations like, "It is more blessed to give than receive." The Internal Revenue Service encourages contributions to charitable projects by allowing you to deduct some contributions from your gross income. Each week our mail is filled with appeals from various groups for our money.

As we believe that celebration is a necessary part of life, we also believe that giving (self, money, and things) is necessary and good, so long as it is life-supporting. Unfortunately, *giving* has gotten out of hand in our society. In a real sense, "give until it hurts" best describes our current practices. Materialism, pollution, the rape of the Earth's resources and the continuation of colonialism are the fruits of our celebration process. The alternatives of celebrating simply, making gifts, buying from self-help craft groups, diverting money to people- and Earth-oriented projects represent a new philosophy of giving. That is what the *Catalogue* is all about.

Simply put, the philosophy affirms that we are struggling to:
1. Be sensitively aware of the effects of our giving or nongiving on people and the Earth and insist that they be life-supporting and conserving.

Giving and Gifts

2. Commit ourselves to simplified living which makes more of our income available for giving.
3. Rediscover that creating gifts with our hands (instead of depending on machines) makes us and the gift more humane.
4. Remember that one purpose of celebrating and gift-giving should be the enrichment of human relationships, a process which requires more than something material: the most important ingredient is the investment of self.
5. Experience the power of our purchases to produce justice.

As you begin to reexamine your giving patterns these alternatives should be helpful.

No-interest Loans—Groups like Koinonia Partners receive contributions for their Fund for Humanity in the form of no-interest loans. The donor can "call" the loan at any time. This arrangement allows the construction of housing for rural black families without the usual high interest-bearing mortgage and cuts the actual owner cost of the house in half.

Interest-bearing Loans—Groups like the Southern Cooperative Development Fund pay interest on long-term loans. The money is then loaned out to people for self-help development projects at 10 percent. Individuals and groups having funds currently drawing interest in savings and loan accounts or banks might consider the human justice factor of depositing money in this Development Fund.

Gifts in Life Estate—Your lawyer can tell you how to make gifts of property to tax-deductible groups by which you are allowed to use the property and the income until your death, after which the property goes to the group.

Alternate Gift Certificate—This method allows you to give gifts in a way which supports people and the Earth at the same time that it retains the recipient's freedom to choose how the gift is "spent."

Supporting "Pioneer" Projects—Operating on the assumption that the majority of people will give money to the old-line established organizations, some people have adopted the habit of giving only to smaller ventures which are breaking ground in an area that the giants won't touch.

The amount of your income which is available for giving depends largely on what you require for your lifestyle. So long as the way one generates income is not harmful, some "simple living" folks believe, "make all you can, live on as little as possible, and give away the rest." Others advocating simple living believe that we should make only that income needed to live simply.

On Creative Deprivation

For the past few months, a number of merchants and other sellers have been poking into my privacy by mailing to my home their Christmas gift catalogues for children. After sinking a plumb line of curiosity to measure the new depths of crassness to which these catalogues have sunk, I throw them away.

Children have little need for and most of us have little money for the marketplace temptings the catalogs advertise, no matter how "innovative" these playthings are said to be. (How cleverly the manufacturers play

on the potential guilt-feelings of parents, as if we are brutalizing our kids psychologically if we dare give them a non-innovative toy; our little achievers might not be achieving for a few minutes of the day.)

As a substitute for the ethic of commercialized Christmas giving, there is the alternate tactic of creative deprivation. It is not the ideal solution—as nothing is this side of the Apocalypse—but as a way of keeping children on the ground and in some kind of value balance, creative deprivation has a number of advantages.

By definition, to creatively deprive children means to keep their senses and minds free of material goods that overwhelm them, the kind soon to be washing in from the immense commercial ocean of Christmas. How can children not be emotionally drowned when wave after wave of toys rolls over them?

How can a child have a sense of value for any one toy when so many are given at once? How can the potential of one gift be explored when the attraction of so many others is pulling? The whisper of newness becomes a deafening roar. It is hard to imagine how this surfeit of Christmas toys can lead to new levels of playfulness.

By refusing to smother children with material goods—it goes on at other times besides Christmas—the two goals of creative deprivation may be accomplished. First, the child's imagination can be kept fresh. An afternoon in a woodland, for example, provides more excitement for a child's mind that a week of afternoons in a playroom crammed with toys. Parents who regularly take their children to woodlands know this to be true, even for the 3-year-olds.

What is a mechanical wind-up squirrel compared to a real one ten feet away? True enough the real squirrel is not able to be touched or held, but the lesson of the creature's independence is one that children need to learn.

The day in the woodland is not isolated, but can be prolonged through the use of picture books and story books that tell about squirrels. This is a genuine feeding of the imagination, a nutrition of the mind that no innovative toy can ever provide. It is a way that children learn that humankind shares the earth with the animals and plants rather than controls it. Ironically, the dullest kids in the neighborhood concerning wildlife are inevitably those whose playrooms and bedrooms are lined with stuffed animals. To deprive children of such is not to stifle them but to lead them to nonmaterial pleasures that will never rust or break: pleasures of the imagination, the senses, and the spirit.

All of life's best and deepest moments come from creative uses of the imagination, whether such activity produces only the child's mudpie or a lone citizen cupping his or her hands to call out in joy above the din of social absurdity. Jung insisted that "the creative activity of imagination frees man from his bondage to the 'nothing but' and raises him to the status of one who plays." What right have we to take this rich capital of a child's playfulness and spend it recklessly on spiritless toys from a factory?

The second goal of creative deprivation is to inform the child that life is often defined by limits. Can the lesson of limitation be learned from parents who insist on giving their children the proverbial and unlimited "everything?" America is filled with parents who look on their own deprived childhood and vow that their children will never be deprived, these parents forgetting that perhaps one reason they succeeded in the world was precisely because they grew up not getting everything.

It is an easy mistake to make, especially for parents who are career-preoccupied. Thus, Christmas becomes the season of making up to the kids via store-bought litter all the emotional support that was absent the rest of the year. It is a buy-off. But, as social scientist Thomas Cottle perceptively notes, children are "brilliant readers of parental intentions." In the case of unlimited Christmas generosity, the intention is not so much giving as obscuring—obscuring the neglect of the previous year and all too predictably the coming neglect of the next year.

Limiting the number of Christmas gifts—even to one toy from both parents—is telling the child not only that

she or he can't have everything but also that you can't give everything. This is a hard notion in a country where many people have known little sacrifice of material goods. For us, nothing is off limits and all limits are off. We elected and re-elected a President who delights in telling himself and us that America is Number One in the world, first in wealth, first in power. With this going for us, the least we can do is give our children everything.

And risk ruining them. It is a risk because we have no exact sociological proof that too many Christmas gifts cause damage. Even to suspect that they might opens one to charges of eccentricity. But each parent must make the choice. The conventional folklore is that Americans love their children, but the evidence in some areas—clothing them in flammable pajamas, feeding them sugared foods that rot the teeth, exposing them to the lies of some TV advertising, spending more money on war than education—questions the quality of this love.

In the end, there is only one gift to our children, to be given at Christmas, Chanukah, on the way to Mecca, or whenever: the treasures of our time and talk, exactly what children want the most.

Colman McCarthy
The Washington Post/Potomac
December 2, 1973

Plants:
A Gift of Life

Plants are a gift of life. Their bright blooms and fresh foliage cheer us; we breathe the oxygen they produce. Unlike antique vases or elephant-foot umbrella stands, plants require care and nurturing: they need us as we need them.

Gift plants may be purchased commercially or grown on your window sill. If you go the route of a neighborhood greenery, the following guidelines are useful in selecting a plant and avoiding catastrophe.

COMPATIBILITY WITH ITS PROSPECTIVE HOME AND FAMILY

All plants have basic requirements, especially of light and water. If you're uncertain of its final location, a plant that tolerates low light is a better choice than one needing full sun it may not get. Exotic or unusual plants often demand special care. Keep the "prima donnas" of the plant world as gifts for experienced indoor gardeners.

Try to include authoritative information on the plant and its needs. *The World Book of House Plants* by Elvin McDonald (available in paperback from Popular Library for $1.25) is a must. It has information on plant maintenance, problems, propagation, and pests—as well as a section describing a multitude of plants and their care requirements. Care cards on a wide variety of plants are being marketed by a Washington, D.C., plant shop. *Write The Third Day, 2001 P Street NW, Washington, D.C. 20036, for further information.*

For children, the Ladybird book *Indoor Gardening* is an excellent and inexpensive introduction to a wide range of topics and experiments. Written by J. Griffin-King, it is published by Wills & Hepworth Ltd. in Loughborough, England.

If a plant's recipient has children or pets with a penchant for nibbling, avoid dieffenbachias, English ivy, Jerusalem cherry, poinsettia, and oleander. These plants are *poisonous*: ingesting some or all parts of them produces unpleasant to fatal results. (In place of the traditional poinsettia as a holiday plant, try Christmas cactus or Christmas kalanchoe—both of which have striking blooms.)

GENERAL STATE OF HEALTH

Healthy plants are happy-looking plants: they may not have cold wet noses but they do have perky foliage with a good luster. A few bruises and abrasions are natural, but be wary of unnaturally pale foliage or yellowing/browning leaves.

Inspect plants carefully for bugs. Aphids come in a variety of colors and are often found on new growth; scale appears as shell-like growths on stems and branches. Both of these insects leave a sticky residue which denotes their presence. White flies cluster on the undersides of leaves; mealybugs resemble tufts of white cotton. Red spider mites are almost invisible but leave a white dustlike substance (discarded shell casings) along veins on the undersides of leaves.

These practices should be routine when selecting plants. They are practical, yet they also remind us that plants are not merely "decorative ob-jects" but living entities with wants and needs.

The following list is divided into those plants which must have at least a half day of direct sun to survive or look their best (full sun); those plants which will be perfectly happy on less than half a day of direct sun (partial sun/bright light); and those which do nicely in dark corners (shade). Some of the plants in the last three categories will actually burn if given too much or any direct sun. Plants that are exceptionally difficult to grow are marked (d); those which are exceptionally easy are marked (e).

FULL SUN
(4 hours or more direct sun—south window)
(e) Cactus
(e) Jade and other succulents
(e) Wax begonia
(e) Coleus
     Areca palm
     Croton
     Wandering jew (*Zebrina pendula*)
(d) Gardenia
(d) Citrus

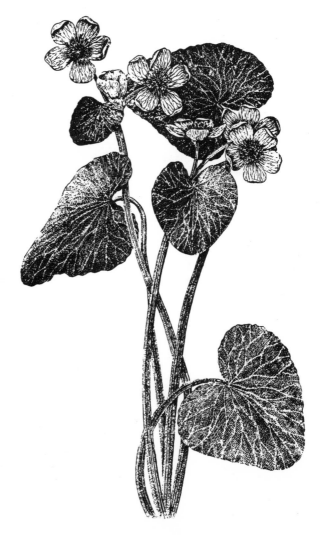

BRIGHT LIGHT
(consistent filtered sun—north window)
- (e) Grape ivy
- (e) Prayer plant (Maranta)
- (e) Nephthytis—"arrowhead plant"
- (e) Dracaena marginata—"dragon tree"
  Spathiphyllum
  Creeping fig
  Piggyback
- (d) Ferns—"Boston fern" and its varieties, or "table" or "pteris" ferns
- (dd) Maidenhair fern (Adiantum)

SHADE
(interior of a room)
- (ee) Sansevieria—"snake plant" or "mother-in-law's tongue"
- (e) Philodendron
- (e) Devil's ivy—"pothos"
  Parlor palm
  Chinese evergreen
  Aspidistra—"cast iron plant"

PARTIAL SUN
(up to 4 hours direct sun or consistent indirect sun—east or west windows)
- (e) Iresine—"bloodleaf"
- (e) Peperomia
- (e) Dracaena sanderiana
- (e) Spider plant
  Asparagus sprengeri—"asparagus fern"
  Asparagus plumosus
  Swedish ivy
  Gynura—"purple passion" or "royal velvet"
  Ivy (*Hedera helix*)
  Norfolk Island pine
  Rubber tree (*Ficus elastica decora*)
  Podocarpus

Grow your gifts this year—it's an inexpensive way of sharing the joy and excitement of your own plants. Cuttings from some of the most colorful house plants root well in water. These include wandering jew, gynura, iresine, coleus, and wax begonia. Such green standbys as philodendron, creeping fig, Swedish ivy, and nephthytis are also easy to root.

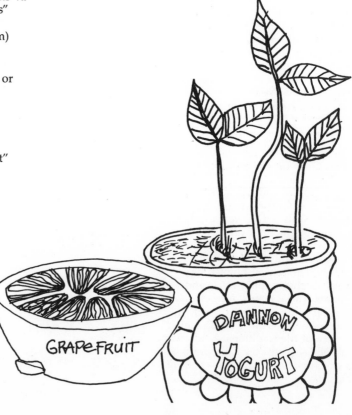

GRAPEFRUIT

DANNON YOGURT

Start your gift plants in the spring and summer. Plants have cycles, and one which roots easily in water in June may rot in December. If some cutitngs don't root after several attempts, you may not be using the proper propagating method.

Cuttings rooted in water or propagating medium (peat moss, perlite, vermiculite, or sand) should be several inches in length. Cut them just below a leaf or stem node, with a few bottom leaves or stems stripped off so one or two nodes are submerged. Cuttings should be kept out of strong sunlight while rooting.

Sand is best for rooting cactus or succulents. Leaf or stem cuttings from these plants should be left exposed to air for several days before going into the sand.

Newly propagated plants need a substantial root system on them before being potted in soil. Avoid overpotting: pots should be just large enough to contain the roots plus a bit of room for growth.

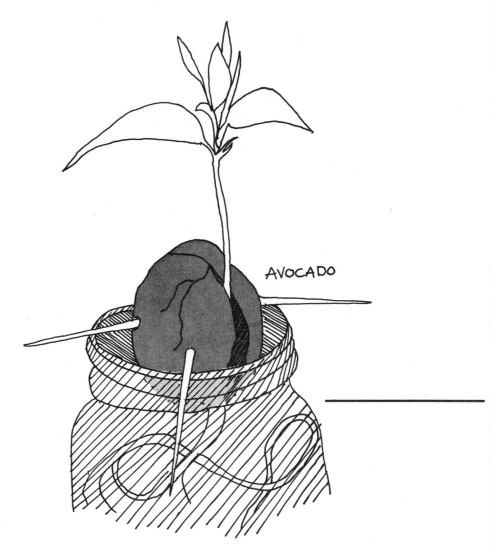

AVOCADO

Oranges and grapefruits are a goldmine of potential present plants. Soak the seeds for several days, then plant a half-inch down in rich sandy soil. Plant a quantity of seeds, as not all of them will make it. Keep young citrus in good sunlight and well-watered, since any wilt is likely to be permanent.

A well-written book for children (and adults), *Growing Plants from Fruits and Vegetables* by Jane Sholinsky, is available in paperback by Scholastic Book Services for 95¢.

Start now with the fruit salads and the pruning shears and any celebration can be brighted by a bit of green gifting.

Seeds and pits from dinner-table fruits and vegetables are another fun way of growing your gifts. Guacamole fanatics could easily present everyone they know with an aspiring avocado tree. Even an occasional salad will provide a pit for planting—or check local health food restaurants for discarded pits. A simplified strategy for avocados is as follows:

- Remove skin and insert toothpicks around the pit's midriff so that it will balance on top of a glass or jar of water.
- Keep the base half of the pit submerged in water. (The base is the end with the dimple in it.)
- After the stalk has emerged and grown several inches, pot the pit in a 6" to 8" diameter pot, leaving the top third to half of the pit above soil. (Several pits potted together will produce a forest effect.)
- When the shoot is about six inches high, prune it back to two or three inches. Traumatic as it may be for you, pruning forces the avocado to branch.

WANDERING JEW

MORE IDEAS

1) Packages of seeds—radishes, carrots, etc.—along with peat pots and soil.
2) Packages of midget vegetables seeds, a bucket or box to plant them in, and a copy of *Growing Midget Vegetables at Home* by Grant and Holly Gilmore, published by Lancer Books for $1.95.
3) Herb seeds or plants and any one of a number of plant books or cookbooks available on herbs and cooking with herbs.
4) Make a gardener's "diary" with pictures cut from seed catalogs to match the seeds given, leaving space for the grower to keep tabs on his/her indoor gardening efforts.
5) Bulbs—narcissus, hyacinth, crocus—for forcing, a bowl, and pebbles.
6) Current seed catalog and "gift certificate" or a "gift certificate" for a trip/purchase at the recipient's favorite plant store or greenhouse.
7) Clean out (with water and baking soda) and decorate a spray bottle (the type window cleaners come in) for use as a mister.
8) Decorate a coffee can and put in it: sharp paring knife, small scissors, small soft paintbrush, magnifying glass, and a supply of fertilizer (organic, please) as a plant owner's "tool kit."
9) Offer repotting or plant-sitting services.
10) Magazine subscriptions:
Horticulture
Horticulture Subscription Service
125 Garden Street
Marion, Ohio 43302
$8/year in USA and Canada
Published by the Massachusetts Horticultural Society
Organic Gardening
33 East Minor Street
Emmaus, Pennsylvania 18049
$6.85/year

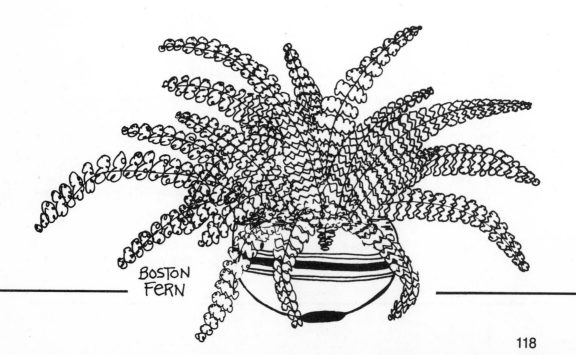

BOSTON FERN

Recyclables from around the home:
- Clear glass jars, brandy glasses, abandoned aquariums, or fish bowls for terrariums.
- Bowls for forcing bulbs or a single cup for one bulb.
- Plastic coffee can lids—good for under clay saucers to protect furniture tops from moisture.
- Jar and can lids for saucers.
- Plastic and Styrofoam meat trays for saucers.
- Coffee can or milk cartons as containers for potting soil.
- Gallon milk jugs—especially plastic ones—make good watering cans.
- Styrofoam cups for rooting cuttings.
  Wendy Ward

Give a Tree!

A real "gift of life" for many celebrations is a tree which is planted in someone's name. Think of this alternative for births, birthdays, and adoptions when a tree would grow as a child grows—reaffirming the vital balance between nature and humankind. At Easter, a new tree is a lasting form of new life. Trees can also be planted as a meaningful memorial to a deceased friend or relative. There are many groups throughout the country which have tree-planting programs of all sorts, either locally or internationally. Contact the Sierra Club: on the East Coast at P.O. Box 32, Sommerville, Massachusetts 02144; and on the West Coast at 220 Bush Street, Mills Tower, San Francisco, California 94104. The Heschel Memorial Forest Fund collects money to plant trees in Vietnam, and can be contacted at 211 Florida Ave., NW, Washington, D.C. 20036. Another project to consider is Save-the-Redwoods League, to which gift memberships are $5 a year. Their address is P.O. Box 38146, San Francisco, California 94138.

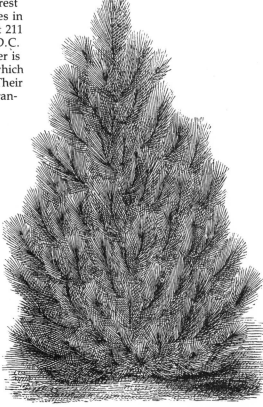

Books for Children: Beyond Disney, Star Wars, and ... Toward Shalom

Before I suggest some ways for readers to use their power and influence, let me tell you that I've been looking everywhere for a long time. What a celebration when occasionally I see it—find it!

I've been on a young children's lifestyle resources search for years. I'm a Christian educator and curriculum writer looking for resources that connect life experiences and values of the Christian faith. I'm a parent with a nine- and five-year-old, and I want the children's environment to be consistent with the values we try to live.

Our environment shapes us. We become what is around us. Therefore, parents want to share their values with children in natural, casual ways as well as through planned activities and discussions.

When values that parents wish to pass on are not readily accessible through the culture of which they are a part, through the media, the books, toys, and records that surround parents, there's an uncomfortable silence. There's a dissonance—a lack of affirmation of one's own values and an implied affirmation of other values. For a parent working to share particular values with one's children, that's a lonely place to be. It feels as though you are against everything that everyone else is for. It makes you ask whether you're making a "big deal" over something that's not so important. Parenting toward shalom values would be easier if the songs, stories, and toys that surround our children were consistent with what we're trying to teach.

In my lifestyle resources search I look in all kinds of bookstores—from university to small town and big city, in various parts of the U.S. and Canada—read reviews and descriptions, search libraries, and talk to people about what they've found. I'm looking for resources that imply:

- It's ok to be different.
- We are people of many cultures.
- Children and parents of both sexes can do anything.
- Winning and being first are not our goals in play.
- Eating healthful foods is enjoyable.
- We are capable of choosing.
- We don't have to have everything just because others have it.

- Kindness, sharing, and friendliness are a normal way for children to relate.
- Sharing is appropriate.
- We can measure history by periods of peace and human achievement as well as by periods of war.
- We can communicate in some ways even when our languages are not the same.
- Living a responsible lifestyle is okay even if it is different from other's lifestyles.
- This is how advertising and marketing work so don't just let them "do it to you." You can make decisions for yourself instead of having others tell you what you want and need.
- Conserving and recycling are a natural part of life.
- It makes sense to buy certain kinds of items that have already been used.
- We can be involved in some social action regardless of age. For example, even preschool children can dictate a letter to a TV station and receive an answer.
- Repairing items for continued use rather than buying another is a natural part of life.
- Persons of minority cultures live now in contemporary settings. They are not just part of past history.

What can be found on these subjects is so minimal that when I do find a book or record, I usually buy it. I want to make such ideas a part of my home surroundings so that the children can pick them up to read or listen to as casually as they can pick up a picture book of animals.

All around us—in grocery stores, drug stores, record stores, bookstores, department stores, discount stores—are resources promoting the lifestyles of the latest fad characters, or of the updated versions of "old favorites." "Why do adults buy and use these resources with young children?" one asks. Because they are very available! Adults want to share with the young children they love and they share what is available.

Adults don't share as often the resources described in this article because many of them are not easy to obtain. "You have to order them." "They're out of stock but will be available in three months." For average busy people who love young children there are too many roadblocks to obtaining stories of responsible lifestyles. So the T-shirts, mugs, placemats, records, Disney, Sesame Street, Star Wars fads continue and grow—without alternatives. All that would be necessary for other resources to be used is their easy availability.

Those adults who are experiencing the inconsistency and frustration of trying to attain consistency between family lifestyle and stories on the children's home bookshelf are waiting to respond with their purchasing power to appropriate resources for sharing their lifestyles. Providing the books and records for home use that families want can be commercially feasible. Even the families that have not consciously made lifestyle choices related to a shalom vision will obtain stories related to these values if they are readily available. Three things are necessary to develop this market:

1) research to find the resources
2) creativity to develop the resources
3) marketing that is sufficiently committed to a shalom vision to promote what is wanted as well as (or instead of) what is presented by the usual sales representatives.

Certainly denominational outlets and religious bookstores are beginning places for making these appropriate lifestyle resources available for use in homes by young children.

Children need to see evidence of a shalom vision in print. Print legitimizes these ideas. Books and records can reinforce what the children hear and experience at home.

The same kinds of books and records are needed to supplement church school studies. When they are available in the church, they reach more children, parents, and teachers with lifestyle alternatives that are legitimized by print.

To describe the search for lifestyle resources for young children is not to say that there aren't lots of good children's books on many subjects. It is to say there is a definite scarcity of resources that include naturally the details of responsible lifestyles. *Our children's literature is too much a reflection of the majority culture.* Just as minorities are not receiving appropriate attention in the literature, minority lifestyles are not affirmed, acknowledged, or included.

We need to change that. We need to distribute broadly what is available. We need to bring the lack of desired resources to the attention of libraries and bookstores. We need to write the books and make the records and games—or encourage our talented friends to do so. We can't just wait for them to appear on the market. (That's how the resources on children with handicapping conditions, for example, have appeared—the ones who work with them care, see gaps, and write books.) We are people with power to choose to use our influence.

That time of influence has come for me:

1) I've talked to bookstore owners and they have stocked some Lollipop Power books.
2) I've bought books for my family and then taken them to the local children's library to show to the librarian. She has ordered them.
3) I've listed supplementary resources as I've written curriculum resources.
4) I've served on the United Methodist Church's General Board of Discipleship in its section on Hunger and Value Formation and heard members talk about the need for assisting people to live responsive lifestyles. I spoke in committee meetings about my concern for more resources for use in homes. I suggested topics for those resources. The next time the group met, I brought records from home and showed them to staff and board members and said, "This is what I mean."

Eventually a staff committee formed to investigate the possibility of providing lifestyle resources for young children's use at home. I celebrated!

The board engaged Janet R. McNish to research what was available related to issues with which we were concerned. After contacting over a hundred publishers she came to the same conclusion I had. There

is little! There are so few resources that we certainly cannot flood the market. There are many topics on which new books and songs could be developed but we don't have to wait for those to become available before we take action on this issue.

I urged the Hunger and Value Formation Task Force to select some already available items and market them assertively right away. The staff has selected and is distributing "Gifts for Life"—a small selection of books and records. Sales brochures* describing these resources have been circulated broadly within the United Methodist Church.

You can help "Gift for Life" get around. You can support informal learning of responsible lifestyles in homes. You can support parenting that creates responsible lifestyles. You can enlarge the network of persons working toward a shalom vision. You may purchase some of the resources below. You may ask bookstores and libraries to carry some of these resources. You may use your influence with writers, publishers, and institutional structures to enable alternative

lifestyles to become an option. You may discover appropriate books, games, and records and tell Alternatives about them.

How will you use your influence?
Carolyn Hardin Engelhardt, a consultant and trainer in education and program ministries in Cheshire, Connecticut.

YOUNG CHILDREN'S LIFESTYLE RESOURCES:

Boys and Girls, Girls and Boys, Eve Merriam. New York: Holt, Rinehart and Winston, 1972.
**Martin's Father,* Margrit Eichler, Chapel Hill, N.C.: Lollipop Power, 1977.
Where's My Hippopotamus? Mark Alan Stamaty. New York: Dial Press, 1977.
The Sand Lot, Mary Blount Christian. New York: Harvey House Publishers, 20 Waterside Plaza, New York, N.Y. 10010
Songs of Nature and the Environment, Children's Songs by Gerry Axelrod and Robert Macklin. Folkways Records, 43 West 61st St., New York, N.Y.
Songs for Young Children, Dandelions, and *Peaceable Kingdom,* Mary Lu Walker. Available from K and R Music, Inc., 112 East Main Street, Trumansburg, N.Y. 14886.
I Learn About Sharing, Harriet A. Roorbach New York: Abingdon, 1968.
***World, World, What Can I Do?* Barbara Shook Hazen. New York: Abingdon, 1976.
Just One More Block, Patrick Mayers. Chicago: Albert Whitman, 1970.
Jo, Flo, and Yolanda, Carol De Poix. Chapel Hill, N.C.: Lollipop Power, 1973.
Many Hands Cooking: An International Cookbook for Girls and Boys, Terry Touff Cooper and Marilyn Ratner. New York: Crowell for UNICEF, 1974.
***The Super Food Cookbook for Kids,* Sherry Garrison Loller. Washington, D.C.: Review and Herald Publishing Assoc., 1976.
Loaves and Fishes, Linda Hunt, Marianne Frase, and Doris Liebert. Scottdale, Pa.: Herald Press, 1980. (A Love Your Neighbor Cookbook).
***Nobody Stole the Pie,* Sonia Levitin. New York: Harcourt Brace Jovanovich, 1980.
Waste Not Want Not Energy, Anne-Marie Constant. London and Toronto: Burke Books, 1976.
The Lorax, Dr. Seuss. New York: Random House, 1971.
Waste Not Want Not Energy, Anne-Marie Constant. London and Toronto: Burke Books, 1976.
Joshua's Day, Sandra Lucas Surowiecki. Chapel Hill, N.C.: Lollipop Power, 1977.
Kids Are Natural Cooks, Parents' Nursery School. Boston: Houghton Mifflin, 1974.
What Can You Decide? Lois Horton Young. Valley Forge, Pa.: Judson Press, 1970.
The Biggest House in the World, Leo Lionni. New York: Pinwheel Books/Knopf/Pantheon, 1973.
Grownups Cry Too, Nancy Hazen. Chapel Hill, N.C.: Lollipop Power, 1978.
*Available from Discipleship Resources, P. O. Box 840, Nashville, Tennessee 37202.
**Also available from Alternatives Resource Center. For a description of these and other resources for children, including board games, write for a book list.

Choosing & Using Toys

Even when the toy maker and the toy buyer work together to assure children of toys that are well made and appropriately chosen for their ages and skills, buying a toy is not always easy. When the interests of the toy industry and the toy buyer are at odds the problems multiply. Huge conglomerates and retail chains now dominate the industry, and the mom-and-pop stores, which once placed restraints on what was sold, have been killed off like the buffalo. The hard evidence is that the industry's "best toy" is the one that sells best and makes the most profit rather than the one that brings hours of safe, creative enjoyment to a child. As a result, parents must face problems with unsafe toys, misleading toy ads, toys which grate against the values many of us hold—realities few of us are armed with when we go in a toy store.

The toy buyer should also know that no matter what the problems, appropriate toys *can be found,* and the toy industry's practices can be improved by consumers who will accept no substitutes for what they need.

The most serious problem facing the toy buyer is that of safety. The toy market is still far from hazard-free, though the establishment of a Consumer Product Safety Commission and the issuance of some standards for quality have improved the situation in recent years.

The buyer should be able to expect that any toy marketed is safe. But the reality is that toys are safe enough if used only as directed, or if they don't break or operate defectively. The toy with glass parts (yes, they still can be found) won't cut unless the glass is broken. The projectile toy with the rubber tip injures no one if the rubber tip remains in place and the projectiles aren't fired at human beings. The electrical toy—essentially a small appliance not designed for constant use and

consequently cheaply made—may not develop a short and shock a child, or worse. Small toy parts present no hazard to a school-aged child, but a younger sibling may swallow them or get them stuck in the ears or nose. Painted toys are a problem for children at the age when they put everything into their mouths.

Even when toys are reasonably safe, parents and guardians must exercise responsibility in choosing them and in guiding play.

Because some children are well-coordinated and have good balance while others do not, buyers should be careful to choose movement toys appropriate to the child in question. Roller skates that are fun for one may be dangerous or frustrating for another. The heavily marketed and glamorous skateboard fad has led to many injuries for both children and adults. If skateboard play is approved, helmets and pads should be mandatory and extreme care should be taken to find a safe skateboarding place free of traffic, rough surfaces, and pedestrians. Other movement toys such as bicycles and tricycles should be carefully investigated for balance, braking, and reflective material—if the child is old enough to use the bicycle after dark.

Parents also need to be aware constantly that injury is most likely to occur when directions for using toys aren't followed properly. The quiet play offered by a craft or science kit can be dangerous if the child is not mature enough to use it. Because of their immaturity children cannot be counted on always to use toys in the proper way, so adults must be on their guard when there is a potential problem.

Another hazard buyers should beware of is the emotional ploys advertisers use to sell their products. Advertising research has plumbed our deepest yearnings to find out what triggers the urge to buy. It has used sophisticated

psychophysiological testing equipment to measure such subliminal body reactions as eye movements and sweating palms to see what makes us tick. (Some questions might be raised about the ethics of using methods of psychological investigation in the interests of a commercial third party. A certain amount of probing is appropriate in the hands of trained personnel if the object is to give an individual insights that could lead to better self-knowledge and adjustment, but the same techniques become insidious when they are used to influence an individual for another's gain.)

The toy industry pours millions of dollars into advertising to get parents and children to choose a certain toy out of a possible 150,000 on the market. In 1977, for instance, more than $109 million was spent on local television spot advertising during the Christmas season. As much as $100,000 may be spent in planning the promotion of a single toy even before air time is purchased. And the adult who makes toy-buying decisions on the basis of emotion rather than reason may be easy prey. At this season especially, it is difficult not to give in to the nostalgia for a childhood when the pace was slower, extended families lived near each other, and family rituals and familiar things gave a sense of comfort and well-being. We wish to create a similar atmosphere for our own children and are led to believe that things will do it—calico decorations, old-style puzzles and games, or new ones which "give a sense of unity to the family that plays them together." We must understand that our yearnings are not for things but for human relationships—the sharing in wreath or cookie or gift making rather than the objects themselves.

Another advertising problem is the difference between what a toy appears to be and what it is. Although the code of the National Association of Broadcasters on children's advertising has eliminated most of the obviously deceptive practices in the preparation of advertising copy, it does not cover whether or not the toy will perform as well as it appears to on television. A study done recently by the Engineering Department at the University of Georgia showed that only two of the ten toys most widely advertised on television performed as described in the ad, and one of these was a doll. Close-ups, camera angles, and other techniques may enhance the toy's

performance. For instance, cars go much faster when viewed from the bottom of an inclined plane. Or, though the toy is shown in one scene with the child to establish its actual size, other shots may counteract that impression. Also, children do not usually comprehend the statement "assembly required" (which most advertisers use) though they know very well what "you have to put it together" means.

Toys based on television characters may be the biggest cheat in town. Several product lines have been designed based on the attraction of a show's popularity rather than the toy's playability. Often they amount to nothing more than character dolls one is encouraged to put through the motions of the same story plots again and again. They are generally far more expensive than the products merit—after all, the makers had to pay for the rights to use the television characters as well as the cost of heavy promotion for the toys.

One advertising practice that adults need to watch carefully is the beaming of the products and the product type directly to children. Even at its best—and it has some way to go—advertising toys to children on television creates a value system in which certain needs can be satisfied only by the purchase of things. The ads sell an idea that money can buy happiness, that owning rather than doing is the way to feel good about yourself, and that we are somehow not complete without this or that. And if that weren't enough, the commercials

show a heaven on earth where no one gets angry or hurt, where parents are always loving and responsive, and where the lifestyle of plenty has erased every care. A child's own family cannot compare to this and may even seem different and shameful. If a child is part of a poor family, these messages can increase the sense of inadequacy and isolation to the point of hopelessness. Or low-income families can feel forced to purchase expensive items to prove that they are as good as anyone else.

These messages presumably are more influential than many others because most of the consumers in the two-to-eleven-year-old market have a limited understanding of what advertising is and how it fits into their lives. Much still needs to be learned about how children process the information in advertisements, according to social science research abstracts on children and advertising collected and published in 1977 by the National Science Foundation. In the meantime, the Federal Trade Commission Staff Report has suggested that programs for preschool children be run without advertising on the grounds that children of that age are not capable of making consumer decisions. The toy industry, of course, vigorously defends children's rights to receive product information, but it provides little information on the functions of buying and selling or on such points as the recommended age range for particular toys. Adults who are concerned about this advertising practice can choose not to buy any product that is advertised to children rather than adults. They can also let the manufacturers know why they made their decisions in the hope of influencing future advertising practices.

Advertising directed to adults can also be misleading. For instance, many adults are conditioned to think well of a toy labeled "educational." We all want to see our children learn new things and develop skills they can use later in school or in life. But the toy labeled "educational" and put in a fancy package may be similar, except in practice, to any other construction set, puzzle, or game. Celebrity endorsements and the use of characters from educational television shows like "Sesame Street" may add nothing at all to the play experience of the item. Adults should remember that child development experts still say a set of plain wooden blocks is one of the best toy investments that can be made.

Another problem parents face when buying toys is that many of those which are most widely sold grate against their values. Parents can and should hold out for toys which support their values.

If we want our children to grow up peace-loving and cooperative, we do not need to give in and allow submachine guns, tanks, pistols, or any of the other toys that encourage children to think that disputes and differences are best settled by force, or that the world is divided up into good guys and bad guys: *us* and *them*. Gun play and war play can trivialize a child's understanding of the value of life. Does a thirteen- or fourteen-year-old who pulls a trigger and shoots someone have any idea of

the gravity of the act or is it just an extension of play? The Mr. Rogers question "What do you do with the mad that you feel?" has many positive answers but violence is not one of them.

Children do need to learn how to deal with aggression, but there are more constructive ways to do this than through war toys. Practice in solving problems through talking things out or negotiating compromises is one way to develop skills in coping with aggression. Sports and games also provide ample opportunity for the expression of aggression within set boundaries. If one kicks the ball and runs as fast as one can, this is aggressive and competitive play. But it is conducted against opponents rather than enemies, has standards and rules and develops physical skill. Playing cowboys and Indians with toy guns does none of these things; moreover, it is deeply offensive to Native Americans.

Toys that support stereotypical views of sex, race, ethnic heritage, or age tend to restrict a child's play opportunities and personal growth rather than open them up. Therefore, care should be taken in examining toys for evidence of these stereotypes.

Some toys are still advertised and packaged showing only one sex, yet research has shown that sex stereotyping is detrimental to both boys and girls because it robs both sexes of full development. Masculine and feminine elements both are included in a well-developed personality—strength and vulnerability go side by side; nurture and discipline overlap in the parental role; boys and girls, men and women are much more alike than they are different. Yet, when asked why a certain line of transportation toys included play scenes from one of the few all-male fourth grades in the country, the manufacturer's reply was, "We wouldn't sell as many toys if we used a group of girls." And women in toys and games continue to be depicted in relation to dating, baby care, and a few traditional women's jobs rather than in the whole range of life activities which they share with men.

Racial and ethnic stereotyping is a disservice to both minority and nonminority children. Yet virtually all the Native American character dolls continue to be clothed in beads and feathers, the Spanish-speaking ones in sombreros, and the Chinese in coolie hats. Also, even now we continue to see whole lines of toys showing only fair-skinned white children and excluding Black Americans and other minorities. It is important for minority children to feel they are represented in all aspects of our society. It is also important for nonminority children to see other racial and ethnic groups included to reinforce the concept of a diverse population and to lay the groundwork for feeling comfortable in multi-racial communities.

Age stereotyping is also a problem in toy design and packaging. In spite of the general distaste for toys based on television series, Grandma and Grandpa Walton were a welcome first step on the doll shelf. It is desirable to show the world as it really is, with people of all ages. Why shouldn't grandparent characters be shown as they are, ranging from people in their early forties on up? Grandma may not have her hair in a bun and wear long dresses; she may go to work in a business suit. And Grandpa may not hobble around with a cane; he may be on the golf course, or volunteering with ACTION. Grandparents may not be white either. They come in the same variety children do. Why don't we see it?

Another point to remember in choosing toys is that the best ones usually foster open-ended play and have multiple uses. The complicated toy with a single use will not retain a child's interest very long and may leave both the adult and the child feeling bad about the choice. Toys that do it all for the child contribute little to growth. The sad jokes about the parent who buys a large, expensive toy for a child and finds out that the child would rather play with the box are too often true. Sometimes an adult and a child have very different ideas about what toys are fun. It's a good idea to ask ourselves whether we think a toy would be fun for the child for whom it is intended or fun for the child in us. If the second is more to the point, maybe two toys are in order. Adults can play too.

Age appropriateness is another important consideration. If a toy is too far behind or ahead of a child's stage of development it will not be a good choice. Some of the better toy companies are including some mention of age range on the packages, but they do not do it often enough or consistently. Even when the age range is given, it may not be appropriate for a particular child. Children develop large and small muscle control, a sense of color and shape, and skill in manipulating objects and concepts at varying rates. Therefore, the buyer needs some sense of the individual child and a knowledge of the general range of toys for that age in order to make wise choices. Local early childhood educators may help make appropriate decisions if the task seems difficult.

One thing we toy buyers should keep foremost in our minds: as consumers, *we are in charge.* Whatever toys are offered us, it is our responsibility to decide which are appropriate and to refuse to buy those which aren't. Children need toys that foster growth, add to a sense of skill and mastery, expand creativity, develop positive self-images, and encourage interaction between adults and children or among children. They need a mix of active toys and quiet toys, toys which encourage both nurturing and competition, that stimulate both muscles and minds. These are the toys we should insist upon; we cannot settle for any substitute for what our children need; and we *can* find the toys they need if we refuse to take anything else.

Allenna Leonard of Columbia, Maryland, is a member of P.A.C.T.

OUR TOY SELECTIONS WHETHER THEY ARE GIVEN AS HOLIDAY OR BIRTHDAY PRESENTS... ...HAVE A SUBSTANTIAL IMPACT ON THE VALUES WE COMMUNICATE TO THE CHILDREN WHO RECEIVE THEM

7.

Gift Making

How many of the gifts you've given or received are still used, or even remembered, with pleasure? My own list would include several store-bought items—one of those popular and durable enameled cast iron skillets, a favorite dress, the complete works of Robert Frost, a fascinating recording of frog calls with a written description of the habitat and habits of each frog. But the majority of those I've enjoyed most are handmade—a large conch shell filled with pansies, a baby doll fashioned from a turkey wishbone and bits of fabric, three handcarved wooden birds balanced delicately in a mobile, a candle made by my five-year-old niece, a jar of calamondin marmalade, a poem, a small bookshelf for my desk.

It's difficult to stop naming them once I start and, thankfully, impossible to stop the warm

Making Gifts

feelings for those with whom the gift is associated. There is something about a handmade gift that has been designed and created with care, something that strums on the heartstrings long after the gift is given, and both giver and receiver hear it echoing within them.

Most of you probably have discovered the joy of gift making—the act of creation itself, with its satisfactions of self-expression and achievement, and the thrill of seeing someone else's reaction to your work. If you haven't, gather up your excuses and throw them out the window, try making something, and see what happens. You *do* have the time. Your first effort may not be "nice enough," but chances are it won't matter. Often, it really is the thought that counts. And you *can* learn how to create something beautiful or useful, just as others across the country are doing.

In recent years interest in making various gifts has mushroomed. For various reasons—seeking to regain a measure of control in their lives by reducing their dependence on machines and advanced technology or, ironically, to fill the leisure time these made possible; evading the "buy now" pressures of mass advertisers; creating islands of identity in a sea of anonymity—people have flocked to enroll in arts and crafts courses and to read books and articles on gift making.

Whatever you want to make, you probably can find through your libraries or community education centers some resource which will help you begin. But we would like to share some books we've found intriguing. Some have been recommended by experts in the field; others appear to emphasize values we believe in; still others introduced new ideas that sent our minds on an adventure. We hope you'll find among them several that pique your interest.

Our thanks to the reference librarians in the Jackson, Mississippi, library system and to the following craft book services for sharing with us their views of "the best of the bunch": Book Barn, Box 256, Avon, Connecticut 06001; Museum Books, 48 East 43rd St., New York, New York 10017; The Unicorn Craft and Hobby Book Service, Box 645, Rockville, Maryland 20851.

If a bibliography leaves you confused, ask a local expert in your field of interest for suggestions of books or articles s/he has found helpful. And if there are subjects you don't find here, head for the reference section of the closest library. *The Reader's Guide to Periodical Literature* will point you to magazine articles, while *Books in Print* will give you titles of any book on your subject that is in print. Your library's card catalog may include some valuable references that are out of print, and the librarian may have clipped some exceptionally useful articles for the "vertical file," so ask about that, too.

A word of caution as you journey through the world of gift making. Commercialism has crept in before you and is waiting to con you, so beware. Those clever kits you buy at craft shops or through magazine ads are generally more expensive, and probably no more helpful, than the kit or completed item you make from scratch. The crafts course at the local arts center may be more expensive and no more useful than a series of gift making sessions you and your friends plan, with the help of a few books and articles or a knowledgeable neighbor. And you don't have to buy a book unless you discover it's one you want to use often—libraries, after all, are organized on the principle of sharing resources.

Some principles of gift making that seem essential if you're serious about conserving resources and creating a world where peace and justice prevail:

1. Use your imagination and make something from "nothing." In other words, share yourself. Write a poem or a song, give yourself as servant-or-playmate-for-a-day, weed the garden, clean the house, take your child for a nature walk, pick a single flower and take it as you go to share an hour with a shut-in or an elderly friend. To keep friends who are accustomed to receiving "things" from being disappointed, make a card or write a note or find some other way of communicating why you chose to give yourself, why you feel that you and your time are more valuable gifts than money or things. You may help liberate them from the trap of materialism. Even if you don't, the way in

which you joyfully give yourself to them will create an atmosphere for better understanding between you.

2. Use materials from nature, but gather them thoughtfully. It is one thing to pick up a piece of driftwood or a beautiful stone and quite another to gather all the sea grasses in sight. Don't be greedy. If you know a resource is rare, or if it appears to be, leave it to replenish itself or to be enjoyed by others who see it in its natural habitat. Perhaps you think you are only one person, and what harm could one person do. But if you think instead of what would happen if everyone who walked by did the same thing, you'll be more likely to use nature thoughtfully.

Also, don't buy natural materials. It encourages the rape of the land and the sea. Someone innocently sees a chance to make a little extra income and starts selling shells or raffia, and before you know it, commercial harvesters have almost depleted a resource. That's the sort of unthinking behavior that has made sea oats a rare plant, done irreparable damage to the coral and tropical fish populations of the world, and nearly killed off certain species of birds whose plumes were once widely sought for pens and hats. In buying natural materials, we may unwittingly create more demand for them than can be satisfied.

Besides, why buy when you can find something beautiful on almost any outing—stones and shells to share as they are or paint and glue into "pets" or flowers, driftwood, garden vegetables, fruits and flowers, cones, nuts, grasses and grains, dried plant materials, perfectly preserved butterflies, fibers to weave and the plants to dye them with.

3. Recycle materials you've already had to buy. Make new garments from old. Use newspapers for papier-mâché crafts; metal or plastic containers for jewelry, fake flowers, or objets d'art; ice cream sticks and burnt matches for clever trivets and decorative boxes. Art teachers and early childhood educators are excellent sources for attractive ways to recycle materials, and magazines like *Woman's Day* have run monthly columns of prizewinning new-from-old creations from their readers.

4. Don't buy raw materials unless you have to, and when you do, take the time to find the best bargain possible. Share a portion of the money you save with organizations like those in the *Catalogue*. Take another portion and use it, along with your gift of time, to adopt a family or community organization. Do it with the same attitude that goes into gift making for your relatives and friends—that you will benefit from it as much as the receiver—and see what happens.

5. Share your philosophy of gift making and giving with your family, friends, and acquaintances. Spread the "alternatives" message and help create an alternative society.

Making Gifts at Home

"WOODS TREASURES"

My favorite things to use for making gifts at home are little treasures that you can find in the woods, on the desert, in a field, or in your own back yard. There are so many things worth gathering, just waiting to be put together to brighten up a spot in someone's home. I start by gathering bits of bark, flowers, mushrooms, moss, leaves, and rocks. Then I dry them, and my process is simple. I just gather them and let them sit. Some may not make it, but most do. For drying flowers, I put them between the pages of a book.

Woods-treasures baskets are small baskets, 1 to 1½ inches in diameter, filled with a bouquet of small seeds, dried leaves, twigs, berries, vines, and flowers. For a basket I use the cap from a large acorn, or any other small cap. If I use an acorn cap, I sometimes use a finish on it for a slightly glossy effect. I fill the bottom of the basket with something like floral clay or Styrofoam to hold the arrangement. After I've arranged and glued all the tiny pieces to suit me, I glue the basket on a small piece of bark (pieces of bark with bits of moss attached look great).

A similar bouquet in a small vase is a little variation to this. I use any bottle that's handy; food coloring bottles work well. Or, lacking the right size bottle, I just wad papier-mâché into a vase shape and make a hole in the top for an opening to hold the arrangement. I cover the bottle with paint, and finish. Here again I use a small piece of bark for a base.

Many times when I find a really great looking piece of wood, bark, or gnarled root, I'll work with that to make a miniature forest floor. For this I might use lichens or small mushrooms (which will dry by themselves in a matter of days).

Dried flower plaques are a little more time-consuming, but tremendously satisfying. I buy unfinished wood plaques, stain the outer rim with a wood finish, and paint the middle flat surface with a few coats of black paint. I use dried flowers, stems, grasses, ferns, and leaves. I set and reset them, until I find the arrangement that I like. Then, using a small artist's brush or a toothpick to dab the glue, and tweezers to hold the small things in place, I glue them to the plaque. Then I gently press them down to the plaque with my finger and wipe away the excess glue.

I like using woods treasures to make *miniature wreaths* out of small acorns, berries, seeds, etc. These tiny versions are great, inexpensive, and easy to do. I cut out a 3-inch circle of cardboard for a base, and glue an ornament hanger or a paper clip at the top for a hanger. Then I just start gluing on whatever dried things that I have around. On some, I use just acorns; on others, a combination of things. Then I coat it with any varnish or clear plastic spray and add a tiny red bow at the top. I have done a few wreaths with shells; while they're not as traditional looking, they are rather nice. I've also tried tree-shaped and ball-shaped arrangements.

I've always liked *stained glass,* but the real way of making it seems expensive and complicated. So, I tried something different. From a glass company, I get a number of large, broken pieces of cathedral glass in many colors, for *free.* And I buy, for very little cost, some sheets of plain glass cut into circles and rectangles. Then I crack the large pieces of colored glass into smaller fragments by putting them into a heavy sack and tapping it with a hammer. I pick out pieces in the right shapes to put together in a flower. After the flower is shaped (jigsaw puzzle fashion) I fill in the rest of the plain glass in the same fashion using only one color of glass and glue all the pieces to the plain glass, making sure to press out the air between them (otherwise the glue might not be transparent when it dries). A hanger of some sort (small wire loop, perhaps) should be glued between the cracks at the top. Then I mix the grout and rub it into all the cracks. (You usually mix grout with a little water; I mix mine with black poster paint or acrylic. This makes the grout black and eliminates having to paint the areas of gray when it's dry.) Using my fingers to fill in the cracks works best. After filling in all the cracks on the surface, I smooth a border of grout around the edge to give it a finished look. Then I put a coat of finish over the whole thing.

I've made small *papier-maché Easter eggs* for several years now. I simply ball up some used foil to mold the egg shape, and cover it with papier-maché. After it dries (in a low oven) I paint it a solid color, then decorate it with tiny flowers or something using a fine brush. Then I put on a coat of finish. These are especially pretty nestled in a bed of moss or leaves, rather than dime-store "grass."

Mary Norman DeLaughter

CLOWN MOBILE

The clown mobile shown here can be made with any amount of variation, encouraging the creativity of the children to give the clown another personality if they wish.

You will need:
- Cardboard or posterboard (for hat, mouth, and bowtie), painted with brightly colored poster paints.
- Ping-pong balls for the eyes (painted with black dots on both front and back of each ball) and nose (painted with red paint or whatever).
- Black thread to tie the pieces together (which is nearly invisible, even at a short distance). Run a long threaded needle through the balls and individual pieces, and tie a knot in thread so it won't slip through.

WALNUT-SHELL TURTLES

Walnut-shell turtles can be made to dress up packages or to pin on a shirt, and are very simple for children to make, perhaps as a "no-special-occasion gift" for friends.

All you need is:
- Green felt, cut like the illustration.
- Walnut shell, to glue on top of felt.
- Felt-tip pen to draw lines on the shell of the turtle.

STUFFED ANIMALS

There are many patterns available for stuffed animals and pillow-toys. These toys can be stuffed with non-allergenic stuffing, which is washable and can be found in local stores. Simple embroidery can be used for eyes, etc., to eliminate the danger of a small child detaching the button eyes. These animals have much more personality than the manufactured toys; they are softer, and show more of a personal effort on the part of the giver.

GINGERBREAD PEOPLE

Making cork gingerbread people for Christmas ornaments is another project that the whole family can participate in. The gingerbread people can be made with a lot of variation, perhaps dressed in clothes made from scraps of material from which a child's dress was made. You could have one gingerbread person to represent each family member.

You will need:

- Gingerbread cookie cutter to trace around.
- Sheet cork (⅛ inch thick) which can be bought at an art supply store.
- Rickrack, or whatever trim you wish.
- Felt pieces for the eyes, nose, and mouth.
- Ribbon for loop hanging it up.

For gift-making ideas for and by children, write to:

Women for a Peaceful Christmas
Box 5095
Madison, Wisconsin 53705

Ask for a booklet called:

"No More Shopping Days Till Peace"
20 cents plus postage

Association for Childhood Education International
3615 Wisconsin Avenue
Washington, D.C. 20016

Ask for a booklet called:

"Bits and Pieces"
$1.25 plus postage

EGG TREE

Egg trees are something that delights everyone as a symbol of new life that comes with the spring.

You will need:

- A branch of a tree that has fallen in the woods. Stand it up with soil or small rocks in a decorated coffee can.
- Collected egg shells, blown out by poking holes in either end.
- Dye the egg shells by soaking onion skins (all colors) and then dipping eggs in until desired color appears.
- Paint the egg shells with whatever decoration you wish (enamel or poster paint work well).
- Hang the eggs with wire or string with button at the bottom to hold string.
- Top each egg with a bow of satin ribbon or colored string.

CLOTH PICTURE BOOK

1) Find some sturdy white cotton material, such as duck, denim, or Indianhead.
2) With pinking shears, cut 10 or 12 "pages" a suitable small size, like 7″ × 7″.
3) Draw with bright permanent markers simple line drawings of familiar objects, such as ball, boat, house, cup, doll.
4) Print the word beneath the drawing.
5) Print a title, such as "Andrew's Book" on the first page.
6) Assemble pages and sew together on machine with heavy thread many times.

   Carolyn and Mary Kate Willet, Larchmont, New York.

BABY BLOCK

1) Machine stitch bright squares and rectangles together until you have a patched piece big enough to cover a brick-size foam block.
2) Sew the letters of the baby's name at random in the squares using tape, braid, or a zig-zag stitch.
3) Cover the foam block with the patched piece. Stitch securely. Block is machine washable.

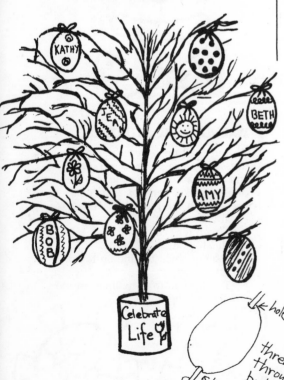

POTATO PRINTING

A neat way to make sure that no one is left out in the planning work for your next celebration is to form a committee to make a potato rubber stamp. All you need is a few cut-in-half potatoes, dull butter knives, poster paints, and paper towels. Just carve out letters, words, designs, etc., in bas-relief (what you don't want goes, what you do want is left raised). Make several "stamp pads" by covering folded paper towels with bright poster paints. Press the potato down on the pad and then onto the desired paper, card, or whatever. Unless the letters and words have been carved backwards, there will be a secret message that will have to be held up to the mirror to be read. If your celebration is centered around a particular person, a special presentation of the stamps (and perhaps one with the person's name on it) would be in order. It's also a good way to teach the young children about mirror reflection and printing presses.

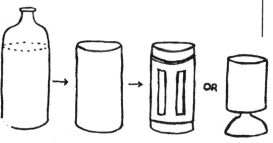

SET OF GLASSES MADE FROM BOTTLES

Inexpensive bottle cutters are not hard to find. Use the cutter to remove the tops of the bottles for the size glass you want. We use non-returnable root beer bottles with straight sides, but any shape will do. The sharp edges can be smoothed down with emery paper. We decorated our glasses by wrapping them with carved leather holders.

By putting the top underneath and applying some silicon glue, you've made a candle holder or wine glass or planter.

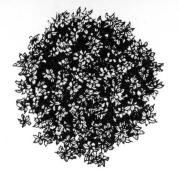

Note: live in-door trees make great Christmas trees with the addition of colorful bows or decorations.

CANDLE FOR A WEDDING GIFT

Use a wedding invitation to decorate a candle. Cut around the printed part of the invitation. You should be able to shape it into an oval. Glue the oval to a wide candle. With a match held near the edges of the invitation, let wax seal the edges. For an added touch, put the candle on a stand and surround it with flowers.
Janet Herringshaw, Akron, Ohio

RAILROAD SPIKE PAPERWEIGHT

Plan one of your next picnics to take place near an abandoned railroad station. A walk around the station or a short hike along the tracks will soon reveal a few discarded railroad spikes (usually pretty dirty and rusty). Scrub them with SOS/Brillo pads or a steel wool brush. Soak them overnight in the strongest cleaning solution that you have or that you can concoct from available kitchen supplies. Repeat the process as needed. You'll end up with a fine quality, rustic-looking paperweight. For those so inclined, a library book or Boy Scout handbook will show you how you can electroplate your steel expedition remembrance.

FOR AVID CROSSWORD PUZZLE FANS

Gather crossword puzzles, cutting them from various periodicals and newspapers which you are sure that the recipient does not see. Paste them on 8½ × 11-inch cutout pages of grocery bag paper or some other paper that can be recycled. Using a clipboard that has a cover folding over it, secure the mounted puzzles under the clip. Paste or glue an attractive print or drawing on the front of the clipboard cover.
Hope Scrogin

FOR A BABY GIFT

For a family with a new baby, how about making a calendar with large spaces to record daily happenings or brief remarks.
Carol A. Watson, Inglewood, California

CHESS SET

The board is made of leather glued with contact cement to a piece of plywood. The squares are marked and gouged out, then stained black or natural with a lacquer finish over the top. The pieces are made by screwing various sizes of square-headed wood bolts into blocks of wood. To further differentiate the pieces, designs can be cut into the heads of the bolts with a hacksaw.

REVIVING TREASURED DRAWINGS

For a gift for your parents (or from parents to their children), get a drawing that you did when you were young, one which is treasured by your parents (or done by your now-grown daughter or son). Use carbon to trace the drawing into linen and then embroider the drawing. They can be completed by using a chain stitch, or satin stitch in the colors that the child chose to use in the original drawing. They make nice pillows or can be framed as pictures.
Carol C. Keane, Mililani Town, Hawaii

RECIPE BOX

Provide small 3 × 5 or 5 × 8 index cards for the children. Have the children copy and illustrate their favorite child-tested recipes. This makes a nice gift from one child who cooks to another child, or from a parent to a child who is learning to cook.
Therese VanHouten, Washington, D.C.

Mrs. Tiggywinkle is a favorite creature of mine from the Beatrix Potter story.

You get a ball of clay and wedge it up so that there are no air bubbles in it, because if there are it will explode. You wedge it by banging it on the table in a few places. Then you pull little bits of clay out of the top of the ball for prickles. You can make indentations for eyes by pressing with your thumb and draw lines for eyelashes with a pencil or knitting needle. Then pull a nose. Draw a line or something for a mouth with any interesting thing you can find. Press your thumb in and down for "feet." Last of all you stick your thumb up the middle inside leaving at least ½ inch of clay at the top. You can decorate it with anything (like paint, glaze), fire it or put it in the oven depending on the type of clay you use.

Libby Scribner, 13

Ideas from the Kids

Handmade gifts are always special but there's something extraordinary about gifts made by children. They may not be as polished as the work of a more experienced hand, but the knowledge that a child spent long hours patiently sanding or painting something just for you adds a different kind of luster to the finished work. The sense of accomplishment when the gift is presented makes all the effort worthwhile.

This section on gift making would not be complete without gifts made by children. They are presented here in the words of the individuals, but since it was technically impossible to reproduce the drawings that accompanied them, our artist has drawn the illustrations based on the children's work.

This Christmas, when I was taking industrial arts at school, I decided to make my family a creche. I used 3 sides of an old drawer for the base, then nailed 2 pieces of plywood for a slanted roof, found some bark and glued the bark to the roof. I cut a star out of Plexiglas to hang over the creche.

You could make creche figures to go with the creche by making simple standing shapes out of clay. Paint faces and clothing on after the clay has baked.

Anne Scribner, 14

I made an obstacle course for my brother's birthday party out in the backyard. I used logs, a sawhorse, trash can lids, anything I could find.

David Scribner, 12

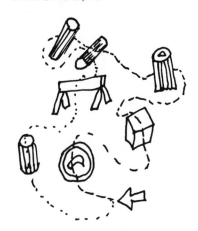

YARN PICTURE

Find a piece of cardboard any shape or size and draw a picture on it. Your picture can be of anything, but the bigger the better. Then pick out the colors of yarn you want.

Put glue on the outline of your object, then take your yarn and put it where the glue is. Put glue on the inside of your object and glue yarn down. Use as many colors as you like. Do the same for your background. You can make a frame out of yarn, by gluing a piece of yarn around the edge. Make a loop out of a piece of yarn and tape on the back of the top of the picture for hanging.

Libby Scribner

I made a Styrofoam print of our dog and gave it to my family for a present. I made a mat for the print out of cardboard.

Bobby Scribner, 10

leave open for stuffing

RAG DOLL

Make a paper pattern for a rag doll. Pin it on cotton material and cut double. Turn both wrong sides out and sew all around the eges, leaving a hole for stuffing. Right side it out and stuff with cotton or foam if you want to wash it. Sew up hole and sew on eyes, nose, mouth, hair. Make clothes out of scrap materials.

You can make nursery rhyme characters like Little Miss Muffet, Humpty Dumpty into dolls.

Collette Surla, 14

GINGERBREAD PEOPLE

Gingerbread people are fun and easy to make. Make an ordinary gingerbread recipe and make it any shape, a man, a woman or anything else. You can use raisins, chocolate chips, or nuts for eyes, noses, buttons, etc. You can make confectioner's sugar frosting and decorate. Roll up a piece of paper from corner to corner so there is one small end. Put some of the frosting in the container and squeeze it so it comes out the small end. You can make lots of different designs with the frosting such as hair, lace, a mouth and many other things. Add anything else you want and give as a birthday or Christmas present ... Have fun!

Allison Barlow, 12

Make a personal T shirt for a present. Draw on a white T shirt with felt markers. The design will not wash out.

Lisa Hay, 12

Make Your Own Greeting Cards

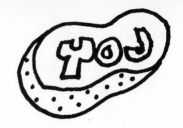

Using our own experiences, our eyes, our hands, our thoughts, we can wish joy, love, laughter, godspeed, get-well, peace, with our own handmade greeting cards. We put technology aside for a minute and simply share a feeling. It's exposure of the best kind. Nature provides us with color, shape, rhythm, and line. Our own backyard jungle might make a watercolor birthday card for a grandparent who lives far away; a leaf from a favorite tree could be used for a graduation card rubbing; the sun suggests a string relief for a birth announcement. Folk traditions provide us with a wealth of techniques such as Polish paper cutting, German Scherenschnitte, block-printing, stencil cutting. By searching out our family traditions, by listening to our children, we can also find what to make.

To avoid the last-minute rush to the card store, clear a space, possibly a kitchen shelf, for card-making materials. Store rubber cement, paper, scissors, magic markers, paints, a ruler, sponges, cardboard. Experiment with different ways of printing, papercutting, stenciling, painting, until you find a method that's fun for you. Here are some successful ways to make cards, invitations, and announcements. Send us some new ways for next year's catalog.

PRINTING

COLLAGE RELIEF

Materials: brayer, ink, scrap wood, cardboard, burlap, lace, leaves, feathers, any textured material.
Methods: Choose different textures and shapes to make a design. Feathers make beautiful prints. Glue final design on a piece of wood. Roll a brayer in printing ink. Roll paint on design. Lay paper on design. Rub with ball of a spoon. Remove print. Re-ink as often as needed.

STYROFOAM PRINT

Materials: meat Styrofoam trays, water-base printer's ink, brayer, cookie tray, colored paper cut into rectangles, squares folded to make a card, a dull pencil or dried-up ball point pen.
Method: Cut Styrofoam (can be washed in the dishwasher) into desired shape. With dull pencil or dried ball point draw design on Styrofoam, pressing down hard enough to make a clearly indented line. Squeeze some ink on cookie sheet. Roll out with brayer to even the ink on the brayer. Using the inked brayer, roll ink onto the Styrofoam design. Press the inked design onto a piece of thin pastel construction paper. Lift up. You can glue this print onto a folded piece of construction paper or you can print directly on the card.

Experiment with colors of paper and ink. Make as many prints as you like, re-inking your design each time you print.

This is a good method for making bookmarks, notepaper, invitations, and prints to hang on the wall.

VEGETABLE PRINT

Materials: potato, craft knife, paper, sponge, poster paints.
Method: Slice potato in half. Carve a simple design—a holly leaf, a diamond, a circle, a pumpkin. Press potato shape onto sponge that's been soaked in paint (or if you can, dip into the paint in a pan). Print on paper. For greeting cards, you might use construction paper, note paper, rice paper, drawing paper. For wrapping paper decorated with the potato method, use brown paper, newspaper, or ask a printer for offcut scraps. After you've experimented with the potato in repeat patterns try printing with half an onion, an apple, a carrot or any odd object—a jar lid, a child's block, a straw, a meat tenderizer or other roller, your thumb.

ANIMAL ERASER PRINT

Materials: art gum eraser, paper, stamp pad, craft knife, pen.
Method: Trace around eraser on scrap paper and practice drawing some simple animal shapes inside the lines. Cut out final animal shape and trace around it with pen on the eraser. With a craft knife cut away from center of animal and remove all sections you do not want to print. Press eraser into stamp pad and print on paper. Repeat the print on the same card. Try different repeat patterns. A heart print could be repeated for Valentine's Day, a ladybug for a birthday or notepaper gift, a candle for Hanukkah, a bell for Christmas. Erasers print more clearly than potatoes.

PAPER CUTTING
SCHERENSCHNITTE, GERMAN PAPER CUTTING

Materials: white paper; black origami paper; small, sharp embroidery scissors; glue; pencil.

Method: Measure white paper with ruler, cut and fold for card. Cut black paper a little smaller than the front of the card. Draw an appropriate design, for instance, a wreath, candles in a candle-holder, a pot of flowers, or a pumpkin, on the white side of the black paper. Carefully cut out design (this take practice). When completely cut out, apply glue and center the design on the card and press down. This black and white silhouette makes a striking celebration card. Designs are usually more naturalistic than the Polish cuttings, but the technique could be adapted to a fanciful silhouette. Experiment.

WYCINANKA LUDOWA, POLISH PAPER CUTTING

Materials: gummed paper, scratch paper, small embroidery scissors, a pencil, mounting paper.

Methods and history: For several hundred years, Polish peasants have made papercuts of birds, leaves, flowers, abstractions of swirls and angles and used them as decorations on their white-washed houses in the springtime, for greeting cards and notepaper, for decorating Easter egg pitchers. The rooster and bird trees are favorite designs.

Practice drawing simple outlines of a flower. Cut out a card from white drawing paper. Cut a piece of gummed paper and fold in half lengthwise with gummed side out. It should be nearly the same size as the card. With a pencil draw a flower on the folded paper.

Carefully cut it out and open gently. Center on card and stick. This is your basic design. Choose another color and repeat this procedure using the same design, but smaller than the first one. Paste the second layer over the first.

Each additional layer is another color. You can also add a wing to a bird, a leaf to a flower in another color. Try origami paper for its brilliance. The technique could be adapted to hearts for Valentine's Day, or pumpkins for Halloween.

RUBBINGS
GRAVESTONE RUBBING

Materials: masking tape, large pad of newsprint or bond, black marking crayons, or thick children's crayons in dark colors.

Method: Make a small gravestone rubbing of an angel, bird, or other design for a Christmas card, or make a rubbing of the complete gravestone as a gift or souvenir of a trip. Make sure the stone is clean. Tape paper to the top of the stone and make sure it is stretched taut, smoothing with your hands as you tape the sides and the bottom. Using the broad edge of the crayon, rub lightly from the center out. Stroke in the same direction. Your strokes should gain momentum and get darker until you are happy with the result. Try mounting smaller rubbings on colored paper.

LEAF RUBBING

Materials: leaf, crayons, rice paper.
Method: Put leaf under a piece of rice paper that is to be the front of the card. Rub the paper with crayon until the outline of the leaf is clearly visible.

ALTERNATE GIFT WRAPPING IDEAS

Wrapping gifts is festive. It makes a gift a gift. Most of our traditional gift wrapping forms must be considered a frill and a waste in this age of approaching scarcity. How can we present our packages attractively without plundering the Earth's resources (and going broke doing it)? Here are some suggestions:

WRAPPING PAPER

1. Last year's paper
2. Newspaper—Colorful week-end comics, the Sports page, the Family Living page (collage of recipes, perhaps), a foreign language newspaper (especially Chinese or Russian).
3. Shiny illustrated magazines.
4. Grocery bags—plain or decorated.
5. Homemade wrappings (from grocery bags or butcher's paper) using block prints; finger paints; draw, color, magic marker, paint, marbleize; collage.
6. Fabric—a yard of new denim which a teenager can use for a project, scraps of leftover fabric, old sheets, batiked or tie-dyed.
7. Kitchen or bath towel to be useful for itself.
8. Decorate the box itself—paint, draw, paste wrapping paper right on box.
9. Add your own ideas.

BOWS AND DECORATIONS

1. Last year's ribbons and bows.
2. Cut strips of comic paper with pinking sheers and roll them into "bows."
3. Leftover yarn.
4. Pom-poms with scraps of yarn.
5. Pinecones, acorn (tops filled with pom-poms), milkweed pods, etc.
6. Fruit.
7. A small toy (truck, doll).
8. Add your own ideas.

DECORATIVE CONTAINERS (useful in themselves)

1. Put the gifts in a woven basket to be used for bread, planter, etc.
2. A decorative and useful flower pot.
3. Decorative department store box.
4. Fabric bag.
5. Canister or cookie jar.
6. Add your own ideas.

SOME GIFTS DON'T NEED WRAPPING

1. Canned food with a bow around it is festive and beautiful enough.
2. Dolls may greet children, unwrapped, under the tree with simply a note saying Hello, Merry Christmas!

Holiday Gifts from the Kitchen

Save your quart jars, fill them with homemade granola, type or print the recipe on an index card, and tie up with a ribbon for a helpful gift.

GRANOLA

1—1½ lbs. rolled oats
2 cups wheat germ
1 cup brown sugar
1 cup unsweetened coconut
1 cup nuts
½ cup sesame seeds
½ cup sunflower seeds
1 cup oil (corn, peanut, sunflower, soy)
1 tsp. sea salt

Mix with hands to get lumps out. Roast for one hour at 325°, stirring every ten minutes. Store in refrigerator in air-tight container. Add diced apricots, figs, raisins, according to individual preference.

HERB VINEGARS

Save jars and bottles, and put your choice of flavoring in them. Then fill with cider or wine vinegar, cap, and store in a cool, dark place for 4 weeks. Then the vinegars are flavored and ready to use. They don't spoil, either. Put in whole sprigs of herbs or spirals of citrus rind for the most attractive effect. Possible combinations are: garlic-chive white wine vinegar, thyme and rosemary vinegar, basil and oregano vinegar, orange and cinnamon (stick) vinegar, lemon and mint vinegar. You can also add several peppercorns, grapes, cloves, or dried currants to the combination for added flavor. Make the labels for the jars yourself.

Pami Bush   La Jolla, California

LIPTAUER CHEESE

Makes approximately 2 cups
8 ounces cottage cheese
8 tablespoons (1 quarter-pound stick) unsalted butter, softened
1 tablespoon sweet Hungarian paprika
Freshly ground black pepper
¼ teaspoon salt
2 teaspoons caraway seeds
1 teaspoon dry mustard
1 teaspoon chopped capers
1 tablespoon finely chopped onions
½ cup sour cream (plus ¼ cup if a dip is desired)
3 tablespoons finely chopped chives

With a wooden spoon rub the cottage cheese through a sieve into a mixing bowl. Cream the butter by beating it against the side of a mixing bowl with a wooden spoon. Beat in the cheese, the paprika, a generous grinding of black pepper, the salt, caraway seeds, mustard, capers, onions, and sour cream.

Continue beating vigorously with a wooden spoon or by using an electric mixer at medium speed until the mixture forms a smooth paste.

If the Liptauer cheese is to be used as a spread, shape it into a mound and decorate it with the chives, or shape it into a ball that may be rolled in the chives. Refrigerate it for 2 hours, or until it is firm.

To make a Liptauer dip, stir the extra sour cream into the paste with a wooden spoon or beat it in with an electric mixer. Sprinkle the chives over the dip after it has been poured into a serving bowl.

Here are two delicious salad dressings that will become the staples of your friend's recipe collection.

LEMON FRENCH DRESSING

1 clove garlic, split
1 cup salad oil
1 teaspoon salt
¾ teaspoon sugar
⅛ teaspoon freshly ground black pepper
⅓ cup fresh lemon juice

Combine the salad oil, garlic, salt, sugar, and pepper. Let stand at least one hour. Remove the garlic, add the lemon juice and beat with a rotary beater.

GARLIC FRENCH DRESSING

1 teaspoon dry mustard
1 tablespoon water
1 small clove garlic, finely minced
1 teaspoon sugar
1 teaspoon salt
1 cup salad or olive oil
1 teaspoon grated onion
3 tablespoons cider vinegar
2 tablespoons lemon juice

Mix mustard with water and let stand 10 minutes. Combine with garlic, salt, sugar, oil, and onion. Let stand one hour. Add vinegar and lemon juice. Beat with rotary beater.

Here are some delicious spreads which could be used for any holiday celebration when friends get together, or given as a gift. Accompany with whole wheat crackers or assorted raw vegetables.

HUMUS (CHICK-PEA SPREAD)

Makes 3 cups
2 cups cooked chick-peas (*garbanzos*) freshly cooked or canned
3 cloves garlic, finely chopped
1½ teaspoons salt
½ to ¾ cup vegetable oil
¼ cup fresh lemon juice
2 tablespoons coarsely chopped parsley, flat-leaf type preferable, or 2 tablespoons chopped mint

If the chick-peas are canned, drain them in a sieve and wash them under cold running water until the water runs clear. Spread them on paper towels and pat them dry. Freshly cooked chick-peas need only be drained and cooled.

To make the *humus* in a blender, place the chick-peas, garlic, salt, ½ cup of oil, and ¼ cup of lemon juice in the container and blend at high speed for 10 seconds. Turn off the blender and scrape down the sides with a rubber spatula. Blend again at high speed, adding as much oil as you need to prevent the blender from clogging. The finished *humus* should be a very smooth puree. Taste for seasoning and add more salt and lemon juice if you like.

BLUE CHEESE AND CHEDDAR SPREAD

¾ lb. aged cheddar cheese, coarsely grated
¾ cup beer or ale
⅛ lb. blue cheese, crumbled
1 tablespoon soft butter
½ teaspoon dry mustard
2 dashes Worcestershire sauce
1 dash Tabasco
1 teaspoon coarsely chopped chives or onions

Put the beer or ale and the cheddar cheese into a blender and blend for 20 seconds, or until smooth. (If you don't have a blender, beat together until smooth). Add the remaining ingredients and blend or beat until smooth and well mixed. Spoon into a crock or serving dish and chill. Garnish with chopped chives before serving. Makes about 2½ cups.

YOGURT DIP

6 walnut halves
1 tablespoon olive oil
1 clove garlic
1 cup yogurt
¼ cup very finely diced peeled cucumber
½ teaspoon lemon juice or vinegar
Whole grain crackers

Place walnuts, oil, and garlic in an electric blender and blend to a paste. This can also be done in a mortar and pestle.

Stir into the yogurt with cucumber and lemon juice or vinegar.
Chill and serve with crackers as dippers.
Yield: Four servings.

Still another present would be to find some inexpensive crocks or pottery jars and fill them with cheese spreads such as the blue cheese and cheddar spread.

This easy but especially rich bread is delicious at breakfast during the holiday season.

RAISIN-ALMOND BREAD

1 pkg. yeast
4 cups unbleached flour or wholewheat
½ cup water
½ cup milk
½ cup butter
¼ cup sugar or brown sugar or molasses
1 tsp. salt
½ cup ground almonds
½ cup chopped raisins or candied fruits (I add a bit of rum or whiskey)
2 eggs, slightly beaten
2 loaf pans

Mix 2 cups flour with the yeast. Stir water, milk, butter, sugar, and salt over low heat until butter melts. Cool five minutes, add flour and remaining ingredients. Knead until smooth and elastic. Divide dough and place in oiled loaf pans, cover, let rise in warm place until dough has doubled. Bake at 375 degrees, for 35 minutes.

GROWING YOUR OWN SPROUTS

SPROUTS

Grow your own fresh sprouts and give an ancient gift. Sprout-growing dates back to 2939 B.C. in China. A prime source of nutrients, "sprouts" are seeds or legumes that have germinated and converted their fats and starches into vitamins, sugars, and protein. Sprouted lentils, alfalfa, and soybeans are high in protein, inexpensive, and easy to grow. They can be eaten as a snack, used in a main dish as a natural "stretcher," or served in salads and sandwiches. They are naturally processed in your kitchen and make a cheery winter garden in a jar.

After experimenting with different seeds and flavors, give a sprout jar and some favorite beans or seeds for a winter birthday gift, or a spring Mother's or Father's Day present. A sprout kit might be especially appropriate for someone who cannot grow a garden, an apartment dweller, or a house-bound person in the wintertime.

EQUIPMENT
   wide mouth mason jar
   piece of screening, aluminum or
      copper
   metal ring to hold the screen
   ¼ cup of mung beans

BASIC METHOD
Wash beans. Put beans in the jar and water to cover. Place screen and metal rim on jar. Leave overnight in a dark place. The second day rinse the beans with fresh cool water. Drain well. Seeds should be damp, not soaked. Lay jar on its side in a spot with indirect sunlight, or make a stand out of blocks and invert jar on blocks to drain well. Repeat the rinsing 2 or 3 times each day. Sprouts will appear on the second day and are ready to use by the third or fourth day. A small amount of mung beans, lentils, soybeans, or alfalfa gives a high yield of sprouts.

If you're still not convinced about the gift-food from the earth try the Golden Temple Sandwich: layer avocado and tomato slices, tuna fish (optional), sprouts, and grated cheese on a piece of whole-grain bread. Place in oven on a cookie sheet until the cheese melts.

NUT BREAD

Bake in greased coffee can; cover with plastic top and decorate or label. If necessary, use a can opener to remove the can bottom before serving.

Combine:
1½ cup whole wheat flour
⅓ cup powdered milk
2 tsp. baking powder and 1 tsp. salt
Add 1 cup milk or water
1 cup nuts
2 tbsp. oil
⅓ cup honey
½ cup wheat germ
Stir briefly. Fill can or 1 loaf pan. Push dough into corners and make indentation in top of loaf. Bake at 350° for 45 minutes.

APPLESAUCE NUT BREAD

Stir together to moisten:
2 cups flour
¾ cup sugar
1 tsp. baking powder
1 tsp. salt
½ tsp. soda
½ tsp. nutmeg
1 cup nuts
1 beaten egg
1 cup applesauce
Bake 1 hour at 300°F.

8.

Drawings by Steven Johnson

Architect remodels old house, installing roof-mounted solar collectors, windmill, and greenhouse.

Reprinted by permission from The Futurist, August 1977.

Voluntary Simplicity:
Lifestyle of the Future?

*Duane S. Elgin and
Arnold Mitchell*

In the years ahead, millions of Americans may move beyond materialistic values and choose an outwardly more simple and inwardly more rich lifestyle. This phenomenon could foreshadow a major transformation in Western values, with wide implications for future developments in business, technology, and society at large.

Newspapers and magazines publish occasional articles about people abandoning the "rat race" pursuits of Western society and seeking a simpler lifestyle, less frenetic in its demands and less tied to today's high-consumption, money-oriented civilization.

We believe that these press reports reflect a major social movement which has the potential of touching the United States and other developed nations to their cores. This movement is toward what Richard Gregg, many years ago, described as "voluntary simplicity"—a way of life marked by a new balance between inner and outer growth. We also believe that voluntary simplicity may prove an increasingly powerful economic, social and political force over the coming decade and beyond. It could represent a major transformation of Western values and signal shifts not only in values, but in consumption patterns, institutional operations, and national policies.

Although there are many precursors and contributing streams to this social flow (environmentalism, consumerism, consciousness movement, etc.), there is little direct evidence to

Beyond Celebrations

measure the magnitude of this way of life. This discussion, then, is *not* intended to be predictive or definitive; rather, as social conjecture and pattern recognition, it is inherently speculative and intended to provoke further thought and comment regarding voluntary simplicity.

WHAT IS VOLUNTARY SIMPLICITY?

The essence of voluntary simplicity is living in a way that is outwardly simple and inwardly rich. This way of life embraces frugality of consumption, a strong sense of environmental urgency, a desire to return to living and working environments which are of a more human scale, and an intention to realize our higher human potential—both psychological and spiritual—in community with others. The driving forces behind voluntary simplicity range from acutely personal concerns to critical national problems. The appeal of simple living appears to be extraordinarily widespread, even gathering sympathy among those who are not presently attempting to simplify their own life patterns. Voluntary simplicity is important because it may foreshadow a major transformation in the goals and values of the United States in the coming decades. Although a social movement still in its early stages, its practical and ethical positions seem well enough developed to permit useful analysis of this way of life.

Voluntary simplicity is not new, but the conditions and trends which appear to be driving its contemporary emergence do seem new in their magnitude and intensity. Historically, voluntary simplicity has its roots in the legendary frugality and self-reliance of the Puritans; in Thoreau's naturalistic vision at Walden Pond; in

Emerson's spiritual and practical plea for "plain living and high thinking"; in the teachings and social philosophy of a number of spiritual leaders such as Jesus and Gandhi.

A uniquely modern aspect of voluntary simplicity is that it seems to be driven by a sense of urgency and social responsibility that scarcely existed 10 or 15 years ago. This sense of urgency appears to derive from many serious societal problems, including: the prospects of a chronic energy shortage; growing terrorist activities at the same time that developed nations seem increasingly vulnerable to disruption; growing demands of the less developed nations for a more equitable share of the world's resources; the prospect that before we run out of resources on any absolute basis we may poison ourselves to death with environmental contaminants; a growing social malaise and purposelessness which causes us to drift in our social evolution; and so on. These are but a few of the elements which converge to make voluntary simplicity a seemingly rational response to the current world situation.

VALUES CENTRAL TO VOLUNTARY SIMPLICITY

The social movement toward voluntary simplicity is very rich and highly diverse. Yet there seems to be an underlying coherence to the rich diversity of expression of this way of life. Among the values which seem to lie at the heart of this emerging way of life are: (1) Material Simplicity, (2) Human Scale, (3) Self-Determination, (4) Ecological Awareness, and (5) Personal Growth. Let us examine each of these in turn:

Material Simplicity. Simplification of the material aspects of life is one of the core values of voluntary simplicity. The American Friends Service

Committee, long a leader in exploring a way of life of creative simplicity, defines simple living as a "nonconsumerist lifestyle based upon being and becoming, not having."

Living simply implies consuming quantitatively less (particularly items that are energy-inefficient, non-biodegradable, nonessential luxuries, etc.), but it does not mean that the overall cost of consumption will go down drastically. Living *simply* need not be equated with living *cheaply.* The hand-crafted, durable, aesthetically enduring products that appeal to frugal consumers are oftentimes purchased at a considerable premium over mass-produced items. Therefore, although the quantity of consumption may decrease and the environmental costs of consumption may be considerably moderated, the overall cost of consumption may remain relatively high since our economy is not oriented to producing the kinds of products which fit these criteria. Material simplicity will thus likely be manifest in consumption styles that are less *ascetic* than *aesthetic,* that is, the emphasis will not be on a strictly enforced austerity (doing without material goods) but rather on creating a pattern of consumption that will fit, with grace and integrity, into the practical art of daily living.

Human Scale. A preference for human-sized living and working environments is a central feature of voluntary simplicity. Adherents of this values constellation tend to equate the gigantic scale of institutions and living environments with anonymity, incomprehensibility, and artificiality. The preference for smallness implies that living and working environments (which have grown to enormous levels of scale and complexity) should be decentralized into more comprehensible and manageable entities. Each person should be able to see what he or she contributes to the whole and, hence, have a sense of shared rewards and shared responsibility. Reduction of scale is seen as a means of getting back to basics by restoring to life a more human sense of proportion and perspective.

Self-Determination. Voluntary simplicity embraces an intention to be more self-determining and less dependent upon large, complex institutions. Self-determination manifests itself as a desire to assume greater control over one's personal destiny and not lead a life tied to installment payments, maintenance costs, and the expectations of others. To counterbalance the trend towards increasing material dependency people may seek to become more materially self-sufficient—to grow their own, to make their own, to do

HOW TO MAKE A CANDLE FLASHLIGHT / FROM *LIVING FOR SELF-SUFFICIENCY*

"For this you need an old can, about one-pound size or bigger, with the top and bottom removed. Then cut a cross with a sharp knife in the middle of the side, and push your candle up through the center of the cross until the wick lies almost exactly in the center of the can. Make two small holes in the top and fit a wire handle ... [It] gives something like a lantern beam, and only the strongest of winds out-doors will ever blow it out. One of them can save you a lot of flashlight batteries when you go out to put the hens to bed."

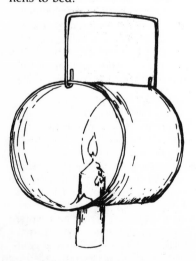

without, and to exercise self-discipline in their pattern and level of consumption so that the degree of dependency (both physical and psychological) is reduced.

Self-determination shows up in production as a counterbalancing force to: combat excessive division of labor. Instead of embracing specialization, a voluntary simplicity (VS) adherent may seek greater work integration and synthesis so that the contribution of his work to the whole enterprise is more evident.

In the public sector, the drive for greater self-determination is revealed by a growing distrust of and sense of alienation from large and complex social bureaucracies. The VS adherent seems to want to take charge of his or her life more fully and to manage his or her own affairs without the undue or unnecessary intrusion of a remote bureaucracy.

This dimension of voluntary simplicity may explain some of the unusual political coalitions that seem to be emerging between the right and left, coalitions that oppose the further intrusion of big institutions into people's lives, and seek greater local self-determination and grass-roots political action. The aversion to being controlled by increasingly distant bureaucracies is reminiscent of the stubborn independence out of which was born the American revolution.

Ecological Awareness. A sense of ecological awareness which acknowledges the interconnectedness of people and resources is central to voluntary simplicity. From this awareness emerge a number of themes that are hallmarks of this way of life. For example, ecological awareness prompts recognition that our earth is indeed limited, with all that implies for conservation of physical resources, reduction of environmental pollution, and maintenance of the beauty and integrity of the natural environment. Importantly, this concern often extends beyond purely physical resources to include other human beings as well. The philosophy of "welfare" espoused by Gandhi—*sarvodaya,* or not wanting what the least of the inhabitants of this earth cannot have—seems to spring, in large measure, from this intimate sense of felt connection with those who are less fortunate than we. The growth of an ecological awareness expands the vision of voluntary simplicity outward and brings with it a strong sense of social responsibility and worldly involvement to what

otherwise could be a relatively isolated and self-centered way of life.

Some of the more concrete expressions of this awareness might include: a willingness to share resources with those who are disadvantaged; a sense of global citizenship with commensurate adjustments in lifestyle, social vision, and political commitments; a preference for living where there is ready access to nature; and a desire to foster human and institutional diversity at a grass-roots level.

Personal Growth. For many persons taking up a materially simple way of life, the primary goal is to clear away external clutter so as to be freer to explore the "inner life." The themes of material simplicity, self-sufficiency, a more human scale to living and working, and an ecological awareness are, in a way, devices to sweep away impediments to inner growth. The goal, then, is to free oneself of the overwhelming externals so as to provide the space in which to grow—both psychologically and spiritually.

Simone de Beauvoir succinctly stated the rationale for this desire for self-realization when she said: "Life is occupied in both perpetuating itself and in surpassing itself; if all it does is maintain itself, then living is only not dying." In the view of many adherents to voluntary simplicity, contemporary American society is primarily occupied in perpetuating itself and living has become "only not dying." They seek an outlet for their growth potential.

A concern for the subjective aspect

The author comments: "Voluntary simplicity seems to constitute a broadly-based attempt to moderate, in the short run, and transcend, in the long run, the industrial world view. VS implies going beyond material growth to include evolution among more subtle dimensions of life.

"A second pattern revealed by this table is that the values cluster embraced by voluntary simplicity represents at least as coherent a world view as the industrial world view (which has powered our social vision and industrial development for nearly two centuries).

"Lastly, voluntary simplicity does not appear to be a movement whose domain of social impact can be narrowly defined; rather, it reaches out and touches a great many aspects of life."

of experience and for the quality of human relationships has been reflected in a number of developments over the past 15 years—the emergence and proliferation of the "human potential movement"; the emergence of "transpersonal psychology" coupled with a rapid increase of interest and involvement in many Eastern meditative traditions; the growth of feminism; a cultural fascination with psychic phenomena; developments in brain research that confirm a biological basis for both the rational and the intuitive side to human nature; a growing interest in sports as both a physical and spiritual process (e.g., the "inner game" of tennis); and more.

Without the compelling goal of exploring inner potentials, it seems unlikely that there will be sufficient motivation to adopt voluntarily a lifestyle of material simplicity. Without greater simplicity, we probably will not be able to cope successfully with scarcity and other problems. Finally, unless inner learning expands, it seems unlikely that we will develop the degree of internal maturation necessary for the human species to act as wise trustees of conscious evolution on this earth.

Our analysis still has not penetrated to the roots of the connection between personal growth and voluntary simplicity. For an adequate explanation of that connection, we must look to a deeper underlying vision. It is an old vision—perhaps as old as civilized humans—but an enduring one that seems destined to be rediscovered again and again. The nature of this vision is succinctly summed up by historian Arnold Toynbee:

CRITERIA FOR SIMPLICITY

The authors report that a group of Quakers have identified four consumption criteria which evoke the essence of voluntary simplicity:

- Does what I own or buy promote activity, self-reliance, and involvement, or does it induce passivity and dependence?
- Are my consumption patterns basically satisfying, or do I buy much that serves no real need?
- How tied is my present job and lifestyle to installment payments, maintenance and repair costs, and the expectations of others?
- Do I consider the impact of my consumption patterns on other people and on the earth?

CONTRASTS BETWEEN THE INDUSTRIAL WORLD VIEW AND THE WORLD VIEW OF VOLUNTARY SIMPLICITY

Emphasis in Industrial World View

Value Premises

Material growth
People over nature
Competitive self-interest
Rugged individualism
Rationalism

Social Characteristics

Large, complex living and working environments
Growth of material complexity
Space-age technology
Identity defined by patterns of consumption
Centralization of regulation and control at nation/state level
Specialized work roles through division of labor
Secular
Mass-produced, quickly obsolete, standardized products
Lifeboat ethic in foreign relations
Cultural homogeneity, partial acceptance of diversity
High pressure, rat-race existence

Emphasis in Voluntary Simplicity World View

Value Premises

Material sufficiency coupled with psycho-spiritual growth
People within nature
Enlightened self-interest
Cooperative individualism
Rational and intuitive

Social Characteristics

Smaller, less complex living and working environments
Reduction of material complexity ("Ephemeralization")
Appropriate technology
Identity found through inner and interpersonal discovery
Greater local self-determination coupled with emerging global institutions
More integrated work roles (e.g., team assembly, multiple roles)
Balance of secular and spiritual
Hand-crafted, durable, unique products
Spaceship earth ethic
Cultural heterogeneity, eager acceptance of diversity
Laid-back, relaxed existence

These religious founders (Jesus, Buddha, Lao Tse, St. Francis of Assisi) disagreed with each other in their pictures of what is the nature of the universe, the nature of spiritual life, the nature of ultimate spiritual reality. But they all agreed in their ethical precepts. They all agreed that the pursuit of material wealth is a wrong aim. We should aim only at the minimum wealth needed to maintain life; and our main aim should be spiritual. They all said with one voice that if we made material wealth our paramount aim, this would lead to disaster. They all spoke in favor of unselfishness and of love for other people as the key to happiness and to success in human affairs.

The foregoing five themes do not exhaust the range of basic values that may emerge as hallmarks of the way of life termed voluntary simplicity. Moreover, these values will surely be held to differing degrees and in differing combinations by different people. Nonetheless, these values possess an underlying coherence which suggests that they have not arisen randomly but rather as a mu-

tually supporting set or pattern. Just a few moments of reflection reveal how powerfully reinforcing these values are; for example, personal growth may foster an ecological awareness which may prompt greater material simplicity and thereby allow greater opportunity for living and working at a smaller, more human scale which, in turn, may allow greater opportunity for local self-determination. No one value theme alone could create the vitality and coherence that emerges from the synergistic interaction of these values. These values combine to form a practical "world view"—a coherent pattern of perception, belief, and behavior which could provide an important bridge between the traditional industrial world view and an uncertain and difficult social future.

Communalized Townhouses

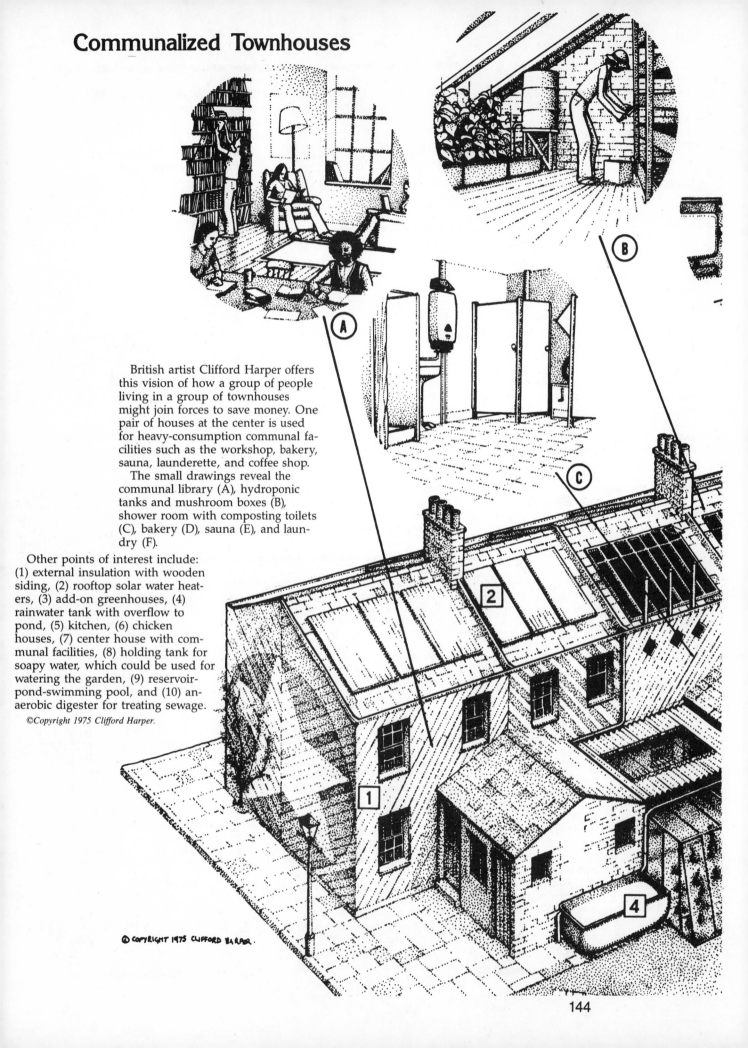

British artist Clifford Harper offers this vision of how a group of people living in a group of townhouses might join forces to save money. One pair of houses at the center is used for heavy-consumption communal facilities such as the workshop, bakery, sauna, launderette, and coffee shop.

The small drawings reveal the communal library (A), hydroponic tanks and mushroom boxes (B), shower room with composting toilets (C), bakery (D), sauna (E), and laundry (F).

Other points of interest include: (1) external insulation with wooden siding, (2) rooftop solar water heaters, (3) add-on greenhouses, (4) rainwater tank with overflow to pond, (5) kitchen, (6) chicken houses, (7) center house with communal facilities, (8) holding tank for soapy water, which could be used for watering the garden, (9) reservoir-pond-swimming pool, and (10) anaerobic digester for treating sewage.

Grandmother teaches grandaughter the art of canning cherries.

WHAT VOLUNTARY SIMPLICITY IS NOT

We have been trying to define what voluntary simplicity is. We can also get a sense of voluntary simplicity by suggesting what it is not.

- *Voluntary simplicity should not be equated with a back-to-nature movement.* Although an historic shift in net population migration towards small towns and rural places is underway, the large majority of people continue to reside in urban environments. Voluntary simplicity seems perhaps as compelling for this urban majority as it does for the rural minority. An urban existence need not be incompatible with voluntary simplicity; indeed, many of the experiments with appropriate technology, intensive gardening, and such have been conducted in urban contexts.
- *Voluntary simplicity should not be equated with living in poverty.* Indeed, impoverishment is in many ways the opposite of simple living in that poverty tends to make life a struggle to maintain oneself and provides little opportunity to surpass oneself.
- *Voluntary simplicity is not confined to the United States.* Virtually all of the developed Western nations seem to be moving in a somewhat similar direction. Many European nations, with more limited land and resources, have been learning how to cope with scarcity for far longer than the United States has. And there is evidence that other nations may be opting for voluntary simplicity rather than endure the stress of striving for affluence. For example, a recent poll in Norway found that "74 percent of the total sample claimed they would prefer a simple life with no more than essentials (these were, however, not defined) to a high income and many material benefits if these have to be obtained through increased stress."
- *Voluntary simplicity is not a fad.* Its roots reach far too deeply into the needs and ideals of people everywhere to be regarded as a transitory response to a passing societal condition.

THE PUSH TOWARD VOLUNTARY SIMPLICITY

Despite the strength of the pull to voluntary simplicity, there is little reason to think that this way of life will grow to embrace substantial proportions of the population unless the *pull* is matched by substantial *pushes.* The twin elements of push and pull need to be considered if we are to assess the likelihood that voluntary simplicity will gather social

momentum in the future. Let us therefore consider whether societal problems will push us in a direction similar to that exerted by the pull toward voluntary simplicity.

The range and diversity of contemporary societal problems is enormous. Space does not allow more than a cursory glance at some of the more prominent problems which may, in their eventual resolution, push us towards a simple way of life. These problems include:

- The prospect of running out of cheaply available, critical industrial raw materials.
- The prospect of chronic energy shortages and a difficult transition to a much more energy-efficient economy.
- The growing threat that we will pollute ourselves to death with the intrusion of many thousands of hazardous substances into our living environments and food chains.
- Rising material demands of the third and fourth world, coupled with climatic changes which may induce periodic but massive famine in certain areas. The growing threat of terrorism (nuclear and biological as well as conventional), coupled with the growing vulnerability of the highly complex and interdependent technology (e.g., communications, energy, and transportation systems) common to the developed nations.
- The changing balance of global power, as nuclear weapons proliferate.
- The poverty of abundance: a growing dissatisfaction with the output of our industrial society as the sole or even primary reward and reason for our individual existences.
- Apparent loss of social purpose and direction coupled with rising levels of individual alienation.
- Chronic and pervasive fiscal crisis of many of our largest cities, coupled with an historic and unexpected turnaround in migration patterns (the net flow is now to small towns and rural areas).
- Decline in the expected number of meaningful work roles, coupled with growing levels of automation, coupled with chronic underemployment and unemployment.
- The prospect that we have created social bureaucracies (at the federal, state, and local levels) of such extreme levels of

scale, complexity, and interdependence that they now exceed our capacity to comprehend and, therefore, to manage them; coupled with growing protests that we are becoming an excessively overregulated society, coupled with growing demands upon government at all levels.

- Growing demands that domestic economic inequities be moderated, coupled with the prospect of a little or no-growth economy in the foreseeable future, yielding the specter of intense competition for a fixed or slowly growing pie.

Resolution of the foregoing problems will likely push our society in a direction which is more ecologically conscious, more frugal in its consumption, more globally oriented, more decentralized, more allowing of local self-determination, and so on. Solving these increasingly serious problems will probably push us in a direction at least similar to that implied by the pull toward voluntary simplicity.

TYPES OF VOLUNTARY SIMPLICITY

We think there are at least two very distinct kinds of people fully living the VS way of life. The first consists of families and individuals who have voluntarily taken up simple living after years or decades of active involvement in the mainstream. The motivations of such people tend to be

Retiree learns bee-keeping to supplement retirement income and provide his family with fresh honey as an alternative to sugar.

highly private and specific—a desire to escape the "rat race," personal disillusionment, boredom with their jobs, a wish to live a more "meaningful," less artificial life, and so on. Such changes in lifestyle make good copy and hence this type of phenomenon gets much publicity. In terms of numbers, this group does not appear very significant, but, as a model for others to emulate, it may be profoundly important.

The other type tends to be younger, more motivated by philosophical concerns, and more activistic. Since no survey has yet been made explicitly for the purpose of defining the demographics of adherents to VS, we are forced to surmise their characteristics based on the attributes of related groups (such as environmentalists, consumerists, members of "human potential" movements, those operating Briarpatch businesses, etc.) on which some data are available. Based on this kind of inferential evidence, the second group of adherents to voluntary simplicity appear to be:

- Predominantly young, the large majority being in their 20s or 30s.
- Evenly divided among the sexes.
- Preponderantly single, although many young families are included.
- Almost exclusively white.
- From middle- or upper-class backgrounds.
- Exceptionally well educated.
- Bimodal in income, over a fourth (mostly students) having annual incomes under $5,000 and another fourth having incomes over $15,000.
- Independent politically— uncomfortable with the standard labels.
- Largely urban residents, although many would like to live in small town or rural environments.

NUMBERS AND DEGREES OF VS

We have found it useful to think in terms of four distinct categories of voluntary simplicity.

1. *Full Voluntary Simplicity.* Our best guess is that only four to five million adults (3 percent of the adult population) fully and wholeheartedly live a life of voluntary simplicity. These people constitute the active, leading edge of the trend toward simple living and are found in all parts of the country.

If we had to draw a caricature of the life-activities characteristic of this group it would include: organic gardening, recycling, natural foods,

Housewife tries out her mail-order spinning wheel in the living room of her urban area apartment.

simple clothing, biking to work, backpacking on vacations, engaging in meditation or other growth processes.

2. *Partial Voluntary Simplicity.* A second group may be described as partial adherents to voluntary simplicity. This group is probably about twice as large as the first and includes some eight to ten million adults. These persons adhere to and act on some, but not all, of the basic tenets of voluntary simplicity. These persons are scattered throughout the adult population—probably a greater proportion of them are middle age and middle class, but they are still predominantly white and predominantly urban.

3. *Sympathizers.* Polls cited later

The Best Way to Travel

"The best way of getting from one place to another is not to go. We've now got so used to easy travel that journeys have lost their significance. Whether we like it or not, they're going to get it back. It's a safe bet that never again will we be able to move so freely about the Earth's surface as we were in the 1960s. And, in some ways, a good thing too. Most of the places people really liked to go to have been ruined beyond repair simply because they went there so often."

From Building for Self-Sufficiency

suggest that a large fraction of the total adult population—almost surely exceeding one-third and perhaps as large as one-half—sympathizes with many values associated with voluntary simplicity, but, for one reason or another, this group does not presently act on this sympathy. We call these people sympathizers toward voluntary simplicity. The sympathizers will play a pivotal role because their numbers are so large that a small amount of swing represents a major shift in American values.

4. *Indifferent, Unaware, or Opposed.* Finally, we estimate that at least half of the population falls into the category of being indifferent to, unaware of, or opposed to voluntary simplicity. This group draws its numbers from both ends of the income spectrum. There are those who are involuntarily simple—that is, who live in poverty and have not yet experienced the life of abundance. These people may oppose voluntary simplicity because they are unwilling to forego the opportunity to strike it rich. At the other income extreme, there are those who are strongly achievement-oriented and see simple living as a threat to their style of life.

The dimensions of voluntary simplicity are most clearly indicated in a variety of opinion studies. A few of these are summarized below:

1. In a poll published in May 1976, the Roper organization found that 51 percent of Americans believe the nation "must cut way back" on production and consumption to conserve resources and keep the economy strong. Only 45 percent felt that traditional lifestyles can continue unchanged.
2. Pollster Louis Harris reported in May 1977 that the American people have begun to show "a deep skepticism about the nation's capacity for unlimited economic growth and are wary of the

benefits that growth is supposed to bring."
Other findings:
- 79 percent of Americans would place greater emphasis on "teaching people how to live more with basic essentials" than on "reaching higher standards of living."
- 76 percent prefer "learning to get our pleasure out of nonmaterial experiences" rather than on "satisfying our needs for more goods and services."
- 59 percent would stress "putting real effort into avoiding doing those things that cause pollution" over "finding ways to clean up the environment as the economy expands."
- 82 percent would concentrate on "improving those modes of travel we already have" to "developing ways to get more places faster."
- 63 percent feel that the country should emphasize "learning to appreciate human values" rather than on "finding ways to create more jobs for producing more goods."

Harris said that the poll suggests that "a quiet revolution may be taking place in our national values and aspirations."

3. Earlier, in late 1975, Harris reported the following results from his polls. To reduce consumption of physical goods and products:
- 92 percent of Americans are willing to eliminate annual model changes in automobiles.
- 91 percent are willing to forego meat for one day a week.
- 90 percent are willing to do away with annual fashion changes in clothing.
- 82 percent are willing to reduce the amount of advertising.
- 73 percent are willing to wear old clothes (even if they shine) until they wear out.

- 73 percent are willing to prohibit the building of large houses with extra rooms that are seldom used.
- 57 percent are willing to see a national policy that would make it much cheaper to live in multiple-unit apartments than in single family homes.

Harris concludes: "When the alternative is posed between changing our lifestyle to have less consumption of physical goods, on one hand, and enduring the risks of continuing inflation and unemployment on the other, by 77 percent to 8 percent, the American people opt for a change in lifestyle."

Concern with the inner life also has a very broad base of support. For example, the firm of Yankelovich, Skelly, and White finds that some 80 percent of the population is interested in developing better self-understanding through the inner search for meaning. A 1975 poll conducted by the National Opinion Research Corporation found that over 40 percent of American adults have undergone what they regard as a genuinely "mystical" experience. In 1974 Roper found that 53 percent of Americans believe in the existence of ESP—a belief, incidentally, that correlates strongly with education and income. A 1976 Gallup poll found that 12 percent of the American people are "involved in" or "practice" some mystical discipline.

The foregoing data seem to indicate (1) a receptivity on the part of Americans to a change in lifestyle, (2) sympathy for values and attitudes congruent with voluntary simplicity, and (3) a wide base of interest in the inner dimension of life.

PROSPECTS FOR GROWTH

We estimate that the maximum plausible growth of VS as a way of life would yield the following figures:

Reasons for Choosing a Simple Lifestyle

The Center for Science in the Public Interest in Washington, D.C., has suggested the following reasons for living simply:

- Naturalistic—helps us appreciate the serenity of nature, its silence, the changes of season, and its creatures.
- Symbolic—promotes solidarity with the world's poor, and reduces the hypocrisy of our current overconsumptive lifestyle.

- Person-oriented—affords greater opportunities to work together and share resources with one's neighbors.
- Ecological—reduces our use of resources, lessens pollution, and creates an awareness that we must live in harmony with our world.
- Health—lessens tension and anxiety, encourages more rest and relaxation, reduces use of harmful chemicals, creates inner harmony.

- Economic—saves money, reduces the need to work long hours, and increases both number and quality of jobs.
- Spiritual—allows time for meditation and prayer, and rejects materialistic values.
- Social—induces frustration with the limited scope of individual action and incites us to move to social and political action levels.

From *99 Ways to a Simple Lifestyle* by the Center for Science in the Public Interest, Washington, D.C.

Maximum Growth of Voluntary Simplicity (VS) (Millions of Adults)			
	1977	1987	2000
Full VS	5	25	60
Partial VS	10	35	60
Sympathizers	60	50	25
Indifferent or Opposed	75	60	55

These figures suggest that possibly 10 million adults follow VS tenets today (if we assume five million "full VS" plus 50 percent of "partial VS"). Their combined numbers could exceed 40 million by 1987 and 90 million by the year 2000. This would be an extraordinary rate of growth for a basic sociological phenomenon. Even so, less than a third of the adult population would be fully living this way of life 23 years from now.

To attain the degree of growth shown in the table, we think several conditions would have to be present.

- *The push pressures described earlier would have to continue to mount rather than decline.* Efforts to overcome them would have to fail, for whatever reasons. At the same time, however, the nation would have to avoid a truly severe economic depression or else *in*voluntary simplicity (i.e., poverty) would largely replace voluntary simplicity.

- *VS would have to prove a rewarding and nourishing way of life to many millions of people who have little experience with the day-to-day realities of living simply.* Attempts to live simply are sometimes abandoned because it doesn't yield the expected inner rewards, because it is too demanding or too lonely, or because changed family circumstances (e.g., having children) require a return to a less extreme lifestyle. Some observers feel that VS makes such large demands on both inner and external resources of people and is at such profound odds with traditional American achievement and material values that only a relative few will be able to live the simple life happily. Hence, they argue, VS will not prove a viable national solution to the problem it addresses. Other observers have no such doubts.

Father and son asemble solar heater from a kit. The father is attempting to establish a business operated from his own home so as to minimize daily commuting and have more time with his family.

- *Perhaps most important, a mass production, high-productivity sector of the economy will have to coexist with the VS sector in order to maintain standards of living; otherwise, the aggregate decline in living standards could be so great as to invite social and economic revolution.* There appear to be no mechanical reasons why frugality and simplicity cannot coexist with high technology and the profit motive. However, it is not clear whether or not antagonisms between the two life ways would permit the minimal—but essential—levels of cooperation.

Even if voluntary simplicity does expand in the coming eighteen years to the degree indicated, it is not likely to emerge in the smooth fashion suggested by the numbers in the table. Rather, it will develop (to whatever extent) with jumps and drops and plateaus, reflecting a variety of specific events, perceptual insights, charismatic leaders, and many types of regulatory and legislative policies. It is also possible that voluntary sim-plicity will progress unobtrusively in the form of countless millions of small, unannounced decisions made so inconspicuously that almost no one is aware of the total effect until, suddenly, it is clear that a major values transformation has occurred.

FUNDAMENTAL CHANGE IN VALUES

The long-run social ramifications of voluntary simplicity—if it develops into a major social movement—are enormous. The eventual result could be the creation of a social order that is as different from the present as the industrial era was different from the Middle Ages.

The reason that the potential social implications are so vast is that voluntary simplicity does not represent merely an internal readjustment of the prevailing values pattern but rather constitutes a fundamental shift in that pattern. Widespread adoption of this way of life could launch our society on a new developmental trajectory.

We are by no means suggesting that voluntary simplicity offers the

AQUARIAN AGE
BLACKSMITH
SHOP

Young member of an enthusiastic communal enterprise offers services derived from an earlier rural economy.

only approach to a viable cultural and economic future. However, the United States and many other developed nations seem to be in a period of social drift. They appear to be losing both momentum and a sense of direction. People seem to be waiting for some leader or chain of events to make clear the nature of an alternative social vision. The uncertainty, indecision, and growing anxiety over appropriate social direction has prompted a new willingness to "think the unthinkable," to deeply consider what life means and where we wish to go. Voluntary simplicity

as a coherent, broadly relevant, practical and purposeful world view could provide an important point of reference or anchoring point as the U.S. begins searching for and experimenting with new social forms.

ALTERNATIVE FUTURES

Although VS as a way of life may have great and obvious long-run significance, it seems at present to be struggling to achieve a critical mass of social awareness and acceptance. We have said that it could grow to major proportions by the year 2000. On the other hand, under some circumstances the movement could fade away. If we are to understand the prospects of voluntary simplicity, we must attempt to understand the nature and dynamics of the larger social context out of which this way of life could emerge.

There is great uncertainty regarding the future course of social evolution in the United States, but we have identified four alternative

The Story of the Shakertown Pledge

It happened at the site of a restored Shaker village about 40 miles south of Lexington, Kentucky. A group of religious retreat center directors and their staffs had gathered for a few days of comparing programs and renewing old friendships. But at this particular meeting, which began on April 30, 1973, something different occurred.

"The talk turned to the alarming statistics about world need and our possible response as Americans and Christians," recalls one participant, Adam Daniel Finnerty.

"When we were only a few minutes into the discussion, I suddenly realized that the atmosphere had changed from the lightheartedness with which we had begun. Some people seemed bored, some angry; some had become intensely serious, and still others seemed quietly agonized.

"I had seen similar reactions before, particularly on those occasions when the focus of the discussion had been on how each of us was conducting our own life in the light of the very real needs of the world."

Finnerty says the participants felt

guilty about being members of a privileged minority in a nation that was guilty of overconsuming the world's resources and recognized that "our own lifestyles were part of the problem." But the group members were unsure whether changing their lifestyles would help improve the global problem.

"If I eat less, how do I know that someone else will necessarily be able to eat more? If we spend less, won't that harm our economy, and perhaps bring its collapse? How could that aid anybody?"

Sam Emerick, the conference chairman, told the group that he had been agonizing over the problem for a long time and wanted to do something. A number of other members of the group felt likewise and they agreed to meet again. After a follow-up meeting and a period of correspondence and of drafts and redrafts, the group agreed on a common pledge. "We called it the Shakertown Pledge," Finnerty reports, "in honor of our original gathering place and because the Shaker community had believed wholeheartedly in lives of 'creative simplicity.'"

THE SHAKERTOWN PLEDGE

Recognizing that the earth and the fullness thereof is a gift from our gracious God, and that we are called to cherish, nurture, and provide loving stewardship for the earth's resources,
and recognizing that life itself is a gift, and a call to responsibility, joy, and celebration,
I make the following declarations:
1. I declare myself to be a world citizen.
2. I commit myself to lead an ecologically sound life.
3. I commit myself to lead a life of creative simplicity and to share my personal wealth with the world's poor.
4. I commit myself to join with others in the reshaping of institutions in order to bring about a more just global society in which all people have full access to the needed resources for their physical, emotional, intellectual, and spiritual growth.
5. I commit myself to occupational accountability, and so doing I will seek to avoid the creation of products which cause harm to others.
6. I affirm the gift of my body and commit myself to its proper nourishment and physical well-being.
7. I commit myself to examine con-

futures which suggest the range of social possibility over the next several decades. These are:

1. Technological Salvation: This is a future where, with good luck and great ingenuity, we find the social will and technological know-how to cope with critical national problems and continue along a trajectory of relatively high material growth. This future assumes that the value premises of the industrial era (rugged individualism, rationalism, material growth, etc.) will withstand current challenges and provide people with meaningful and workable living environments.

2. Descent into Social Chaos: This is a future in which society is torn by divisions and tensions among competing interest groups. There is no cataclysmic demise—just the grinding, unrelenting deterioration of the social fabric as crisis is compounded by crisis amidst diminishing public consensus as to how to cope with it all. Inept bureaucratic regulation and

unforeseen events (such as severe climate changes) could change the drift toward social chaos into a rush.

3. Benign Authoritarianism: Despite the growing public pressure for and acceptance of the need for fundamental social change, the large, complex and highly interdependent bureaucracies in both public and private sectors could thicken and, like slowly hardening concrete, lock people into an inescapable net of regulations and institutions. The new order could be a benign authoritarianism which emerges from the unstoppable logic of well-intended bureaucratic regulation which seeps into nearly every facet of life.

4. Humanistic Transformation: One expression of this alternative could be a future in which the underlying value premises shift and two closely related ethics emerge. The first is an ecological ethic that accepts our earth as limited, recognizes the underlying unity of the human race, and perceives humans as an integral part of the natural environment; the second is a self-realization ethic which as-

serts that each person's proper goal is the evolutionary development of his or her fullest human potentials in community with others. Each ethic could serve as a corrective for possible excesses in the other. A humanistic transformation might substantially embrace voluntary simplicity or some similar way of life that, though materially more modest than current lifestyles, is overall more satisfying.

These four thumbnail sketches of alternative futures present an enormous range of social possibility. Yet, to the extent that each of these is a plausible future, its seeds must exist in the present. Therefore, they need not be mutually exclusive social futures. For example, we can imagine a plausible future marked by both a humanistic transformation and by technological success (although it may be "appropriate" rather than "high" technology that underlies that success).

One way to test the viability of voluntary simplicity as an emergent way of life is to assess the extent to

tinually my relations with others, and to attempt to relate honestly, morally, and lovingly to those around me.

8. I commit myself to personal renewal through prayer, meditation, and study.

9. I commit myself to responsible participation in a community of faith.

Finnerty says that people have reacted most strongly to the two "sacrificial" points (numbers 2 and 3). "Declarations of world citizenship are not new," he says. "What is 'new' in the Pledge—and what gives it impact—is the firm declaration that personal piety, social conscience, and a simple life-style are all essential parts of a religious life that possesses integrity."

See *No More Plastic Jesus: Global Justice and Christian Lifestyle,* Orbis Books. Adam Daniel Finnerty. Maryknoll, New York 10545: Paperback, 223 pages, $3.95. Comment: "This book is a shocker. In an age that has become increasingly immune to excesses of sex and violence, the stripping away of one's own illusions can still provoke a reaction. This book must be X-rated not only to the religious people who cherish cloistered virtues in million-dollar cathedrals, but also to the vast range of middle-class people who think that they are enjoying the good life."

What It Means to Take the Shakertown Pledge

Two points of the Shakertown Pledge have caused the most controversy. The sponsors offer the following explanation of what these points mean:
I commit myself to lead an ecologically sound life.

Through this we pledge that we will use the earth's natural resources sparingly and with gratitude. This includes the use of the land, water, air, coal, timber, oil, minerals, and other important resources. We will try to keep our pollution of the environment to a minimum and will seek wherever possible to preserve the natural beauty of the earth.

Concretely, this should mean that we will try to correct wasteful practices in our communities, schools, jobs, and in our nation.
I commit myself to lead a life of creative simplicity and to share my personal wealth with the world's poor.

This means that we intend to reduce the frills and luxuries in our present lifestyle but at the same time emphasize the beauty and joy of living. We do this for three reasons: First, so that our own lives can be more simple and gracious, freed

from excessive attachment to material goods; Second, so that we are able to release more of our wealth to share with those who need the basic necessities of life; Third, so that we can move toward a Just World Standard of Living in which each person shares equally in the earth's resources.

Concretely, anyone who takes the Pledge should sit down with their family and review their present financial situation. Each item of expenditure should be looked at carefully, and unnecessary luxury items should be reduced or eliminated. The surplus that is freed by this process should be given to some national or international group that is working for a better standard of living for the deprived. This surplus should be a regular budgeted item from then on, and each member of the household should endeavor to see how this surplus can be increased. In the future, families and individuals who have taken the Pledge might consider meeting together in "sharing groups" to discover new ways in which community and cooperation can free up more resources for the poor.

151

which it could assume a significant role in all four of these futures. In other words, is VS a social movement that has relevance only in the context of a future humanistic transformation, or could it plausibly play a major role in the other three futures as well?

A future marked by "technological success" would probably still require people to attack the problems of resource scarcity, environmental pollution, and global economic inequities by consuming less. To the extent that there is a continuing need to approach these and related problems from the demand side, there will be a corresponding role for voluntary simplicity even in this materially successful scenario.

In a society of growing internal strife and tension, voluntary simplicity could, in the short run, exacerbate that conflict. In the longer run, however, VS might help to alleviate social tensions. To the extent that voluntary simplicity provides a way of life that transcends traditional interest group conflicts and provides a meaningful and workable response to a worsening social condition, it might alleviate tensions by directing social energy in a more coherent and harmonious direction.

In a society marked by growing bureaucratic regulation and erosion of democratic processes, voluntary simplicity (with its emphasis on local self-determination, human scale, and self-sufficiency) could provide a healthy corrective and counterbalancing force. Voluntary simplicity could provide an important source of grassroots innovation and vitality to what otherwise could be an increasingly rigid and somber society.

The important point is that voluntary simplicity fits into many alternative futures and therefore it is unlikely to disappear soon from the social landscape.

SOCIAL IMPACTS

What kind of society would emerge if voluntary simplicity were to become the predominant way of life? A partial answer to this question can be found by examining stereotypical contrasts between the value premises and social characteristics of the industrial "world view" and the voluntary simplicity "world view."

If this way of life were adopted by a majority of the population, we could anticipate certain long-run directions of social change that seem congruent with voluntary simplicity, including:

National Tenor: A society in which a large proportion of the population adopts voluntary simplicity would probably have a uniquely different "feel" to it. Such a society might possess a greater sense of frontier spirit, a feeling of continuing challenge at the prospects of forging new, evolving relationships among individuals, societies, nature, and the cosmos. Although some would likely view this as an escapist retreat from problems or a faddish response to soon-to-be-solved difficulties, the VS-oriented society would have a higher degree of cultural cohesion, social maturity, and social consensus. People would likely be settling in for the long haul and hence would have a greater sense of future destiny and the conviction they were working on behalf of future generations as well as for themselves. The culture would likely be more open, less tense and serious, and more tolerant. There might be a higher degree of and delight in social diversity. There would likely be a rebirth of a sense of geographic community and regional spirit and a grass-roots renaissance in the arts.

Material Growth: Society would tend to move from a goal of material abundance to a goal of material sufficiency. What level of material sufficiency is appropriate would largely be decided by individual choice constrained by resource availability and prevailing cultural norms. Clearly, this presumes a strongly cultural context with widely shared beliefs as to what constitutes appropriate levels of material sufficiency. Although material growth may tend toward a steady-state condition, this need not imply a materially static society. With selective growth, some sectors of the economy would grow rapidly while others would contract. For example, growth in appropriate technology might be rapid while production of items of conspicuous consumption declines.

Human Growth: The society would tend to transfer its growth potential and aspirations from a material dimension to an increasingly nonmaterial dimension. This shift would be of the highest import if, as many suggest, our present problems arise in part from a gross disparity between the relatively underdeveloped internal faculties of humans and the extremely powerful

The Cowboy Economy

The Cowboy—long viewed as a hero—is becoming something of a villain, in the new perceptions of certain radical economists.

The near-extinction of the bison was an early warning of what might happen if resources are plundered for whatever immediate gain might be realized, and devil take the consequences. His profligate ways are now memorialized in the pejorative phrase "the cowboy economy."

"The basic objective of the Cowboy Economy," according to a team of Library of Congress researchers, "is to maximize the flow of production, to expand, to grow. The key measure is, therefore, production of goods and services, expressed in economic terms as the Gross National Product (GNP). The key to expanding production and growth is technological advance. In the presence of abundant resources, the Cowboy Economy succeeded well, providing the standard of living that now permits the questioning of its continued value."

The questioning is not all aesthetics and environmental morality, the researchers say. The linear Cowboy Economy is running into problems at both ends. As resources become scarcer, the ability of established technologies to increase the flow of production is diminished. No matter how good the technology, if the oil is not there, it cannot be pumped out of the ground.

"The scarcity of key resources is taxing the system. Capital investments required for expanding the flow of production are pressing the limits of current capabilities. Moreover, the uncertainty of the success of advanced technologies is raising the risks of investment. These problems are beginning to stimulate a search for a restructured or alternative economy."

One alternative to the Cowboy Economy, the researchers say, is what might be called the "Conserver Economy," which would be designed to achieve many of the same qualitative social objectives while minimizing the consumption of resources.

See *Appropriate Technology: A Review,* prepared for the Congressional Clearinghouse on the Future by Wendy H. Schacht and William Renfro with Keith Bea. The Library of Congress, Congressional Research Service, Washington, D.C. 20540.

external technologies at their disposal. Society would attempt to achieve greater balance by fostering a degree of interior human growth that is at least commensurate with the enormous exterior growth that has occurred over the last several hundred years. This implies that the United States would increasingly become a trustee of conscious evolution on this earth, and, in doing so, endeavor to act with a level of awareness equal to the power and responsibility inherent in that role. The implication is that the nation's industrial prowess could provide, with suitable guidance, the material base to support the pervasive and intentional evolution of individual and socio-cultural awareness. Seen in this light, a trend toward voluntary simplicity is a logical evolutionary extension in our civilizational growth.

Life Environment: Society would tend to shift from living and working in large, complex environments to living and working in smaller, less complex environments. Accompanying this might be migration from large cities to small cities, towns, and the country. Such trends would probably stimulate grass-roots social action, revitalize the sense of community, and produce stronger, more distinctive clusters of neighborhoods.

Identity: The VS society would tend to define personal identity less in terms of consumption than in terms of one's awareness—psychological, social, spiritual. For many Americans, consumption is not only an expression of identity but is basic to their sense of identity. The growth of voluntary simplicity would tend to produce a cultural perspective in which identity could be expressed in many other ways, such as experimenting with various forms of voluntary simplicity; developing vital communities through new forms of group and extended family relationships; exploring human consciousness through the hundreds of consciousness expanding disciplines, ranging from meditation, biofeedback, hypnosis, encounter, bioenergetics, and so on.

Technology: Society would tend to move from "high" or "space age" technology to the careful application of "intermediate" or "appropriate" technology. Just as the industrial era was built on high technology, the voluntary simplicity era would likely rely on technology that is explicitly designed to be ecologically sound, energy-conserving, comprehensible by many, integrated with nature, and efficient when used on a small scale.

Engineer communtes to work on a bicycle for exercise and because of his conviction that the automobile has a deleterious effect on the environment.

Politics: If voluntary simplicity were to emerge as a dominant way of life, much of its growth would likely be driven by political activism at a grass-roots level. Extensive decentralization of institutions would require that local communities take much greater responsibility for the well-being of their population. Politics would probably assume a more humanistic orientation as people came to see the intimate connection that exists between the processes of personal growth and social change. Politics would thus be infused with a higher degree of honesty, compassion, and integrity. There might emerge new political coalitions and a greater number of political parties. There would also likely be greater self-righteousness, more frequent appeals to spiritual symbols in attempting to find political consensus, persistent tension between those holding the voluntary simplicity view and those adhering to the industrial world view, confusion concerning the equity and scope of programs conceived and administered at the local level, and so on. Overall, it probably would be a society in which political processes were more experimental, error embracing, and intentionally seeking diversity.

Global Environment: The emergence of an America dominated by the philosophy of voluntary simplicity would undoubtedly lead to many changes in international policies, such as:

- Support for international bodies dealing with issues such as defense, food, energy, conservation, pollution, critical resources, regulation of nuclear activities, and so on.
- Reduction in trade barriers and greater economic and technical assistance to developing nations
- Much more cultural interchange
- Moderation of power politics, with the U.S. attempting to exert moral rather than economic or military leadership.

If U.S. policies were successful, the nation might ultimately emerge as a symbol of human rights, a source of sophisticated aid in technological problems, and the leader in building a worldwide sense of unity among all peoples everywhere.

THE IMPACT ON BUSINESS

The advent of a large segment of the population acting fully or partially in accord with VS tenets would have a major impact on business. The highlights of these implications are sketched below:

Income Patterns: Our back-of-the-envelope estimates are that this way of life would not reduce the gross national product of the U.S. as much as might be expected; adoption of simple living by roughly a third of the adult population (such that their consumption levels were halved) would reduce personal income available to consumers in the year 2000 by only about 15% from what it otherwise would likely be. The biggest effect would likely be on the pattern of aggregate consumption and on moderating the level of growth.

Businesses that view voluntary simplicity as an opportunity rather than a threat might find it to be the fastest-growing consumer market of the coming decades. Our rough estimates (calculated at 100 percent of the spending of "full" VS consumers and 50 percent of "partial" VS consumers) suggest that consumption with a VS orientation could plausibly rise from about $35 billion today to perhaps $140 billion a decade hence, and to well over $300 billion in 2000 (all in 1975 dollars). This growth seems more than ample to engage traditional business and also to support large numbers of new firms that start up to serve VS consumers.

The growth of voluntary simplicity would almost surely lead to an increasingly bimodal income distribution. The enduring disparity between rich and poor in our society would likely grow in magnitude as VS income patterns (although motivationally quite different) would look increasingly like those who were involuntarily simple or poor. How long this gap would persist is an open question. For a substantial proportion of the population—and particularly the poor—we think an equitable redistribution of income would be a precondition for voluntary frugality.

Consumer Markets: VS consumption criteria are significantly different from traditional patterns. The person living the simple life tends to prefer products that are functional, healthful, nonpolluting, durable, repairable, recyclable or made from renewable raw materials, energy-cheap, authentic, aesthetically pleasing, and made through simple technology. Such criteria will adversely affect many products of conspicuous consumption. On the other hand, the VS lifestyle should create an excellent markets for such items as:

- First class durable products, such as solid wood furniture, high quality music and television systems, top-grade hand tools, geared bicycles.
- Sturdy cotton and wool clothing deemphasizing fashion, which can be mended, handed down, and worn for years.
- Do-it-yourself equipment for home construction, home repair and improvements, cooking, gardening, entertaining, and so on.
- Inexpensive prefab "flexible" housing.
- Easy-to-fix autos and appliances, perhaps using modular construction.
- Healthy, "natural," unprocessed foods.
- Self-help medical, childcare, housekeeping items.
- Products for arts and crafts and other aesthetic pursuits.
- Simple, safe, nonplastic, nonmetal toys and games for children.
- Products or services associated with shared tasks in communal living, cooperatives, recycling, and energy-reduction and food-conservation projects.
- Leisure activities geared to country living.
- Imaginative ways of refurbishing old city and country homes.

- Traveling car repair and parts services.
- Machines, equipment, and systems utilizing intermediate technology.

Prices: Many prices would increase substantially to meet the qualitative demands of people; people may be less willing to accept varying profit margins (i.e., profit will increasingly be based on a "cost-plus" basis) and will no longer tend to reflect the market's willingness to pay a premium for style, fashion, or fad. Price will more often be in terms of barter or "energy exchange." Bulk purchasing of nondurables should be anticipated as a frugal market response to unit pricing.

Outlets: A growing and appreciable portion of market activity will take place in the "alternative marketplace": flea markets, garage sales, classified advertising, community bulletin boards. Consumer cooperatives and mail-order operations will increase as VS consumers become less willing to support superfluous merchandising costs. Purchases will be increasingly localized to diminish the costs of transportation and to encourage the utilization of intermediate technology. Specialty stores will likely increase, especially for food (home canning apparatus and utensils for greater self-sufficiency), shelter (energy conservation technology, materials-efficiency guidelines), and clothing (kits).

Promotion: New styles of advertising and promotion will tend to replace traditional types of sensational, emotional, and image appeals. Although an interesting and "aware" image will be important, the aim of advertising and promotion will be to help the consumer gain useful (rather than solely persuasive) information.

The advertising will be more closely associated with the product or service being promoted. False or misleading advertising will be taken not as exaggerated puffery but as evidence of the advertiser's lack of concern for others—a message of "you versus us" instead of "we together." Appeals aimed at product quality, utility, durability, and service will likely be more successful, although the marketplace undoubtedly will have its share of "clique products." Keeping-up-with-the-Joneses will diminish in importance, but popularity or market acceptance of a product will be an important promotional criterion.

Work Roles: In a simple-living society the role of work would be downplayed as a status and power symbol and upgraded as a means of contributing to the collective good. Cooperation rather than competition would be the hallmark of work. Complaints would be directed more toward matters of ethics, social responsibility, and esthetics rather than issues of pay, office size, and promotion. Very likely there would be many more part-time jobs, enabling people to earn enough to fulfill their essential needs and yet have much more free time to pursue personal development and perhaps aid others.

Significantly, management would tend to be highly participative, to be organized around tasks, and to be less hierarchical than at present. Ultimately, the traditional proprietary attitudes of business might yield to greater openness and inter- and intraindustry cooperation. The aggressive expression of the profit motive (exemplified by "making a killing" rather than "making a living")—although it is not likely to vanish in the near future—would likely be a diminishing force in business.

Consumerism: It seems likely the advocates of voluntary simplicity will, as a consumer group, continue to exert political and economic pressure to change business and industrial practices. A trend toward VS implies no abatement of consumer movements directed toward such specific issues as safety, pollution, conservation, land use, ecological balance, and others.

As individuals, VS people may very well try to influence business by

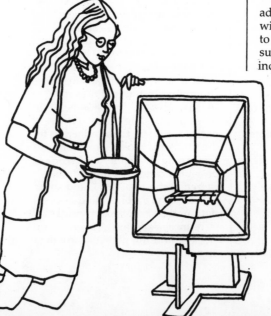

Rural housewife prepares to cook meal wrapped in aluminum foil in her new solar oven. She and her husband are trying to free themselves of wasteful sources of energy, and this sun-powered "appliance" is their first big investment.

154

buying in accord with rating criteria applied to long lists of specific products and specific manufacturers, retailers, banks, and the like. Such activities, accompanied by word-of-mouth publicity, might be one way in which adherents of voluntary simplicity will try to enforce their sense of social responsibility.

VS Businesses: We think it likely that small businesses run by VSers for the VS trade will flourish in many parts of the nation. The Briarpatch network in the San Francisco Bay Area may prove to be one important template. Founded by Dick Raymond only a few years ago, the Briars have established several hundred individual firms in such areas as food and clothing stores, restaurants, book and magazine publishing, auto repair, baking, small-scale manufacture, child care centers, a toy company, etc. The Briarpatch network provides professional advice and services in a variety of domains including finance, advertising, insurance, charter flights, quantity purchasing, accounting and legal services, bartering opportunities, fund-raising skills, and recruitment.

The operating principles of Briarpatch businesses are significant. They include:

- Job sharing, in which two or more people are paid for one position.
- Job swapping, through which people can occasionally try out other positions.
- Multiple jobs or roles, in which a person might be the bookkeeper as well as a board member.
- Functions generally performed without titles. If a title exists, it would probably be facilitator instead of president; "she buys everything," rather than purchasing agent.
- Meditation is increasingly scheduled on the job.
- If there are end-of-year surpluses, they are "recycled" in various ways. But generally there is a desire to help other projects rather than passive investors.
- Directors serving as facilitators rather than watchdogs.
- One favorite practice is to set prices according to the rule that the best price is what you would charge your friends.

LONG-TERM SIGNIFICANCE

The phenomenon that we have called voluntary simplicity appears to be of deep social significance for three fundamental reasons:

First, it is a concept and a way of

Authors Duane Elgin (right) and Arnold Mitchell collaborated on a study of voluntary simplicity for the Center for the Study of Social Policy at the Stanford Research Institute in Menlo Park, California. The Center was founded by Willis W. Harman, author of "The Coming Transformation," which appeared in the February and April 1977 issues of The Futurist. *Elgin currently is a consultant to SRI and is setting up a Center for Tranformational Studies. Mitchell is a Senior Social Economist at SRI.*

life whose time seems at last to be arriving. The idea of voluntary simplicity has been discussed for millennia. However, our present era of relative abundance contrasts sharply with the material poverty of the past. The voluntary assumption of a life materially simple and non-materially rich, therefore, is not only increasingly psychologically acceptable but physically feasible for perhaps the first time in history for large numbers of people.

Second, voluntary simplicity specifically addresses the critical issues of our times—the problems of eco-system overload, alienation, the unmanageable scale and complexity of institutions, worldwide antagonisms, and so on. VS is a creative, comprehensive, and holistic approach to a host of problems customarily considered to be separate. By coping simultaneously with scores of interrelated specifics, voluntary simplicity seems to provide a solution that could not be achieved via the one-by-one route.

Third, it meshes with the eternal needs of individuals to continue to grow. The emphasis on the inner life permits people to grow psychologically even if material growth may be denied by events beyond their control. Further, there is reason to think that the kind of growth fostered by voluntary simplicity is especially appropriate to our times and circumstances. In brief, the need of the individual uniquely matches the need of the society.

Of what other emergent life patterns can these things be said?

CONTINUING RESEARCH ON VOLUNTARY SIMPLICITY

The authors are continuing their study of voluntary simplicity and would appreciate any help that readers can provide. Some specific questions:

1. If you are fully living the VS style, could you say when and under what circumstances you consciously started to live simply? Why did you take up VS? What are the major changes in living arrangements you made as a result? What satisfactions and dissatisfactions do you find associated with this way of life? Do you see VS as a movement that is likely to spread rapidly? Why or why not?

2. If you rate yourself a "partial" adherent to voluntary simplicity, how are you acting in VS style? How are you *not* acting in VS style? Do you expect to become more or less so? Why? What kinds of things would prompt you to embrace more fully a lifestyle of voluntary simplicity?

3. If you are sympathetic to VS but not acting substantially on your sympathy, could you say why you are not and what might trigger you to change your lifestyle in the direction of VS?

4. If you are opposed to voluntary simplicity, could you give us your reasons?

5. Please provide some basic data about yourself: age, sex, education, occupation, approximate income, place of residence.

Please write: Duane Elgin or Arnold Mitchell, P.O. Box 2483, Menlo Park, California 94025.

Suggestions for Further Information on Simple Living

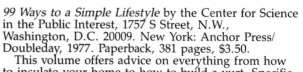

DEMONSTRATION MODEL
NEW AGE STOVES
FROM RECYCLED
55 GALLON DRUM

Former bookkeeper quits his city job and starts his own business manufacturing stoves for cabins and rural homes. The stoves are made from 55-gallon oil drums.

Organizations

Institute for Local Self-Reliance, 1717 18th Street, N.W., Washington, D.C. 20009.

The Institute publishes a bi-monthly newsletter and booklets on such topics as *Neighborhood Technology* and *How to Research Your Local Bank.*

Environmental Action Foundation, 724 Dupont Circle Building, Washington, D.C. 20036.

This organization has a free booklet entitled "The Case for Materials Conservation."

American Friends Service Committee, 2160 Lake Street, San Francisco, California 94121.

This Quaker group has organized a "Simple Living Collective," which has produced a book entitled *Taking Charge: Personal and Social Change through Simple Living, Bantam Books, Inc., 1977.*

Publications

Rain: Journal of Appropriate Technology, 2270 N.W. Irving, Portland, Oregon 97210.

This is a monthly journal specializing in brief notes concerning what is going on in energy conservation, appropriate technology, radical economics, etc.

Undercurrents, 11 Shadwell, Uley, Dursley, Gloucestershire, GL11 5BW, England.

A British journal that publishes articles by E. F. Schumacher and similar-minded thinkers.

Conserver Society/Notes, Science Council of Canada, 150 Kent Street, Seventh Floor, Ottawa, Ontario K1P 5P4.

This is issued as part of a Science Council project exploring the implications of a Conserver Society in Canada, that is, a society that conserves resources rather than consumes them.

Conserver Society News, 512 Boulevard Wilfred Lavigne, Aylmer, Quebec J94 3W3, Canada.

A grassroots newsletter for Canadians interested in developing a society in harmony with the biosphere. The editor is Bruce McCallum, author of *Environmentally Appropriate Technology.*

Briarpatch Review, 330 Ellis Street, San Francisco, California 94102.

This magazine, which styles itself "A Journal of Right Livelihood and Simple Living," is put out by a group of people interested in "simple living, openness, sharing, and learning how the world works through business." *Briarpatch* also specializes in "humanistic management methods and unusual organization solutions."

Simple Living, American Friends Service Committee, 514 Bryant Street, San Francisco, California 94302.

This is a tabloid-style newsletter that reports on the simple living movement.

99 Ways to a Simple Lifestyle by the Center for Science in the Public Interest, 1757 S Street, N.W., Washington, D.C. 20009. New York: Anchor Press/Doubleday, 1977. Paperback, 381 pages, $3.50.

This volume offers advice on everything from how to insulate your home to how to build a yurt. Specific counsels include: "Consume less meat," "Organize a food co-op," and "Join a craft cooperative." Comment: "Packed with useful hints on how to live more simply—and cheaply."

"When examining the definition of 'simple lifestyle,' a number of qualities surface," say the authors. "For example, simple lifestyle practices are less wasteful, less showy and fashion-oriented, capable of reusing items, less consumptive and not addicted to commercialism, not overly mobile, not noisy. They are more natural than synthetic, homemade than factory produced, more personal than institutionalized, with more human involvement than energy use."

Specifically, the team lists the following qualities, which can be matched with sample practices described in the book:

Quality—Sample Practice
Reusable—Mend and reuse garments
Resourcefulness—Save heat and insulate
Not superfluous—Eliminate unnecessary appliances
Do-it-yourself—Keep bees
Stability—Avoid unnecessary auto travel
Homemade—Bake bread
Peace and quiet—preserve a place for quiet
Natural—Eat wild foods
Personal—Care for the elderly and ill
Human effort—Exercise without equipment

How to Live Better with Less— If You Can Stand the People

On March 30, 1973, British science writer Robin Clarke abandoned London to join a rural commune in Wales. What he learned during the experience is the subject of his new book, *Building for Self-Sufficiency*.

Clarke and his associates had bought a 43-acre hill-farm, and their first job was to convert the small and near-derelict stone cottage to a house that could shelter a community of 16 people. Setting themselves up as BRAD (Biotechnic Research and Development), Clarke and his friends planned to turn the site into a research center to investigate such things as wind power, heat pumps, methane generation, etc.

"We wanted to devise a life-style that would be valid, not for just this generation living off a depleting stock of natural resources, but for generations far into the future. So we planned to be self-sufficient not only in food, but also in energy, water, and, eventually, perhaps even materials...

"Someday, one of us will certainly write a book about that community— but that is not my intention here. Suffice to say that I and my family left 18 months later, and another five a few months after that. Nearly all of us left for the same reason: the struggle to do the things we wanted to do against a background of mounting inertia and community dissent proved too great. Just over three years later the community had been officially disbanded, and the farm sold."

But Clarke doubts that anyone involved feels that the experiment could justly be called a failure. "Certainly, I spent some of the most depressing moments of my life at Eithin. But, equally, certainly, I experienced some of the highest points I have ever known, and for at least a year revelled in a freedom of spirit which I had never dreamt was possible. But, above all, I learnt. More, I think, in 18 months than in 15 years of being an editor, journalist and freelance writer."

Clarke and his friends lived, technically, far below the poverty line, "but we were certainly never deprived." The most important discovery for Clarke was his ability to do all kinds of jobs he previously had no idea he could do.

"Concrete-mixing, drain-laying, carpentry, joinery, roofing, plumbing, writing, guttering, rendering, farming, and even vehicle maintenance soon became part of the daily life," he says. "And we did them well. So, I suspect, can everyone else. Yet in our society there is a mystique attached to such crafts which leads 95 percent of us to declare ourselves incapable of them."

The divorce which modern society has effected between the heads and the hands is, for Clarke, its greatest evil. "It turns us all, in the end, into less than half a person. And anyone who learns again to use them together will, I guarantee, experience a rejuvenation not normally associated with the mundane tasks of laying drains and learning to make a ridge ladder. It is all something to do with bringing your life back under your own control. And of spending your time at a number of highly different jobs. The human being, surely, was never intended to do the same thing for hours on end for most of his waking life. There is more to living."

Anyone who really wants to save money should join or found a community, Clarke says. The many obstacles that Clarke had feared would occur—such as failure to get planning permission, or the difficulty of finding community members— failed to materialize. But the one obstacle he felt confident of overcoming proved their undoing.

"We failed to make it as a community. Not all the time, in that I and many others there almost certainly spent some of the best moments of our lives at Eithin. But, in the end, after the first year, those at first intangible differences between us rose up and smote us most mightily."

Within a year after Clarke and his family left, the farm and the house were up for sale.

"With such a history, it may seem strange to urge anyone to join a community. Yet I believe it is a sensible way to live...if you can do it ...

"Most communities, of course, fail in the end through lack of competence, lack of money, or both. That we seemed to have both these problems licked makes our own failures if anything more significant. We didn't have those hard economic facts forever draining away our morale. We were just unable to live with one another as human beings with any enjoyment. It was as simple as that.

"So, if you are planning to do it, what advice could I offer? First, perhaps, never join a community because you want to live in a community, or you think you do. Do so only if you discover a group of people, or even one or two, with whom you positively think a shared life would be a turn for the better."

Building for Self-Sufficiency: Tools—Materials—Building—Heat—Insulation—Solar Energy—Wind Power—Water and Plumbing—Waste and Compost—Methane—Transport—Food, Robin Clarke. New York: Universe Books, 1976. 289 pages, paperback, $5.95. Available from the World Future Society's Book Service. Comment: "Readable and practical, this book is strongly recommended to anyone interested in self-sufficiency, appropriate technology, and communal living."

For a description of Clarke's community by an outsider, see "Communities That Seek Peace with Nature" by John P. Milton in *The Futurist*, December 1974. (The whole issue is focused on appropriate technology.)

BACKYARD AQUACULTURE

Experiments at the New Alchemy Institute on Massachusetts' Cape Cod aim at developing ways to raise table-size fish in an area no bigger than a child's swimming pool during the six summer months, Robin Clarke says in *Building for Self-Sufficiency*.

"The preferred fish is tilapia, a native to the Near East and Africa which grows extremely fast in warm water, is rich in protein, and has a good flavor. And the first thing you need is a pool, approximately 12-14 feet in diameter, and some three feet deep...Over the pool you need to construct a greenhouse of some kind...If you don't have anything suitable, the easiest, most transportable and lightest structure you can make is a dome."

The tilapia can be fed earthworms, which fish farmers can raise on household garbage. (The worms love such items as used coffee grounds.)

"It wouldn't take many people growing fish in their yard to solve the world food problem once and for all," says Clarke.

Why Voluntary Simplicity Won't Destroy Us

What will happen to the economy if everyone starts moving toward a life of greater simplicity and increased self-reliance?

Bankers, politicians, business people, economists, government officals, and a number of sensible and common-sense people think it will go straight to hell. We live in a complex world, they say. We live in a technological age, they say. We live in a world of rising expectations, they say. We must expand our economy if for no other reason than to help the poor, here and abroad, they say. It is only natural that we grow more complex, they say. It's like a law of nature, they say. You can't go backwards, they say. If it weren't for elaborate and elaborated demand, they say, there wouldn't be enough jobs to go around, and unemployment already is a ghastly, growing curse upon us.

Fortunately, there isn't a significant word of truth in anything they say. What they say should be taken seriously only if one can imagine a growing change in the way we live without a change in *anything* else. Unlikely, eh?

Let's start with jobs. The common argument about jobs is that they can be "created" only with the investments of going business, usually the biggest. Wrong. Jobs are created, also, whenever anyone enters into a fairly regular agreement with anyone else to provide goods or services in return for something of value.

Such jobs, incidentally, also create wealth—i.e., new things of value—rather than just swapping dollars as our Big Economy does.

The Big Economy is based upon the exchange of dollar bills or other instruments, upon credit. The dollars we exchange don't represent real wealth. They are not tokens of actual production or minerals or food. They are simply the issued paper of the central bank of the nation state—the Federal Reserve System.

One result of shifting the economy away from money that represents real production to dollars which are just government scrip has been the involvement of more and more of the economy in debt management rather than in production or the creation of value.

Big Business, for instance, has proven singularly *un*-innovative over the past several decades. Technology is developed in very small companies which are subsequently taken over by the big ones. The big ones deal not in bettered production and innovation but in acquisition, accumulation, hoarding on a massive scale. Banks finance their shenanigans along with other purely speculative things more than they finance genuinely new productive operations. And small businesses disappear into the abyss of this financial game playing. Actually, the more Big Business—the top 2,000 corporations (out of several million) which account for somewhere around 90 percent of annual profits and hold about the same proportion of corporate wealth—destroys small business, the *fewer* jobs there are. The growth of the economy along its present lines does not mean more jobs except in the service industries, where jobs increase apace with population.

One of the major impacts simpler lifestyles and more self-reliance would have on the job situation is in agriculture. Our farm population, as everyone knows, shrinks daily under the impact of urbanization and agribusiness. Also, we move toward monocultural growing, or single-crop domination over vast areas. And we increase the use of pesticides, fertilizers and—most significantly—water for irrigation as this process continues. (Having just finished a fairly major research on water supply in America, I can say flatly that unless our agriculture changes drastically we are going to run out of water supplies all across the country. We won't run out altogether, of course, but we will have to start making very hard choices about how we use what's left—and what's left that is fit to use!)

A more self-reliant lifestyle should mean that communities, towns, counties—all local areas—would take a hard look at growing more and more, and ideally *most,* of their food within 50 miles of the point of consumption. Such decentralized agriculture—returning to more traditional diversity of crops; relying more on small, probably organic farms (which, incidentally, can be more nutrition efficient than big, chemical farms)—would create more opportunities for people to work on the land. Jobs would spring up everywhere as farms began springing up everywhere.

But, they say, Americans have become too sophisticated to go back to working on farms. Hah! What do city dwellers almost universally thirst for every weekend? A plot of land to tend. What do corporate vice-presidents do when they are sober? Tend gardens. And what sort of idiot supposition is it to believe that people, poor and battered in the cities, would be worse off independent and farming in the countryside?

Also, in manufacturing, if quality were ever to be emphasized above quantity, jobs would fountain up in a geyser of new prosperity.

The productive bonus of a simplified lifestyle—rejecting the profusion of trivial products which now account for the major space in most stores, such as supermarkets—is that it would focus more creative energy on the design and production of superb, rather than trivial, products. Fine tools instead of junk furniture. Wonderful, energy-light cooking devices instead of TV dinners. Constant local entertainments instead of *Charlie's Angels*. And so forth. Anyone who cannot envision a life of quality as superior to a life of sheer quantity will, of course, not opt for a simplified lifestyle. So? It shouldn't stop you. Your being simple, self-reliant, or free does not shackle someone else.

Only the person prepared to say that we do and should live in a regimented society can say that people cannot turn back their clocks. In a free society they can turn at will. They simply can't *force* anyone else to do it also, or to pay for it or its consequences.

As for the complexity of demand being the key to a healthy society, as some say it is (34 brands of equally innocuous deodorant being thought of as the epitome of "freedom of choice"), the proper answer is that choice to be free is not simply choice *of* things. It also involves the choice *not* to have things. Again, only advocates of a regimented society can make arguments in which freedom of choice is the freedom to choose only what the established authority offers.

Incidentally, my own vision of a simpler life does not happen to be a wholly primitive life in the sense of foregoing knowledge, foregoing tools, etc. I share, rather, the vision of a young physicist who wrote of being able to imagine a time when he could join with friends to do high energy, theoretical research as a cooperative venture; then ride his horse from the lab to a shared community work activity where he and they could produce community wealth (food, objects, art, etc.); and then go to a cabin in the woods where he could read philosophy by the light of a kerosene lamp.

He was simply envisioning a society in which the way people live would blend into their own landscapes, becoming a true and shared culture, rather than an imposed and onerous life of necessity. I do not, in other words, feel that human beings will ever be content, or should be content, with the ultimately simplified life of a grazing animal. Simplicity for humans is not the same as simplicity for antelopes. On the other hand the sheer and mad complexity-for-complexity's sake of today's social organizations, with their wildly artificial and contrived hierarchies, is not a fit human environment either.

The argument that a simplified, self-reliant economy might hurt our ability to help the poor here and abroad is based on the unreal assumption that we are helping them anyway. Today, what we call help—which takes the form of molding the developing peoples in our image and creating economies designed to service our own unwieldy one—simply diverts the poor of the third world from the necessary tasks of securing their own agricultural base and developing, in the texture of their own cultures, appropriate technologies and social agreements. What we are doing now is summed up best by our help in such areas as the Sahel where, by introducing the people to the wonders of modern, monocultural agribusiness, we managed recently to produce the spectacle of thousands of people dying in the agonies of starvation while huge amounts of crops were shipped from the same area to export markets in Europe.

It's the same with the poor in our cities and rural areas. Land—basic agricultural opportunity—would serve as a better base for the liberation of most current ghetto "prisoners" than any amount of continued welfare.

When it comes to technology, should that be of any interest—and it is to me—then rest assured that a simplified and self-reliant lifestyle will not hurt it. At least it will not hurt the development of the sort of technology which is nonlethal, resource conserving, or reusing, capable of being understood and operated by people generally (if they try) and not shielded by artificial complexity or secrecy, and also scaled so that it becomes a tool of the person or persons using it and not a *user of them.*

Such technology is developing quite nicely among people who already are moving toward simpler lifestyles and more self-reliant communities.

Just one of those technologies, solar heating, owes most of its status today to people out of the mainstream of Establishment America. But so do more classically "high tech" developments, such as the amorphous semiconductor, developed by a man without college credentials who is wholly an inventive maverick. Given the development of this technology to date it seems safe to predict that within just a couple of years it will make possible the lowest-cost electrical energy available on the earth, by using semiconductor arrays for the direct conversion of solar radiation into electrical energy.

Or, for those who worry about other high accomplishments in a simpler world, just remember that the most powerful computer on the face of the earth, the Cray I, is built by about 50 people working together on a farm in Chippewa Falls, Wisconsin.

Or, recall that a car which is a cottage industry vehicle compared, say, to a Chevrolet, is still highly regarded: the Rolls Royce.

The point is this: scientists can be scientists without working in great skyscrapers. Most usually are, anyway. Technology can flourish in garage spaces as well as in gleaming, mile-long plants. And it usually does! Jobs can be created by people who work and not just by people who manipulate money markets. And the best ones usually are. And so on.

A few other specifics to calm our fears:

The Sheet Metal Workers Union figures that the installation of solar devices is going to provide 15,000 new jobs for their members in the near term.

Conversion of toilets to waterless composters, which may become necessary as clean-water supplies dwindle, would add jobs.

An agricultural shift, as mentioned, would create

more jobs than anything else. Any move away from massification (even away from mass-consolidated school education, for instance) adds to and does not subtract from the vitality of a truly productive economy and, particularly, a democratic economy in which everyone is invited to share and work.

Self-reliance, of course, means that people, individually and in volitional associations, communities, etc., depend largely upon their own energies, initiatives, and resources for the major portions of their needs. It may also mean that they accommodate needs *to* what they have and can do. At any rate, it surely means turning away from the compartmentalized, production-line, corporate, mystified sort of production that dominates us today. It does not say anything, in particular, about the tools we will use except that we will use them in a different way, a way that gives priority to personal involvement and responsibility, with less room to hide in fancy legal exclusions, like corporate law, or in privileged sanctuaries like universities.

As people become self-reliant, they become, necessarily, more and not less productive in terms of their own needs. They, among other things, remove themselves as a burden on anyone else! At the very least they do that. How, then, do they hurt the economy? The only economy they could hurt would be the economy of nonproducers, of people who expect to get by *without* being self-reliant.

Simplicity, on the other hand, means getting away from the duplicative, accumulative, massified forms of social and production arrangements which, today, are showing every sign of economic bad health: top-heavy and featherbedded managements; large amounts of resources siphoned off to absentee and nonproductive interests; heavy drains to political influence; soaring debts; stagnating techniques of production as well as an increasing bias against innovation; a marketing philosophy that has shifted almost entirely to the merchandising of style rather than substance and toward creating new markets for trivia and tinsel novelty instead of competitively satisfying larger, more serious markets. Simplifying your life in the sense of getting away from that cannot hurt a real economy; it instead helps build one, while the old, sick mass economy putrefies around us.

That economy has killed itself. Worrying about it is to worry about the incurable. It may last, as a terminal patient, for years. If it does, the real economic vitality in the world will be found among the self-reliant and creative. They may weep for the old, but they cannot save it. They must build something new. And I believe they are. I believe we are.

Karl Hess, a former speechwriter for Barry Goldwater, lives in Kearneysville, West Virginia, his base for writing and lecturing.

Models Which Give Direction

You may believe with us that basic structural changes need to take place in the way our society operates and the way we live. Relax if you are apprehensive about what the new forms will look like. There is fortunately no cut and dried blueprint for how life will be celebrated in the age of voluntary simplicity. That's good. The people must invent (or rediscover) values and structures as they go along—and that is happening today. Exciting experimental models are testing what works best to produce a society which is just, gentle and cooperative. We hope you will want to start projects like this in your community.

COMMUNITY LIVING

New ways people are relating to each other is one of the most important pieces in the puzzle of inventing a more livable society. Forging new lifestyles, structures, and values often produces resistance from the rest of society and the solidarity and support of a caring community is vital. Some of the expressions are based on religious beliefs while others have grown from a desire for economic justice, nonviolent social change, or humanistic philosophy. If you want to know more about these groups, write them directly. A stamped self-addressed envelope or small literature contribution would be a helpful gesture.

Reba Place Fellowship

In Evanston, Illinois, the Reba Place Fellowship is an extended family community of more than 130 members living in houses and apartments within a three-block area. Reba Place was formed as a vehicle to give religious expressions a deeper meaning than people were finding in most churches. Members share money, possessions, and social concerns because they feel this style is necessary to fully practice Christian love.

In an interview with *Fellowship* magazine one of the members said: "We have come to realize that there is no way you can really live a set of values different from those of the rest of society unless you have a community, a social network, that will be strong enough to compete. Mainstream social values and the American lifestyle are perpetuated by such powerful institutions as General Motors, the Pentagon, universities, and so on. These corporate institutions keep getting more powerful and more sophisticated. They swallow up the individual ... Reba Place Fellowship is by far the most powerful influence on the lives of members of this community and what we are doing. That kind of shift in power is what has to take place, and that is what community is all about."[1]

Arcosanti—Dream City

On a much larger scale, the work of Paolo Soleri is rising out of the rugged Arizona desert in the form of Arcosanti, the Dream City. An article in the August 16, 1977, *Newsweek* described the utopian architect's vision as "nothing less than a self-contained city, built by volunteer student labor and designed, according to Soleri, to save the planet from its own excesses."

The amazing fact is that Arcosanti does not receive any large government or private funding, depending greatly on the sweat labor and seminar fees of volunteers. The finished city will be a 25-story structure facing south to collect solar heat and the sun's rays for the over 4-acre greenhouse which will produce food for the community. The 5,000 inhabitants will live and work in buildings occupying only fourteen acres, leaving 846 acres of the land preserve undisturbed or to be developed for farming or recreation needs. There will be no absentee landlords; one must live at Arcosanti to share in property use. Automobiles will be banned; people will move up and down by elevators. Soleri sees his city as nothing less than a step in Pierre Teilhard de Chardin's spiritual evolution toward pure mind and spirit. Write to the Cosanti Foundation, 6433 Doubletree Road, Scottsdale, Arizona 85253 for literature.

Community Land Trust

As the population in the United States increases, there are more people wanting a piece of real estate for homes or making a living and this has driven the price so high few people can afford land

anymore. The only ones who profit are the speculators. One alternative to this social problem is the community land trust, a social mechanism which eliminates speculation by holding "land in stewardship for all mankind, present and future, while protecting the legitimate use-rights of its residents."[2] As the authors of *The Community Land Trust, a Guide to a New Model for Land Tenure in America* remind us, "If land is limited, then its use in the face of steadily expanding human demands upon it must be regulated for the long-range welfare of all people."[3]

This new model for land use holds the land in perpetuity—and it probably will never be sold. Parcels are leased to the users as a part of the goal to preserve and enhance its long-range value. Leases are restricted to those people using the land—subleasing and absentee control are not allowed. The residents may build whatever kind of community they desire—one involving common ownership or individual homesteads.

New Communities, Inc., of Lee County, Georgia, is the best U.S. example of a large rural community land trust. Planned as a new rural town

on 5700 acres of good farmland and a number of existing buildings, twelve families now live on the land with hundreds involved in the day care center, farming operation, and roadside vegetable market. For more information on community land trusts write to Bob Swann at Institute for Community Economics, 639 Massachusetts Ave., Cambridge, Massachusetts 02139.

FOOD

Food Fairs

Several years ago law student and organizer Lindsay Jones looked at the food problem holistically and found the survival of the small farmer coincided with the consumer's goals to buy good food at lower prices. Jones's dream and organizing skill resulted in 300 Food Fairs in summer 1977 in Tennessee, Alabama, Arkansas, Virginia, and Mississippi—a simple concept of bringing together consumers and vegetable producers at church parking lots for direct marketing. The alternative distribution system proves that bigness is not better, for the truck farmers average 15 percent more income from Food Fairs and the consumers save 40 percent over supermarket produce prices. Eventually all the Food Fairs will be run by local farmer associations. Ag Marketing would like to help you start a Food Fair in your community: write Agricultural Marketing Project, Center for Health Services, Station 17, Vanderbilt Medical Center, Nashville, Tennessee 37232.

Food Cooperatives

Next to taxes more people probably gripe about the high cost and low quality of supermarket food than any other thing. The alternative food distribution movement, which includes food buying clubs and cooperatives, zero-profit grocery stores, organic truck farms, and trucking collectives, are a part of the cooperative movement which goes much deeper than lowering cost and raising quality.

The goals and operating style of the Southern California Cooperating Community Warehouse are symbolic of the movement (5300 Santa Monica, Los Angeles, California 90029):

We are women and men operating a wholesale food warehouse which serves stores and buying clubs which are not-for-profit. We are a worker-managed business, and after our incorporation we will be consumer owned as well.

We are for low-cost, nutritious food for all people at prices which are determined by all of us acting together as a community. We are for people beginning to take control of their own lives by setting up people's enterprises that

serve our needs according to policy we make as a community ...

We are against monopolies which make a mockery of the term "free enterprise."

We are against big corporations running our lives ...

We support small farmers whenever possible ...

Other examples are included in a resource manual *Non-Profit Food Stores,* published by Strongforce Inc., 2121 Decatur Pl. N.W., Washington, D.C. 20008. A skeptic will become convinced that it is possible for a community of people to create their own food system. Common Market Cooperative, formed in late 1972 as a campaign promise of a campus political party at the University of Denver, now sells nearly one and one-half million dollars a year out of an abandoned Safeway in downtown Denver—the last supermarket in center city. Begun as a small buying club, Common Market now serves the large senior citizen community and college students, operating as a member-controlled consumer's cooperative. For information write to Common Market, 1329 California, Denver, Colorado 80204.

Food Bank
Did you know that tons of edible food are "dumped" every day in our land as a normal and acceptable practice of supermarkets, produce jobbers, growers, and packers? Ten years ago this bothered John van Hengel enough to start St. Mary's Food Bank, the nation's first salvage food agency which today warehouses and distributes 35 percent of Phoenix, Arizona's surplus, outdated, and damaged food to thousands of hungry people. John's dream has spread across the country with many food banks forming a national network. How much edible food is dumped in your city? Bob McCarty can help you start a food bank if you'll write him at Second Harvest, 819 N. 3rd St., Phoenix, Arizona 85004.

Senior Gleaners
One of the reasons so much food is wasted in the fields where it is grown is the lack of a system to harvest the unwanted fruits and vegetables. Sacramento, California, retiree Homer Fahrner thought it was criminal to waste all that food when people were hungry so he organized and trained 1500 fixed-income retirees, made agreements with growers, and Senior Gleaners now picks around 400 tons of food valued at $800,000 (50 percent of retail). The gleaners keep what they can eat and the rest is given to nonprofit organizations. Homer's address is 2606½ J St., Sacramento, California 95816.

INTEGRAL URBAN HOUSE

If the estimate made by Duane Elgin and Arnold Mitchell in "Voluntary Simplicity" is correct most of the 25 million people fully committed to the

simple lifestyle will live in cities. Between now and then these urban dwellers will be learning how to grow their own food, capture the sun's energy for heat, and recycle household waste materials—called by the people at the Integral Urban House in Berkeley, California, "urban homesteading."

A project of the Farallones Institute founded in 1969, the House successfully demonstrates all those novel ideas you read about in a renovated old city dwelling on a lot 60' × 125': two

beehives, chickens and rabbits which produce 130 dozen eggs and 350 pounds of meat a year; an organic garden and fruit trees fertilized by kitchen wastes and animal manure which has been composted into rich soil in three weeks; a fish pond growing native trout and crayfish partly fed with worms grown in chicken droppings; hot water heated by a homemade solar panel; a wood-burning stove and a bottle wall; and a waterless toilet, which turns human waste into rich fertilizer.

One short visit through this exciting experimental house and I knew I had to start one in Jackson, Mississippi! So far I have the bees and the rabbits at my home and plan to work on the other elements of an "IUH" in the years ahead. For literature on the Berkeley House write to Tom Javits, Farallones Institute, 1516 Fifth St., Berkeley, California 94710.

WORK

There has been an evolution of work from pure survival to sweat labor to automation (and unemployment!) And recently there has been growing agreement that *people* are more important than *efficiency.* Most people in our country "work for someone else." A study entitled *Work in America,* published by the Department of Health, Education and Welfare in 1973, discovered a high level of alienation among workers, perhaps some of it caused by lack of control, lack of fulfillment and monotony. Control relates to the work task, division of profits, working conditions and social responsibility. Some people think worker-run factories and businesses are the answer to this problem.

International Group Plan Insurance

It comes as a shock to a lot of people to learn that International Group Plan Insurance Company in Washington, D.C., a 350-employee, $60 million annual volume business, is *worker-owned and self-managed.* The guiding philosophy is that the company exists to serve the working members. All workers from the president to the file clerks have one vote on company policies. Employee committees appoint management, set working hours, and determine salaries. IGP workers, by their own decision, have a 35-hour week with unlimited sick leave and days off with team agreement.

Berkeley Co-op

The Berkeley (California) Co-op is a huge network of retail services which does $78 million sales each year with the help of 800 employees—and it is owned cooperatively by 85,000 families! The Co-op network includes two package liquor stores, four pharmacies, two yard and garden centers, one hardware store, an auto repair store, three service stations, one natural food store, and twelve supermarkets. It is no surprise that it took forty years to develop to its present size.

The purpose of the Co-op is to develop a sense of community, to shape an environment which encourages sharing and responsiveness. Consider a sign in the supermarket: "Eat before you shop. Hungry shoppers buy too much." In the cereal aisle small labels reading "recommended," "not recommended," and "OK" are a shock to first-time shoppers. Community involvement includes special programs for senior citizens, yoga classes, craft fairs, and an annual black history festival. All this plus savings of 50 percent and better on many items.

If you would like to read more about economic democracy for working Americans get a copy of *Own Your Own Job* by Jeremy Rifkin. It's a Bantam book which sells for $1.50.

[1]*"Religious Community: "The Way of Reba Place Fellowship." Fellowship,* April 1975.
[2]*The Community Land Trust,* published by Center for Community Economic *Development, 1878 Massachusetts Ave., Cambridge, Massachusetts 02140,* 1972, page 1.

COMMUNITY ACTION

Community Composting

One hundred acres of abandoned Bronx ghetto land in New York City will be reclaimed for urban agriculture by composting tons of spoiled produce from the world's largest produce market. The Institute for Local Self-Reliance, 1717 18th Street, N.W., Washington, D.C. 20009, can help you organize a community composting project.

Community Gardens

What if you could improve your health, have a lot of fun, and in the process save from $200 to $300 a year on your food budget?

The miraculous activity which quietly hides behind all those benefits is gardening. Yes, gardening—either the at-home variety or on a community plot. And some enthusiasts even say the exercise from a big garden combined with eating more vegetables versus meat and junk foods will make you live longer! If all these bonuses are true, gardening qualifies as a major stewardship activity especially if you use organic insect control and fertilizer instead of chemicals.

Still, can individuals grow enough to make any difference? Considering that most households have enough land nearby (or rooftop space in urban areas) to grow most of their vegetables, the answer is yes! The Institute for Local Self-Reliance told of a study which determined that people in one crowded urban District neighborhood could produce 75 percent of their fresh produce—and most of it grown on rooftops. People in less dense areas have greater access to garden space, including public land and church property.

Another individual who got excited about the benefits of community (shared land) gardening is Tommy Thompson, director of Gardens for All (Box 371, Shelburne, Vermont 05482). Several years ago he started this national project, which publishes materials and provides organizing aid for community garden projects. When asked how popular gardening is, he exclaimed, "There are 300,000 gardeners in the state of Pennsylvania." Publications offered by the group include a basic manual for community gardening ($10) and a fourth-grade gardening level teacher's manual ($2).

All these projects were dreamed up and organized by one person. And they are working to bring bread and justice to our world, even though they are only scratching the surface. You could be that *one person* to give your area the gift of a food project!

Turn Trash Into Cash—Start a Recycling Center!
Recycling almost everything has become increasingly popular—and for good reason. Environmentalists are concerned about nonbiodegradable plastics that litter most locations reachable by "civilized" humankind. Those of us aware of the spiraling prices and growing scarcity of many essential materials would like to recover and reuse what we can. Need I say more?

Recycling can begin as a do-it-yourself project, but usually what you can do yourself is only a first step. You can, of course, promote yard sales as a way to raise money for worthy causes, and you can donate to and patronize thrift shops as a way to recycle clothing, furniture, and housewares. Find the demolition contractors in your city, and hunt in their yards for building materials. If your area, like mine, disposes of trash in "sanitary" landfills, mount a campaign to have these facilities open to the public for salvaging. But what about the real nitty-gritty—paper, cans, bottles? You've heard that there's money in recycling these, but how do you make the connections?

I got some good tips about getting into the recycling business from the president (and paper roll cutter) of a major paper recycler in my town. The most important (and probably first) step is to investigate the potential markets for the goods you recycle. If you're into newspapers—and they're a pretty good thing to be into—find out if there are any paper mills in your general area that would agree to handle your collections. To insure a steady income, even if not a large one, you'd do well to negotiate a contract with a mill, for

instance. Then when the price of paper fluctuates, you are guaranteed a market and a price.

You can start small, as LERN (Let's Each Recycle Now) did in Tucson, with a door-to-door preannounced pickup. A more practical way to operate, however, is to establish locations at which bins can be placed for paper (or whatever you are collecting) and to publicize your service and location so that people will bring recyclables to you. Encourage groups to hold paper drives to raise money. In Tucson, bins to receive paper to be sold for the benefit of the Community Food Bank have been extremely successful.

You need to weigh the advantages of nonprofit operation and a regular business. Nonprofit status helps you to get freebies that can be quite helpful, like advertising. But you need to understand tax laws. Cities are finding, however, that waste is big business. In Odessa, Texas, the city recycles everything—the first American city to do so. Metal is extracted and sold; organic matter is shredded and composted. The sale of the metal alone may pay for the $800,000 recycling plant within five to eight years. And this is in a city of just 90,000! Suggest to your city council that a plan of this sort be tried.

In the above, I've concentrated on paper, mostly because if you do want to do your own recycling thing, paper is probably easiest. Glass is hard to handle and hard to sell. Only glass factories will accept it, and you need to be near one to make such an operation pay off. In a growing number of cities companies like Reynolds Aluminum have weekly pickups of aluminum cans and pay in the range of 17 cents per pound. Some breweries recycle their own cans, so check into that also.

One idea you might try, instead of going into recycling yourself, is to start a recycling hotline as was done in Seattle, Washington. People can call in to find the location of the recyclers nearest them and what they accept. Instructions on separating recyclables are also available. If you are familiar with the companies in your town that accept recyclables, you might want to set up a neighborhood recycling station for all kinds of goods. For a rundown on the Seattle experience, call the toll-free hotline: 1-800-RECYCLE.

Getting it All Together in a People's Yellow Pages
Newcomers and oldtimers alike often don't know what facilities their city has: how to help a transient in trouble; where are the food co-ops and recycling centers; locations of thrift shops, second hand bookstores, etc; low-cost health facilities; skilled or semi-skilled people who are willing to barter for their services; alternative schools and specialized classes; and so forth.

A People's Yellow Pages community access guide should contain information like that just mentioned and other listings that help people to get better acquainted with the city. Often a PYP is selective about the material listed, because it has a focus on empowerment and liberation and helping people to help themselves. Usually a PYP is classified, like Ma Bell's book of the same name, so that readers can more easily find the subject they're looking for.

Almost any city has the beginnings of a PYP somewhere; daily newspapers sometimes print a list of phone numbers of helping services. If there is a food co-op in your community, it most likely has a bulletin board where people offer the kinds of services that might belong in a People's Yellow Pages. Assembling all the information within a time period short enough to insure reasonable accuracy in the final product is a tremendous job. It would be a good idea to put out the word at schools and colleges (this work would make a good independent study project), in the churches, at meetings of community organizations, that you are looking for volunteer researchers. Often a person will have lots of contacts in his/her fields of expertise, and might be able to put together a whole section of your book—health workers, for instance, or handcrafters.

Printing takes money, so you might want to elicit the help of a local bank or merchant to help defray the costs—provided that you do not lose your independence of operation that way. In Tucson, when I was helping with our PYP, I solicited small loans, to be paid back out of sales. The printer was willing to take his money in a couple of installments, and it all worked out fine. The local bookstores, when told of the many workers who had gotten the book together as volunteers, were willing to forego half their usual profit in selling the book.

There are several good sources for details on starting a People's Yellow Pages for your community. The "classic" is from Cambridge, Massachusetts: *Getting Together a People's Yellow Pages: An Underground Overground Toward Social Change*—available from Vocations for Social Change, 353 Broadway, Cambridge, Massachusetts 02139, $1.50. Other than that, I would recommend looking at some good examples of the genre. Contacts are as follows: Seattle, Metrocenter YMCA, 909 4th Ave., Seattle, Washington 98104 (also ask if they'll send you a copy of the procedures they wrote up as they were assembling the book); Los Angeles, Box 24 B15, Los Angeles, California 90024; Tucson, New West Trails, c/o 2237 E. 18th, Tucson, Arizona 85719 (and request a copy of an article from *Communities* No. 28 on the way they did it). When you write the PYP folks, mention the fact that you are interested in doing one yourself and suggest an exchange arrangement—you'll send a copy of yours, when ready, in exchange for theirs. Most are very willing to help in this way.

Give Your Neighborhood a Community Organization
All across America neighborhoods are sick and dying. Mobility means that people have become strangers to each other, even in their own communities. We lock ourselves in our houses from fear we'll be attacked. Bland, corrupt politicians try to fill the void left by citizens who have abandoned public life.

While this may be an accurate description of the general political condition of our land, there is no denying that an increasing number of citizens are responding to the challenge of restoring democracy to America. They take seriously, the old cry, "Don't mourn—organize!"

There is no greater gift a group of citizens can give their community than to restore its political life. In brief, that restoration entails a return of political power to the people who live in the community. The people who are afflicted by political decisions should make those decisions.

But the powers that be won't turn over the reins just because you ask them to. You have to earn the reins by fighting for them. You have to organize.

ACORN (Association of Community Organizations for Reform Now), has learned something about organizing during its eight years of experience in thirteen different states. ACORN now has 13,000 family members who work in their neighborhoods, cities, and states to bring power to low-to-moderate income people.

Before you begin to organize your area you must answer some key questions:

1. Who do you want to organize? Everyone? Poor people? Middle-income people? Those who believe in the same ideas you do? Whom do you stand with? Which side are you on?

2. What kind of a group do you want to build? Do you want to work strictly on material issues? Do you want to work on just one issue (e.g., taxes, nuclear power) or be a multi-issue organization?

3. What is your idea or vision of a transformed neighborhood, city, or country? Would it be enough to clean up all the trash on your block or to win an adequate amount of social services for your area?

4. How will your group raise the money to pay its expenses? Will you have a membership dues system, or will you depend on local sources for donations? Will you appeal to foundations for gifts and grants or come up with internal fund-raising projects?

5. Will you hire a staff or try to wing it with volunteers? The latter is very difficult. Usually, without a paid staff member, the group folds as soon as the energies of volunteers are depleted.

There are five steps to actually organizing a community group:

1. Select a target neighborhood or area. You can't organize an entire city at once. A group of 600—1500 is a reasonable target area.

2. Make a list of everyone who lives in the neighborhood.

3. Visit every one of the people on the list. Tell them why you're organizing a group, what your political vision is, what issues you think are important. Give them a chance to join the new group. Get their ideas for issues to work on.

4. Put together a core group from among the most interested people. Get this group to help you in visiting the rest of the neighborhood. They can also help select the first slate of officers, propose a name for the group, collect dues, etc. They key to organizing is to get as many people invloved as possible.

5. The group should have regular meetings for the entire membership. Remember that the only real democracy is direct democracy. The founding meeting of the group is the most important. Everyone in the neighborhood should be notified and reminded about the meetings by personal visits, telephone calls, and flyers placed in their doors.

There's a lot more to be said about organizing, but these are the bare essentials. If you desire technical assistance on community organizing projects or training in organizing, contact Meg Campbell at The Institute, Inc. If you would like ACORN to work in your neighborhood or city, contact ACORN Chief Organizer Wade Rathke. Both Meg and Wade can be reached c/o ACORN, 628 Baronne, New Orleans, Louisiana 70113.The telephone number is (504) 523-1691.

Joshua Miller   ACORN,
Department of Research and
Publications

Publish a "Local" *Alternative Catalogue:*

Here's How

"Why not create a "local" version of the *Alternate Celebrations Catalogue* in your city? It's a large metropolitan area with many opportunities for redirecting time and money for a people-oriented Christmas."

This was the reply Cleveland's West Side Ecumenical Ministry received when, in 1976, it asked for ad space in the next national *Catalogue.* That reply started people thinking and after months of brainstorming and seeking enabling funds, the answer became "yes" in the form of a tabloid newspaper entitled *The Living-Giving News.*

"ARE YOU BUYING A PET ROCK THIS CHRISTMAS?" This was the headline on the first issue. In eight words it captured the materialistic binge that Christmas has become. The headline sought to bridge the gap between where the readers were in their celebrating and where our hopes for them were by making several guesses about them:

• That you are indeed embarrassed and maybe even angered by pet rocks.

• That you really would like a calmer, less hectic Christmas season.

• That you don't enjoy being told by the ads what you "need" for Christmas.

• That you believe *people* matter more than things.

• That you are tired of the bombardment of just "$19.99" toy ads and the resulting "gimme, gimme" idea of Christmas in your children.

• That you would act to change your lifestyle of celebrating if you knew how.

The Alternate Celebrating idea was briefly stated, and the point emphasized that we were talking about a process of growth, not a dream to be achieved in one year. The editorial ended with this positive note: "Our hope is that the ideas here will be helpful tools for affecting your ways of thinking, spending, and living. Celebrate with us a vision of life-supporting style of celebrating; act

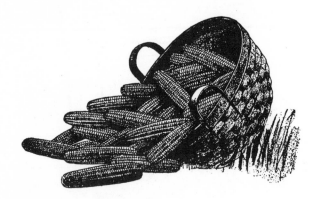

creatively on the dream and than share your experiences with others and with us. Let us celebrate life.!"

Within the pages of this Christmas issue, specific ideas were shared on how to celebrate in a more people-ized manner. A foretaste of the second issue's theme was given in a back-page article on simplifying life—Jorgen Lissner's seven reasons for examining one's own life.

The four-page centerfold invited readers to consider some "living-giving opportunities" in the Cleveland area. Fifteen groups told their story in graphic form and asked readers to redirect some shopping money and/or time to their life-supporting work. Groups included FISH, Meals on Wheels, Inner City Protestant Parish, Greater Cleveland Interchurch Council, Probation Friend Program, Society for the Blind, and Project Friendship.

Also included was a sample gift card on which one said, "I am putting my love for you to work in the world through a gift to_____.

The Living-Giving News No. 2 appeared during Lent, an appropriate time for raising the issue of one's own values and lifestyle. Catching the mood of the winter energy crisis as well as that of the religious season, the headline read, "IF RELIGION WON'T, YOUR GAS BILL WILL." The editorial continued, "Will what? Will cause you to think about your style of life."

In this issue of *Living-Giving News,* we invite you to join others in searching for livable answers to questions of lifestyle such as:
- What guidelines are there for a Christian style of life in a world where natural resources are scarce and where there is a growing gap between our affluence and the poverty and hunger of millions?

- Is progress always our greatest product?
- When is enough, enough?
- What does stewardship of my life and the earth's resources mean?
- Are things my god or my servant?
- What values do I live in the way I spend my money and time?
- Am I primarily a consumer or a producer?
- What do I really need?

Our basic conviction is that life can be richer by being simpler; that by simplifying life we can
- Renew our joy in being and becoming rather than having and maintaining.
- Be freer to use our time and resources for creative response to society's sore spots.
- Focus our lives and take control of them by being less dependent on things for meaning.
- Have more time and deepening our relationships with others.
- Have richer lives with less expense.
- Contribute toward a more just distribution of the world's resources.

The purpose of the paper was reiterated in the final paragraph: *Living-Giving News* wants to be a resource tool—may its contents start you thinking, struggling, dreaming, and living in a lifestyle which, when Spring finally comes, can celebrate the Easter message of the ever-possible renewed life."

Articles in this issue discussed how we discover what our values are, the concept of "simple living," the Shakertown Pledge (one example of a statement of personal commitment), a bibliography, a pictorial presentation of ways to live less wastefully and in a less energy-depleting way, and a consideration of how to celebrate Easter in people- and life-affirming ways. The "stories" were introduced with the statement, "One of the benefits of simpler living is the freeing of more of our time and money for creative response to society's sore spots."

In a somewhat lighter vein, the summer issue of *The Living-Giving News* continued the theme of simpler, more people-oriented living. Articles suggested ideas for vacations in less consumptive ways, for enjoying sights and activities right here in our town, and for recycling furniture, fabric, and "junk" into new creations. One page considered the place of eating in a simpler life and in relationship to the whole problem of world food distribution.

Focusing typical summer celebrations (Father's Day and weddings, for instance) on persons rather than on things was the topic of another page. Funerals were also discussed as a celebration needing rethinking.

Introduced in a book review was a thought-provoking and informative book on the topic of lifestyle—*Enough Is Enough* by Bishop John Taylor. This book furnishes an excellent biblical background for guiding one in search for a responsible lifestyle.

The fourth edition of *The Living-Giving News*

asked, "Is Your Living Thanks-Giving?" The relationship between our celebration of Thanksgiving and our lifestyle and the problem of world hunger was spelled out. The editorial asked, "How would our celebration of Thanksgiving look if we created it out of our own beliefs about life?" Feasting was questioned as an appropriate response, in view of the statistics of world hunger. But, to counteract the temptation to respond only with the feeling of guilt, specific suggestions were given for an Alternative Thanksgiving celebration.

Besides eating, another theme associated with Thanksgiving is the Native-American Indian. Articles in the paper shared an Indian's response to Thanksgiving and the ways in which we might act in response to their needs.

On the issue of world hunger, the work of organizations like Bread for the World and Church World Service was outlined. The creative use of our gift of citizenship was especially emphasized in the Bread for the World article. Readers were informed about local responses to the problem of hunger in articles about an ecumenical Hunger Task Force and its "hunger centers" and a food co-op that had just opened. In hopes of helping readers to understand that hunger is not the basic problem—that behind it is the problem of maldistribution of the world's resources—an article by "experts" Frances Lappe and Joe Collins was included.

Halloween—what kind of treat?—that was the question asked in an article suggesting alternatives to candy handouts.

Humanizing Christmas was the theme again of part of this issue. Ideas of making gifts and being a gift with one's time and talent filled the pages along with several alternative celebration experiences by local churches.

From 2,000 to 2,500 copies of each edition of *The Living-Giving News* were distributed through churches, local people-supporting agencies, and individual subscriptions. Letters to pastors invited them to consider organizing an adult education course around the themes in the paper.

Individual response to the paper's ideas was very encouraging, but we knew that for an individual to make any real sustained simpler living response, he or she would need a support group. As the second issue had stated, "Wrestle with these questions and ideas *with others*—the sharing and testing of ideas and mutual support, in a growth process which can be painful at times, is crucial." Also, the scope of some of the problems—natural resources and hunger, for instance—requires more than individual response.

And so, our efforts after four issues are being directed not to producing more editions, but to getting the four issues used as a study packet by small groups. It is our hope that *The Living-Giving News,* as an offspring of the *Alternate Celebrations Catalogue,* will bear its own fruit in changed lives in the Cleveland area.

Charline Watts   is a Hunger Activist and Alternative Colleague in Lakewood, Ohio

◆◆◆◆◆◆◆◆◆◆◆◆◆◆◆◆◆◆◆◆◆◆◆◆◆◆◆◆◆◆◆◆◆◆

If you're seriously considering producing a local *Catalogue,* here are some facts from the *Living-Giving News* experience which might help you: their total budget was $2000 and copies were sold for 5¢ each. Ads were sold on a sliding scale from $13-$40 to help defray the printing cost. Much of their copy was reprinted with permission from the Third edition of the *Catalogue.* Ms. Watts didn't allow the *News* to be an end in itself—she sent out 600 letters to pastors in the Greater Cleveland area and conducted two workshops to move congregations into the Alternative Celebration Campaign.   **Editor**

Third World Shops

The idea of the Third World Shoppes originated in Holland as a result of the United Nations Trade and Development Conference held in New Delhi, India, in 1968. The developing countries asked the richer countries to lower their tariffs in order to increase trade between the two groups. A Dutch reporter was shocked at the fact the rich countries wouldn't do anything. He got the idea of UNCTAD shops which could mobilize public opinion and put pressure on the Dutch government to take action in behalf of the poor countries. The idea was molded by the people involved in the cane sugar campaign (a publicity campaign to show the unfairness of world trade structures), who were looking for something with which to follow up their actions. The shops grew rapidly with a lot of support and publicity through "peace weeks" organized by the churches.

Now the 150 Dutch shops, called World shops, have become action centers as well as places to purchase so-called "political products" and handicrafts. A typical Dutch shop includes:

170

1. Sales of handicrafts for which (a) the country of origin is of particular educational value for studying the problems of the Third World (those who are poor), (b) the profits have to go to the people who produce the goods (and prices have to be reasonable so they will sell), (c) sales of products should be working to eliminate "unjust world trade structure," and (d) each item should be accompanied by a pamphlet with information for the customer.

2. Distribution of literature and information about world economic and social problems.

3. Sales of "political products" like tea, cane sugar, and coffee which can easily be used as examples of what is wrong with the present world trade structures. For example, under the international coffee agreement countries are not permitted to expand their share of the world coffee market. A poor Latin American country like Bolivia with

coffee as a major crop cannot sell more to feed a growing population. Thus they are forced to try to sell other types of products to the world without any real means of developing new industry and without additional aid from the rich countries who buy the coffee and write the agreement. An even poorer country like Tanzania, with a small part of the coffee market, cannot expand because of the coffee agreement and is effectively cut out of the market. Yet the price keeps rising on these items to the consumer in the rich countries. Neither the coffee drinker, nor the coffee grower, benefits.

The shop idea has since caught on in Belgium, Germany, England, Sweden, and several other European countries.

In the United States many groups are becoming interested in the shop idea as a means of doing something positive about the poverty problem, both at home and abroad. Several groups, some affiliated with existing anti-poverty agencies, some with churches, have developed local "Third World" shops. A national Union of Third World Shoppes has been formed to try to encourage more people to get up local shops and to help those shops that have started. We've found these common goals coming from the existing shops:

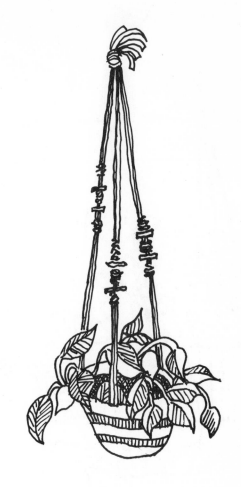

1. A commitment to providing a market for small groups and families who would share in the profits. Wholesale agents (except a few groups like SERRV, Mennonite Central Commitee, and similar humanitarian groups) often buy in large quantities and greatly mark up the retail price, not allowing the artist to share in the profits. Providing people direct outlets will allow the groups to sell their articles at lower rates yet receive more of the profits and avoid the failure rate of 85-90 percent of all small businesses in the first year of operation.

2. A commitment to providing meaningful ways of creating a living and providing for basic needs: food, clothing, housing, and education. Handicrafts are labor intensive, that is, they take little or no tools, and can provide those who have the greatest need with a way of earning a living without losing their dignity.

3. A commitment to the sharing of information through education and action programs (community volunteer work, crafts training, hunger education, etc.) sponsored by a shop. Increased awareness comes through personal contact between the consumer (generally middle class) and the producer (the poor).

4. A commitment to a cooperative or democratic way of making decisions within the local shop program.

Operating on donations and volunteer help, members of the Union of Shoppes and those active in local shops provide the following services in response to needs:

- A catalogue (in the form of a monthly newsletter) of producers, with descriptions of items and literature on them.
- Training workshops in business and marketing techniques, including visits to local groups wishing to set up shops.
- A nonprofit wholesale ordering service to pool small orders—especially from overseas producers.
- Coordination of any national publicity efforts agreed upon by local shops.
- Educational helps concerning craft groups, cultural situations, and world problems affecting the poor.

Also in the planning stages is a revolving loan fund for local groups who wish to begin shops. (We're accepting human interest loans of money for the fund.)

The Union is in a position to provide help to groups who wish to begin shops. We ask that you donate something for the cost of help (like a stamp and large envelope for a reply). We're accepting memberships from shops and individuals for $10 a year. Membership is open to anyone who agrees with our goals. You get the newsletter (catalog) and a chance to participate.

HOW TO SET UP A LOCAL THIRD WORLD SHOP

The most important things needed to start a local shop are goals, a storefront or other means of public access, an initial small group of people who are ready to make a six-month-or-more time commitment, money to buy a stock of goods, and a solid publicity plan. In getting your shop together you must:

1. Hold regular meetings and write out goals for your particular shop. You will have to develop a structure and answer the following questions: who will make the decisions in your shop, whom are you trying to reach, what type of goods will you sell, what type of action and education program will you organize, who will do the work involving bookkeeping, clerking, ordering, etc.? Once you've come past the idea stage, you should write your answers to these questions in a brochure about your shop to give the public whenever they ask "What is the———shop?"

2. You will need a name for your shop or marketing project. The name Third World Shoppes is a registered name of the United States Union of Shoppes. You can either work something out with the Union, get a local organization to sponsor you, or you can form your own organization. Whoever has the name you choose has to make reports to the local, state, and federal authorities, which take time and money. (We are suggesting nonprofit shops since this would help poor craftspeople the most.) In any case, whatever your legal structure is, the main idea is to get the shop going, not to build an empire. If you need advice on this, get it early and save trouble later.

also work in the shop for pay or sell their own products there. It is very important to find workers who will be dependable and be willing to make a commitment on a fairly long-term (6 months or more) basis. A budget of projected costs for people and place should be made, and you should develop a knowledge of purchasing, shipping, inventory, etc. If you don't have a local person who knows about such things, we can help find someone who does to teach you before you spend any money.

5. Contact domestic and international groups and/or individuals who will supply crafts and products. Seek out local artisans to help. However, make sure those you will buy from are truly poor. There is a big difference between the middle-class person who makes and donates things because he or she is handy and has some free time, and the poor person who makes things as a means of support. Be careful of buying through middlemen or dealers. Personal contact is important to get a feel of what producers' needs are and what to expect. The producers will be your strongest supporters—they receive a living from your efforts. Get to know who they are. (Be sure to get in on the Union of Shoppes catalog.)

3. Analyze your community situation to decide how and where a shop might be set up. It could be in a church, youth center, or house. Space could be low-rent or donated. It could be mobile. You will need space to display goods, educational pamphlets, hold meetings, and take care of office functions.

4. Work out the details involving people. A shop has to be specific, have hours and deadlines. Work out the staff, schedules, salaries (if any), and responsibilities. If an all-volunteer staff is impossible, perhaps one or two regular workers could receive minimal salaries. Poor people could

ALTERNATIVES' BOOKSTORE

1124 MAIN STREET

COME IN

GIVE BOOKS FOR GIFTS

& more life-supporting ways to celebrate:
• WEDDINGS
• BIRTHDAYS
• EASTER
• 4th of July
• ORDINATIONS
• FUNERALS

POSTERS

8. Plan everything around your goals and educational ideas. Create an atmosphere in the shop through art, wall hangings, and music. Our shop is arranged by continent with goods from each area labelled. We have lots of maps. Print educational leaflets to describe each item to be sold. Set up a literature section and include information on groups and areas your goods come from. If you create enough interest through education, your sales will take care of themselves.

7. Develop a publicity program which is consistent with the goals of your shop. We (in Fort Wayne) do not have any "sales" in our shop but rather promote our nonprofit, all-volunteer nature. Word-of-mouth advertising, flyers, mailings, and talks before church groups bring more results (and are cheaper) than bland mass media splats. If you qualify for public service ads, you may get some free radio and TV time.

Identify who your supporters are and seek them out. Many people are concerned about poverty. Many are interested in different kinds of crafts, Native American, Asian, or African. Try to get items and give out images to the public that attract those you feel are your supporters. In Fort Wayne, we take the name and address of every customer and send a newsletter before each educational event or project we sponsor.

6. Raise funds to pay for an initial supply of goods and operating expenses. You should have at least the amount of cash available to buy the initial order, which can be from $750 to $7500. There are very few truly poor people who can have goods made available on consignment, so keep this in mind. Figure one-third of the initial order in additional cash to pay start-up expenses: rent, light, heat, brochures, displays, mailings, publicity, for the first month. A commercial shop generally has a year's worth of money on hand before they open. If you don't you had better have a committee of people ready to bring in the customers.

Don't let the immensities of the business or organizing ideas scare you. Think positively. Take one step at a time, and remember, even a small effort can help somebody. You will surely get something out of it for yourself. Courage!

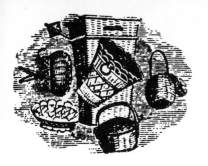

Note: We've written from our experience. We'd like to share information with other groups. To communicate, for help or for more information, please contact us at the address below. Include something about yourself and what you're doing. We have trouble answering postcards with no feelings:

Jim Goetsch   UNION OF THIRD WORLD SHOPPES
428 East Berry Street
Fort Wayne, Indiana 46802
(210) 422-6821

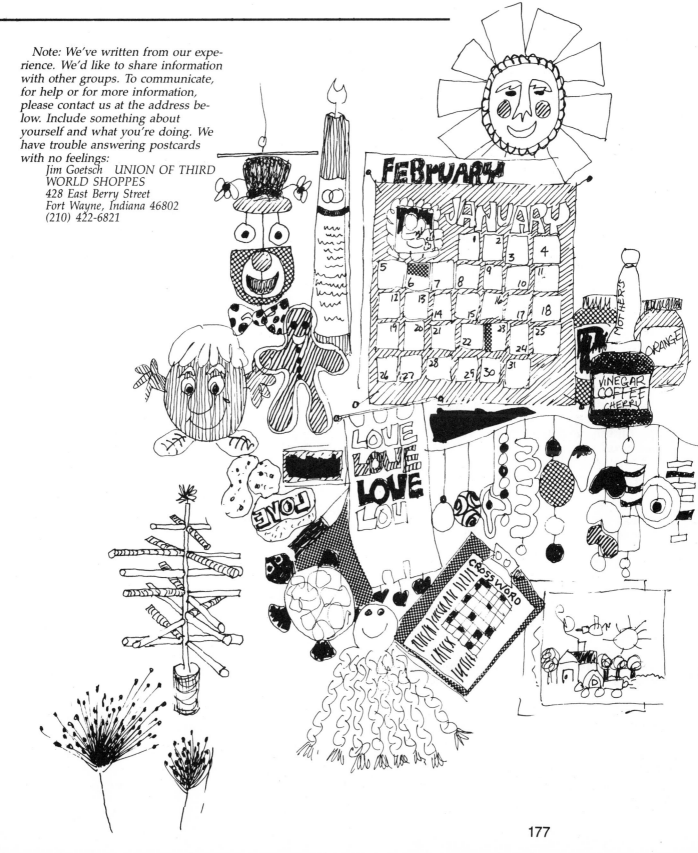

Warning: TV May Be Bad for Your Health

Perhaps no issue in recent memory has been the source of so much public rancor and debate as the controversy over the effect of television on children and adult viewers—and on society as a whole.

From a struggling infancy only a few decades ago, television has risen in dominance to the point where 98 percent of American homes have television sets—more homes than have running water. In the average home the set is on more than six hours a day, seven days a week, and the average child watches nearly three of those hours.

This viewing by children is not limited to programming intended for them—"kid-vid" in television industry parlance. Industry sources have estimated that the under-12 viewing audience does not drop below one million until well after 11:00 P.M. An estimated 100,000 children under 12 watch NBC's *Tomorrow* in the early hours of the morning.

Research findings on television viewing and television content have begun to round out our understanding of the impact this viewing has on children. Both in programs specifically intended for children (cartoon and "live action") and in programs intended for "family" or "adult" viewing, children are being told that society condones violence, relies on violence to solve problems, ties violence to sex, and accepts intimidation and aggression as normative methods of problem-solving and interaction.

These messages regarding violence also can be set in a larger context. They seem to fit within a view of normative lifestyle that condones doing violence to others through our own consumption and waste patterns. These lifestyle messages pervade not only commercials, but also every program where a specific style of living and consuming is illustrated. For example, when we see the overwhelming consumption of hard liquor that occurs on television, we get a very clear lifestyle message. The characters consuming it have credibility for their audience, and thus their actions teach and influence others.

Behavioral research has supported content analysis with findings that such messages can influence young viewers to accept television-mediated ideals and interactions as their own. This learning process has been shown to extend from specific instances of learned behaviors, such as hitting and shoving, through more complex ideals of what society deems acceptable lifestyle and behavior.

Research also tells us that television's effects aren't limited to children. A study of heavy viewers among the adult population (adults who watch more than four hours a day were considered heavy viewers) found that they held views of society more consistent with the world of television than the real world.

Television is a teaching instrument that brings viewers experiences and ideas which are gradually integrated into their view of life and, of course, their view of celebrations.

For instance, television advertising and much of its programming during the Christmas season helps support the "Big Lie"—that in order to have a happy holiday, it is necessary for children and adults to buy certain things. In the 1977 season alone the toy industry poured out $109 million into local television spot advertising. Children in major cities were bombarded with as many as 80 commercials for some product line. Christmas, the ads told them, would not be Christmas without a Farah Fawcett Doll or a Stretch Monster.

Other holidays attract their share of advertising and programming which tell us we can't be happy unless we buy things. It's part of the psychological manipulation carried out in all the media by high-powered advertising and promotion campaigns that help make our tastes a bit expensive, excessively consumptive, and not particularly related to the meaning of celebration.

The reaction of industry to criticism about

violence and other aspects of TV has been mixed at best. At worst, industry representatives have consistently refused to accept responsibility for such "social effects" of broadcast messages. George Heineman, an NBC vice-president, has frequently echoed industry sentiment regarding responsibility. When discussing children's programming at a symposium sponsored by Action for Children's Television in 1975, Heineman cautioned the group "not to forget what business we're in ... *show* business, not education."

I beg to disagree. The television industry is not in the entertainment business; it is in the "audience delivery" business. No one pays a network to entertain. Sponsors pay networks and stations to deliver an audience for their advertising message.

The law of supply and demand, with its mandate to most efficient service of customer needs, has guaranteed us a broadcast industry that is very good at delivering an audience to sponsors. It is less effective, however, at integrating into its standard operating procedures any concern with audience needs and interests.

Thus, violent shows are retained because they deliver audiences, in spite of research evidence that indicates they might have negative effect. With the industry mandate clearly in the direction of gathering the largest possible audience for its sponsors, audiences can expect "gimmicks" that attract the most viewers while offending the fewest. Violence is one such "gimmick." And in the 1977-78 season, with new shows such as *Soap* and *Three's Company* and the renewal of *Charlie's Angels*, networks discovered that sexual titillation might also work as a gimmick.

Another level of concern is the way television has seriously altered American family life. Its value messages have even begun to usurp the influence traditionally held by parents, schools, and the church.

The presence of television has forever altered family interaction patterns. Meal times are changed to accommodate the evening news. Family discussions occur rarely, and often in the midst of television viewing. Visiting with neighbors, once a quite important social function, has dropped off, and when it does occur, it is often accompanied by the faint glow of "the box."

Adults rely heavily (60 percent of them rely *entirely*) on network news for information about current events. Pastors and others involved in marriage counseling are beginning to encounter couples and families for whom television has become a pathological phenomenon similar to alcoholism. Television can be a wedge, an escape, a weapon.

I was surprised at one time to learn that I had been invited to hold a workshop at a local congregation precisely because the pastor had discovered that television was interfering with a number of marriages. After that weekend of examining their viewing habits, a number of families sold their sets or made commitments to change their habits.

Marie Winn, in a recent book, *The Plug-In Drug,* maintains rather convincingly that in television's impact on the family, the problem is not so much with children's addiction to viewing as it is with the use of television by parents as a baby-sitter. Recounting many of the psychological, social and educational effects of television, such as

hyperactivity, poor reading skills, social maladjustment and passivity in learning, Winn places responsibility on parents for allowing their children to get hooked on the medium.

The use of one's time and the stewardship of the family's attention is a serious question growing out of Winn's work. We need to be aware of how our lifestyle is affected on one level merely by the existence of television in our homes, regardless of how "hooked" we may be on it.

An experiment in "unhooking" children was reported recently in *Redbook*. Parents in Connecticut were asked to take their children off television for a month. At first there were the expected fights over viewing, the pleading, the nagging. Parents found themselves having to spend a good deal more time with their children. In the end, the experiment was a resounding success. Both in home atmosphere and school performance, a vast majority noted a great change for the better.

I have noted similar success stories on a limited basis in my discussions with parents. Someone will become slightly misty-eyed and say, "I remember once when the set was broken for a couple of weeks, and it was great. We could eat supper when we wanted, take walks, talk to the kids, play games. We rediscovered our family. Then we got the set fixed ... " I always ask why the set was repaired, and the answer is usually something like, "We felt that we were missing too much."

This is an important point. There is much good on television that would be missed by not having a set. Few people have found that their best relationship to television is no relationship at all, although it is obviously a solution for some.

In many ways, learning to live *with* television is more difficult than learning to live without it. Once you have begun to perceive some of the ways it can affect you and your family, dealing with it becomes a real challenge.

Several church groups have responded to this challenge with a program of Television Awareness Training (TAT). TAT is a human development program which proposes that each of us can be empowered to deal creatively with the challenge of television.

Motivated by their concern with societal values and value development, the American Lutheran Church, Church of the Brethren, and the United Methodist Church based TAT on research findings which showed that parents can be quite effective in mediating television's impact. Certain studies have found that by merely watching with children (even occasionally) and discussing the values presented, parents can be more effective in value development than television can.

Beginning there, TAT involves participants in an active encounter with the variety of value messages television delivers. There are specific sessions dealing with children's television, violence, sexuality, stereotyping, advertising, news, and impacting the system. Participants view films of program excerpts, and within the context of a small group encounter, begin to work at coping techniques and action strategies for responding.

TAT workshops are led by trained personnel, and besides film and process material, involve a text/workbook that is one of the most comprehensive resources available on the subject.

TAT hopes to develop a cadre of people, through training of leaders and participation in workshops, who have some skill and knowledge of broadcasting's effects, processes and feedback mechanisms. Through their activity and "spreading of the word," more and more people can come to have a different relationship to this pervasive medium.

Broadcast reform activity, pioneered by the United Church of Christ, and since joined by other denominations and secular groups, must continue. The economic, political and ideological aspects of American broadcasting communication are a just concern for the church. We should also help individuals assert creative control over television and its influence.

Television may be the most pervasive institution in American society, but that is no reason to surrender our responsibility to make choices about the quality of life we want for our children and ourselves.

Stewart M. Hoover   is a media education and advocacy consultant for Church of the Brethren, Elgin, Illinois.

9.

A Look to the Future

The past ten years have seen the growth of a movement of people who have said "NO!" to mindless consumption, being blind to injustice and quietly tolerating the rape of the earth. As we have learned from their experiments, discoveries and ways of living and celebrating, which have filled this book, they are people who want to give their families and the whole human family a world with a healthful environment, without war, racism, poverty and oppression.

What does the future hold for this movement and the people who comprise it? What is its agenda in the last two decades of the century?

Although it requires a certain amount of presumption to look into the future, it does not take a great deal of wisdom to project present trends and imagine what will happen if those trends are not somehow changed. Assuming that present trends are not altered significantly, by the year 2000 we are likely to see

—A world in which wealth has been concentrated in even fewer hands than at present. The current rate of 70 percent of the world's income going to about 30 percent of the population will likely shift to 75-80 percent of the income going to about 25 percent of the population. That will mean greater affluence for a decreasing minority and greater poverty for an increasing majority.

—A world in which the struggle for dwindling natural resources is pervasive as superpowers vie for control of resources outside their boundaries, as intermediate powers seek to protect their own natural resources and compete with the superpowers for those of smaller nations, and as smaller nations unsuccessfully resist encrochments on their resources.

183

—A world in which the arms race is no longer bilateral (between the U.S. and the Soviet Union) but multi-lateral, including especially West Germany, China and Japan. The proliferation of nuclear weapons will be so widespread that virtually all nations will have them. The possibility of their being introduced into even the smallest scale clashes will be real.

—A world in which transnational corporations will have surpassed all but the major national powers in power and influence. With assets greater than the gross national product of many nations and not subject to regulation by any one nation, the transnational corporations will have almost unlimited resources to influence government policy and be less accountable to the popular will than national governments.

—A world in which poverty and suffering will be dramatically increased because of the marginalization of larger numbers of people through unemployment. Science and technology will have been used to reduce need for human labor, thus increasing opportunity for leisure among the affluent minorities and unemployment among the poor majorities.

—A world in which the borders of the rich nations will be like the Berlin Wall, but to keep the large numbers of displaced poor people out. Border control will become an increasingly significant amount of the defense budgets. Because of

the concentration of wealth, declining natural resources and the conflicts over them, and unemployment, the number of refugees and displaced persons will be in the hundreds of millions rather than the tens of millions at present.

—A world in which air and water pollution have become of such magnitude that new technologies for air and water purification will give priority to purifying small amounts of contaminated air and water for use in enclosed areas by those who can afford them, in effect giving up the battle to clean up the lakes, rivers, oceans and atmosphere. Clean air and water will be like food, oil and other commodities, available to those who can purchase them.

Even without projecting scenarios of massive destruction caused by nuclear accidents or nuclear war, this is not a very positive vision of the future. It is precisely this future that the people in the movement toward responsible living do not want to give to their children.

While some simply refuse to acknowledge that this vision has any basis in reality, others wring their hands over its inevitability. Still others reaffirm their faith that science and technology will, like the cavalry in old movies, save us just before the end. Some see the only solution in a strong central authority where the affluent profit from such a future. Although they take these views seriously, the people in the movement toward responsible living have yet another response.

Tapping the resources of the Judeo-Christian tradition, these people believe that the future is open. There are no immutable laws that have determined the future. Another future is possible and can be created. By the same token, because the future is not determined, the dark vision looms on the horizon if no alternatives are forthcoming. They are committed to creating an alternative future, one in which neither global justice nor ecological balance is sacrificed on the altar of greed. They will work at creating that future in several different ways.

First, they will develop what John Kavanaugh calls a "spirituality of cultural resistance." That is, they will draw on the resources of their faith to resist the pervasive cultural values which make commodities of persons, greed a virtue, and self-gratification a god. Celebrations, especially those which touch the wellsprings of faith, will become occasions which nourish that resistance. Taking action to change one's celebrations so that they are more humane, expressions of solidarity with all the earth's people, and considerate of the earth, are part of developing that spirituality of cultural resistance.

Second, they will endeavor to create the new future in their households. Conserving resources, treating all members fairly, developing higher degrees of community self-reliance, consuming only what is needed, providing appropriate education, and celebrating with integrity, are all elements in creating the future in the household. This is not retreat from the world, not an individualistic approach to change, nor a "model" approach. By taking charge of those areas of our lives where we—with all the persons in those areas—can control, we can create new futures in those places. Experiencing the reality of a new future in the household is integral to creating that future in the community and beyond. Beginning in the household is also an act of integrity.

Third, they will organize in society at large, and support the efforts of others who are organizing, to create an alternative future:

1. They will organize in the *workplaces.* More than organizing for fair wages and benefits, they will organize around issues to make the workplace a more humane setting and reduce the alienation between the household and workplace. The provision of satisfying and rewarding employment will become an important economic objective in itself, the failure to provide it being seen as the greater cost. Some of the issues which will receive attention will be ● dealing with boredom and lack of incentive through job rotation, worker consultation on the production process, new forms of split-time employment (e.g., working half day on an assembly line and half day in a child care center), etc; ● providing on site child care facilities for nursing mothers and parents of young children; ● seeing the importance of people's energies and skills as an important renewable resource, as contrasted with the non-renewable energy and materials required in higher mechanized and capital intensive operations.

2. They will organize for *government issues.* The 1970's saw a burst of growth in citizens' lobbying groups to compete with the lobbying efforts of corporate

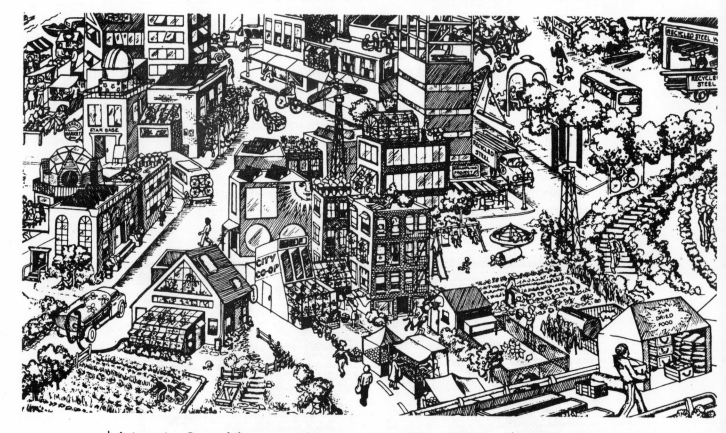

interests. Organizing around voter registration and support for candidates in local as well as national offices will be even more important in the last two decades of the century. Organizing around specific issues of both immediate and long-term consequence at all levels of government will be critical. This will mean organizing around issues like the following: ■ a public referendum in one's community on the safe disposal of hazardous wastes; ■ national land, air and water use policies which set the terms for whom and how these precious resources can be used for the interests of all people; ■ truth-in-advertising issues under review by the Federal Trade Commission; ■ taxing policies which are fair and do not penalize persons with low incomes; ■ budgetary priorities for all levels of government (e.g., the decision by Congress in 1981 to continue federal tobacco subsidies and

reduce them for school lunches, or the high priority given to defense spending).

3. They will organize in the *marketplace*. Consumer organizing for corporate policies and practices which do not compromise concern for global justice and a healthful environment is still in its infancy. "Consumer sovereignty," the notion that the consumer is the ultimate decision-maker about what and how much is produced (the phrase is usually pointed to by business to resist government regulation and intervention), needs to be redeveloped and used. Its redevelopment will involve a clear recognition of the reasons why consumers consume in this society and will be informed by a vision of the future. Some of this organizing will be done around shareholder resolutions in company board meetings, but more often it will take place at the points of advertising and selling. It will mean, for example, organizing to ★ receive equal time in the public media to show the true economic, social and health costs of mindless consumption; resist "single service" and "built-in obsolescence" products and encourage the development of products which use minimum amounts of non-renewable resources, create less waste, and are durable and repairable; ★ oppose the manufacture, sale and use of products whose availability depends on the exploitation of people; ★ decentralize and regionalize all forms of production, especially food production.

In the last decades of this century, the people in the movement toward responsible living will find themselves developing a spirituality of cultural resistance, creating new futures in their households, and organizing in society at large. They will organize where they are and will be supporting the efforts of others in their organizing efforts. This strategy for living responsibly is no guarantee that the dark vision will not come to pass. Indeed, some look at the future we want and say, "It can never be." Others resist this notion. Their answer is, "Why not?"

SOME DAY AFTER
MASTERING THE WIND,
THE WAVES, THE TIDES
AND GRAVITY,
WE SHALL HARNESS FOR
GOD THE ENERGIES
OF LOVE.

AND THEN, FOR
THE SECOND TIME IN
THE HISTORY OF THE WORLD--
MAN WILL HAVE
DISCOVERED FIRE.

TEILHARD de CHARDIN